P. Martin Duncan

Heroes of Science, Botanists, Zoologists, and Geologists

P. Martin Duncan

Heroes of Science, Botanists, Zoologists, and Geologists

ISBN/EAN: 9783337190231

Printed in Europe, USA, Canada, Australia, Japan

Cover: Foto ©ninafisch / pixelio.de

More available books at **www.hansebooks.com**

BOTANISTS, ZOOLOGISTS, AND GEOLOGISTS.

BY

PROFESSOR P. MARTIN DUNCAN, F.R.S., F.L.S.,

VICE PRESIDENT OF THE GEOLOGICAL SOCIETY;
HONORARY FELLOW OF KING'S COLLEGE, LONDON.

PUBLISHED UNDER THE DIRECTION OF THE COMMITTEE
OF GENERAL LITERATURE AND EDUCATION APPOINTED BY THE
SOCIETY FOR PROMOTING CHRISTIAN KNOWLEDGE.

LONDON:
SOCIETY FOR PROMOTING CHRISTIAN KNOWLEDGE;
NORTHUMBERLAND AVENUE, CHARING CROSS;
43, QUEEN VICTORIA STREET; 48, PICCADILLY;
AND 135, NORTH STREET, BRIGHTON.
NEW YORK: E. & J. B. YOUNG AND CO.
1882.

PREFACE.

THERE is no little difficulty in obtaining correct and reliable life histories of most of the greatest naturalists. Many of the men to whom natural history science owes so much, lived extremely retired and uneventful lives; but a few, and as might have been anticipated, the reformers and epoch makers of their respective sciences, have had their most interesting biographies well written. Abstracts of these biographies form a large portion of this book; and the author desires to acknowledge the very copious extracts he has made, from sources which he has recognized in the proper places.

INTRODUCTION.

MOST of us, on leaving school or college, are anxious about our future career in the world, and concerning how we are to live, and what will be our occupations. Some young people who have finished their education, find themselves in comfortable circumstances, and are apt to look forward to an easy life; but the majority have a hard struggle before them, ere they can hope to be free from cares and to be successful. Yet it usually happens, that those youths starting with the very best prospects, do not live so happily, usefully, and well, as those who have to struggle with poverty, and who casting aside inglorious ease, labour on perseveringly. It is hard to believe, until the experience of years brings its very practical proofs that knowledge is more valuable than money; and therefore, how to get rich, is a predominant question with the majority of us. But the history of the struggles and successes of some of the men who have led most useful and beautiful lives, generally shows that industry, perseverance and contentment have served them better than pecuniary wealth, and that this has often been a source of trouble to them. There is no better incitement to a youth who has tried to do his best at school, and who is thinking about leading a useful, successful life, than to read the history of the lives of the men whose names are household words in the branches of knowledge he has learned.

At the present time, much care is taken to instruct young people about the nature and uses of plants, the characteristics of animals and the ancient history of the earth. Museums are readily visited, and little home collections of plants, insects, birds, and fossils are frequently easily made. Natural history, in all its branches, is easily studied; and as one becomes learned in it, the names of many men, constantly, come before the student as the masters of their respective subjects. Who has not heard of Linnæus, Cuvier, and

Lyell? If any young naturalist will read the history of the lives of these great men, he will find much that is very noble in them; he will see that they made their way through great difficulties, by constant and great intellectual labour, and that they led very good, and useful, and happy lives.

It may happen that any one just commencing to study nature, is anxious to make a great discovery and to obtain a great name. The history of the lives of these and other heroes of science, will prove to him, however, that discoveries are not sudden gains of knowledge, but are the result of very slow and gradual accumulation of facts. If he is a real student of nature, he will strive for truth and not for personal distinction; and the truth, brings a better reward than the fleeting praise of man. The true lasts. He will be able to glean that the special gifts of men, if properly fostered and cultivated, advance knowledge in particular directions, and that certain great changes and advances in the method of learning, have been due to men who have begun poor, have laboured hard, have been persecuted and vilified, and who have nevertheless lived happily in their consciences, and have often become great men in every respect.

INTRODUCTION.

The following chapters contain the history of the lives of some of the most interesting men of ancient and modern times—of men who are the heroes of Botany, Zoology, and Geology, and who have added methods of study and many facts to their sciences.

CONTENTS.

CHAPTER I.

THE INFANCY OF THE KNOWLEDGE OF THE SCIENCE OF PLANTS.

Old fancies and notions about plants—Aristoteles, the first botanist—Theophrastus—Plinius—Dioscorides—Their lives, labours, and troubles . . . . PAGE 1

CHAPTER II.

THE RISE OF THE SCIENCE OF PLANTS.

John Ray—Joseph de Tournefort—Their lives . . . 27

CHAPTER III.

THE LIFE OF LINNÆUS.

The science of plants begins to mature, to be reformed, and to be made more exact 52

CHAPTER IV.

THE LIFE OF LINNÆUS (*Continued*).

The publication and reception of the artificial system of classifying plants 81

CHAPTER V.

THE CONSOLIDATION OF THE SCIENCE OF PLANTS.

The life of De Candolle—The Natural System . . . 98

CHAPTER VI.

HEROES OF ZOOLOGY.

The nature of the science of zoology—Great zoologists usually botanists also—Aristoteles as a zoologist—Plinius—The long age of no progress—The life of Conrad Gesner—The zoology of Ray and Willughby—Swammerdam—Réaumur—The zoology of Linnæus 122

CHAPTER VII.

THE LIVES OF BUFFON, PENNANT, AND LAMARCK.

The popular writings of Buffon, and his life—Pennant's life—Lamarck and his life—The rise of popular natural history, and of exact descriptions and philosophical zoology . 144

CHAPTER VIII.

THE LIFE OF CUVIER.

The union of zoology and comparative anatomy, and the examination and study of fossil remains 178

CHAPTER IX.

HEROES OF GEOLOGY.

The rise of the science which treats of the ancient history of the earth—Students of the present changes which are the examples by which the past may be comprehended—The Greeks—The life of Pythagoras; a notice of the geology of Aristoteles—Strabo's life—The nature of fossils and the life of Steno 209

CHAPTER X.

THE LIFE OF HUTTON.

The rise of the modern school of geology—The continuity of the operations of nature and their sameness—The necessity of studying the existing state of things in order to comprehend the past—The denial of catastrophes—Hutton's theory of the earth the foundation of scientific geology . 221

CHAPTER XI.

THE LIFE OF WILLIAM SMITH.

The succession of the strata recognized—Strata known by their fossils, position, and mineral contents—England surveyed by Smith and made the type of the results of the succession of changes studied by geology 236

CHAPTER XII.

THE LIFE OF MURCHISON.

The older rocks of the globe studied accurately and surveyed —The general similarity of the succession of strata in many parts of the world decided—The geology of Wales and Scotland described—The commencement of accurate geological surveys 275

CHAPTER XIII.

THE LIFE OF LYELL.

The study of existing nature and its changes undertaken in order to comprehend the past changes during geological ages—The uniformity of natural operations under law—Catastrophes abolished—The succession of life on the globe, and that of the tertiary ages explained—The antiquity of man and of the great ice age established . 307

HEROES OF SCIENCE.

CHAPTER I.

THE INFANCY OF THE KNOWLEDGE OF THE SCIENCE OF PLANTS.

Old fancies and notions about plants—Aristoteles, the first botanist
—Theophrastus—Plinius—Dioscorides—Their lives, labours,
and troubles.

EVERYBODY likes to gather flowers for the sake of their beauty and scent, and most young people ask the names and the uses of the plants which grow them. These appear to have been the questions that the earliest races of men sought to answer for themselves. They gave plants names, and ascribed some truthful and a great many very curious and false properties to them. Many of the first races of men lived on fruits, vegetables, and roots, and it became important to know good and nourishing plants from those which were poisonous. The ablest men of the tribes, probably, studied the names which had been given by custom to many plants; and the healing power of some plants, and the poisonous nature of others began to be known; the good and ill-disposed amongst men endeavoured to learn all about them. Thus the first steps in the science of plants were to name them, and to ascribe properties to them. It has often been noticed that there is some resemblance between the history of the progress of a science, during all the ages of civilization, and that of the rise and progress of one in the child, youth, and man. The child receives everything that it is told, as a truth, and loves the wonderful; the youth likes to hear of mysteries, and his emotions and poetic feeling lead him to desire general truths; and the man criticizes what he has been told, tries to learn for himself, and longs for exact knowledge and the absolute truth. So in the early days of civilization, men believed in everything that was told them, and ascribed wonderful properties to the nature around them which they saw was so beautiful and yet often so terrible. As the world got older, curious legends were associated with truths and falsities; and with the general diffusion of learning, and the careful exercise of the reasoning powers, knowledge became more exact and useful, and was followed for truth's sake.

All branches of knowledge relating to nature passed through many stages, and were influenced by the prevailing habits and methods of thought of the age. The wonderful, the mysterious, the marvellous, the union of poetry with true and false religion, the struggle between the desire for truth and fear of the persecution of the ignorant, and the victory of cultivated observation and reason, all followed, in order, during the history of the progress of every science. A great writer states that it cannot then surprise us that the earliest lore concerning plants, which we discover in the records of the past, consists of mythological legends, marvellous relations, and extraordinary medicinal qualities. To the lively fancy of the Greeks, the narcissus, which bends its head over the stream, was originally a youth who, in such an attitude, became enamoured of his own beauty. The hyacinth, on whose flower certain markings are to be traced resembling the Greek expression of grief (AIAI), recorded the sorrow of the god Apollo for the death of his favourite Hyacinthus. The beautiful lotus of India, which floats with its splendid flower on the surface of the water, is the chosen seat of the goddess Lackshmi, the daughter of Ocean. In Egypt, the god Osiris swam on a lotus leaf, and the lotus-eaters of Homer lost their love of home immediately.

These legends and odd fancies, although believed in by the populace of the Eastern nations until a late period in history, were of great antiquity; and under different names of gods and plants, heroes and flowers had been handed down from the dawn of civilization. Yet this was not all the knowledge about plants in those early years. The more thoughtful amongst men began to recognize plants by name and to study their uses. Some men were hunters and shepherds, but with them were those who, with gentler spirit, tilled the ground and stored the fruits of the earth. What these were, can be learned from the pictures in Egyptian paintings. The corn of Egypt was wheat and barley, and it is interesting to know that the wheat was of a kind that must have been produced by skilled cultivation.

The vine comes early into notice in the Bible, and it had been studied, for wine was made of its fruit. Solomon loved nature, because it brought him into the presence of truth and beauty, and he " spoke of trees from the cedar tree that is in Lebanon even unto the hyssop that springeth out of the wall." This was part of his wisdom. And the great traveller, Herodotus, shows us that a taste for natural history had, in his time, found a place in the mind of the Greeks—a great race who followed after the first child-like nature-studies of the Chaldeans, Assyrians, and Babylonians had merged into real knowledge. In speaking of the luxuriant vegetation of the plains of Babylon—now dreary wastes—he is so far from desiring to astonish merely, that he says "the blades of wheat and barley are full four fingers wide; but as to the size of the trees which grow from millet and sesame, though I could mention it I will not, knowing well that those who have not been in that country will hardly believe what I have said already." It is clear that when the Greeks were in the child-like stage of plant lore, the older races had passed it, and were successful cultivators of plants that had required much study to turn to use. But the Greeks soon made amends, and the teacher of Alexander the Great, Aristoteles, tried to arrange plants, and to classify them according to their peculiarities. Plants and herbs had been long used as medicine, and the poisonous properties of aconite had been employed to destroy one of the noblest men of old, before this time, so that this celebrated naturalist had the knowledge, which had been accumulating for centuries, to put in order and to arrange.

Aristoteles was born at Stageira, in the year 384 B.C., and it is interesting to note that his wonderful love of nature was fostered by, and, indeed, probably arose from the profession of his father. His father was the physician and friend of Amyntas, King of Macedonia, and his mother was a descendant of the great physician Æsculapius. The young Aristoteles lost both his parents at an early period of his life, but the son of Amyntas, called Philip, was his friend, and kind people brought the boy up. We know nothing of the boy's habits or method of life; but it can be readily understood by those who read these lives, and have had a love of nature, before the experience of such a calamity as the loss of parents, that many an hour of sorrow was shortened and solaced by studying the graceful and blooming plants and the movements and habits of animals.

Certain it is that the boy loved study, and it soon became evident that his loss was compensated, as it is very often in such cases, by a spirit of self-reliance. In his eighteenth year he went to Athens to study the healing art. When Aristoteles was about twenty-one years of age, the philosopher Plato returned from Sicily, and the young man then seems to have cared more for the study of the sciences which were requisite for a polished physician, than for the art of healing. He made his first self-sacrifice, as many a man has done since; he gave up the uncertainties of the art of curing diseases, and learned natural history and philosophy. His eagerness for knowledge and his extraordinary acuteness and sagacity doubtless attracted Plato's notice, who soon called him "the intellect of the school," and said his house was "the house of the reader." As Aristoteles grew up, his early training and his love of the truth seen in nature, began to separate him from the common run of men, and his self-reliance began to make him an antagonist to the teachings even of the great Plato. But this opposition was not that of a vain and conceited young man. Plato had noticed his ability, and he was really a man of mark, whose opinions were valuable. Aristoteles studied facts, and knew many truths about natural history, but his wonderful master cared more for ideas. Such men must always clash, and Aristoteles writes in one of his books about his opposition to the philosophy of Plato, that it is painful to refute the doctrine of ideas, as it has been introduced by persons who were his friends; "nevertheless it is a duty to disregard such private feelings, for both philosophers and truth are dear to me, but it is right to give the preference to truth." Truth! what is truth? said Pilate, and turned from the true. The Creator's light, seen with our longing eyes, precious beyond conception, the sweetest solace of intellect; what is, what was—yet not to be defined by finite man. The very root of science, it is that which we are to hold in our consciences against all opposition. Appreciated by the savage, dear to pagan, the pride of the Christian, the giver of confidence amongst all men. Hard to get at, yet it is at the foundation of all those branches of knowledge which relate to the study of the Creation. Aristoteles studied natural history, that is, the plants and animals which came before him, especially. He recorded their description, noted their reproduction, and tried to make out their resemblances. He noticed the growth of things, and the decay of the surface of the earth, and having the facts and truths before him, he argued upon them. His master, Plato, was not a naturalist, but accepting the truths handed down to him by those who were observers of nature, he generalized about them, and got ideas by thinking out the bearings of the truths. He loved the ideal, and wrote, "Behold this world! You will find that its efficient cause is God, by whom it was brought into being; its moving cause, the goodness of the

Creator." He could no more occupy time by studying the structure of the flowers, plants, and sea-shells, than Aristoteles could in imagining or speculating on the causes of things. Both desired the truth, and tried to get it in different manners; but as at the present day there are moral philosophers and naturalists with totally different kinds of mind and habits of thought, so in those old days the master and pupil never worked together. The master gave way to his grand imagination, and the pupil was strictly a matter-of-fact man.

Aristoteles remained at Athens until he was thirty-seven years of age, when the death of Plato, in 347 B.C., happened. Before that time, however, he had become a man of note, and the Athenians sent him on an embassy to his friend and former patron, Philip of Macedon. It appears that he was able to serve his adopted country; but he made a mistake which all naturalists should avoid—he became a politician. His position at Athens became uncomfortable, and he left the city after the death of Plato, and, accompanied by a fellow-disciple of the great teacher, went into Asia Minor. They were invited by the Prince of Atarneus, named Hermeias, who had received lessons from Aristoteles. This man was once the slave of a banker, and when at Athens received a liberal education. Returning to his native country, he fought for Eubulus, the King of Atarneus, successfully against the Persians. On the death of Eubulus he was raised to the throne, and gladly welcomed one of the men who had given him knowledge, and, therefore, power. The romance of Aristoteles' life followed quickly, for, unfortunately, Hermeias was captured by the Persians under a Greek general, after Aristoteles had been three years with him. He was put to death, and Aristoteles fled to Mitylene, the chief city of the neighbouring island of Lesbos. Hermeias had a sister, Pythias, and Aristoteles, knowing her excellent character and disposition, and being aware of the sad fate which she would suffer, were she to fall into the hands of the Persians, married her, and she accompanied him in his flight. She made him an excellent wife, and Aristoteles had always a fervent and sincere affection for the patriotic and philosophical prince his friend.

After two years' residence in Mitylene, Aristoteles was invited by Philip to return to Macedonia, to superintend the education of his son Alexander, the future Alexander the Great, then fourteen years old. He was with this very able prince during about four years, and instructed him in morality, politics, and natural history. It was a strange position for a student of nature to occupy, and that he did his duty to his pupil is evident. It is the universal opinion that much that was admirable in the character of Alexander the Great was due to the influence of Aristoteles. The great conqueror was fond of literature, delighted in physical and even medical pursuits, sought the intimacy of men who thought, rather than that of men who had no other recommendation than titles and riches, and was devoted to the study of nature. These were the fruits of Aristoteles' instruction, and it must be remembered that Alexander differed entirely in his conduct from the brutal conquerors who have been, over and over again, the scourge and curse of mankind.

Aristoteles lost his wife during this time, and she left him an only daughter. Then Philip was assassinated, and his son reigned at Macedon for two years, and then began his great expedition into Asia. Aristoteles accompanied his pupil to Athens, and parted with him never to see him again, but still to influence him for years. Unfortunately, however, Aristoteles recommended a relation, named Callisthenes, to the young king, and it was the cause of a rupture of friendship in years to come. Left to himself, our hero resolved to open a school for the benefit of the Athenian youth, and to teach good learning in philosophy and nature. He chose a house near a temple of Apollo Lyceius, which was called the "Lyceum," and attached to it was a garden with walks, where the instruction was given. The Greek word for the walks was *peripatua*, and the school was called that of the peripatetics. His habit was to give one lecture in the early part of the day, on the more difficult parts of his teaching, to his more advanced students; and this was called the morning walk, and lasted till the hour when people dressed and anointed themselves. Another lecture, called the evening walk, was on more popular subjects, and to a larger and less select class. It was during these thirteen years of teaching that Aristoteles composed and completed the greater part of his works which have descended to our days. Amongst them are treatises on natural history, the result of his own observations and of the carefully selected works of others.

His great pupil never forgot his master during his victorious career, and Alexander is said to have sent Aristoteles the enormous sum of eight hundred talents to prosecute his studies in natural history. He, moreover, ordered several thousands of persons over the whole of Greece and Asia, who lived by hunting, bird-catching, and fishing, or who had the care of parks, herds, hives, stews, and aviaries, to furnish Aristoteles with materials for a work on animals. Two volumes on plants were written by Aristoteles, but they are lost to us; and he influenced the botanists of his day by his great exactitude of description and observation.

Aristoteles' writings and teaching embraced a great variety of subjects, and they were so genuine that he became the leader of one of the principal schools of Greece; and his method of study and many of his facts and ideas have influenced mankind down to the present day. His works were much studied during the Middle Ages, and although his books on botany have been lost, still he influenced the study of botany through his pupil, Theophrastus, who became the great light of after years.

There is one point about Aristoteles' character which everybody must admire, and it was the gratitude he felt for the good friends of his youth and of the days of struggling upwards in his career. It has been noticed that he was brought up by kind people. They were not relations, but probably were appointed his guardians by his father. They were Proxenus and his wife, citizens of Atarneus, who had left that city and had been long resident in Stageira. Not only were they the good friends of the boy, but they evidently brought him in contact with Hermeias, who subsequently became the prince of the place and Aristoteles' fast friend and brother-in-law. Aristoteles testified his gratitude to his friends by directing in his will that statues of them, as well as of his parents, should be set up at his expense. He likewise educated their son, Nicanor, to whom he gave his daughter in marriage. Whilst growing old he wrote a beautiful poem, which is still to be read, praising the virtues of his friend and patron, Hermeias.

But success in life is sure to produce envy and hostility, and Aristoteles was no exception to this rule. A charge was made against him of impiety, and that he had made a god of his friend Hermeias. Such charges were not uncommon in those days. Socrates, one of the greatest and purest of men, had been accused of impiety a few years before, and that teacher of the immortality of the soul, and the master and friend of Plato, had been condemned and poisoned. The charges were absurd enough, but the judges were ignorant, and sunk in paganism, and almost invariably took the side of the accuser. Indeed, all through the history of the progress of the rise of civilization there were men who teaching a false religion, accused the bright lights of genius, science, and wit, of irreligion. The false priest and the fighting class, with rare exceptions, have always persecuted the leaders in science, and have antagonized progress, except in their own interests.

When the charge was made against Aristoteles, Alexander the Great was dead, and the great teacher, knowing full well what would be the result of the trial, quitted Athens and took refuge in Chalcis, in Eubœa, saying that he wished to prevent the Athenians *twice running against philosophy*, alluding to the judicial murder of Socrates.

But Aristoteles' work was nearly ended, and the slightly made, delicate, and sensitive man sank during the first year of his exile, in the sixty-third year of his age.

A great writer on moral philosophy, the man whose career has just been noticed will always remain a master in natural history subjects also. He was really a greater student of animal life than of plants; but it appears that his method of study of botany, and much of his knowledge, have descended to us, in consequence of his careful teaching, through his pupil Theophrastus. A great writer remarks that "everywhere Aristoteles observes *the facts* with attention; he compares them with sagacity, and endeavours to rise to the qualities they have in common." He found the study of plants in its very infancy and loaded with child-like and wonderful stories, and he rejected the nonsense and studied what was to be observed by any one in nature. In fact, he took the first step which a well-educated boy of the present century does in trying to learn nature unaided. He observed as correctly as possible, took notes of his observations, compared the observations made on one plant with those recorded about another, and tried to explain or discover the things which were common to both. It must not be imagined that the botanical work of Aristoteles exists as part of the systems of botany of the present day; but he clearly gave the method of how to study, by insisting on the superior value of observed facts, over notions and preconceived ideas about things. The childhood of the science passed with him.

The name of Theophrastus has been noticed as that of the pupil of Aristoteles, and it is one which will always be mentioned with respect by students of natural history. He was born at Eresus, on the island of Lesbos; but the date of his birth is uncertain; moreover, nothing is known of his early youth, except that his name was Tyrtamus. His early education must have been good, and he was sent to study at Athens by his father, and to be a pupil of Plato. Becoming a friend of Aristoteles, this great man, charmed with the abilities, and especially with the beautiful pronunciation and oratory of the youth, gave him the name of Theophrastus, or one who speaks divinely. Theophrastus studied with Plato, and on the death of his master, left the academy and mixed with the turbulent politics of the day, but in a truly patriotic spirit. He was absent from Athens for many years, and the historian Plutarch writes that Theophrastus delivered his country twice from the oppression of tyrants. One of the defeated at the battle of Chæronæa, Theophrastus returned to Athens, gave up the military life, and became the favourite pupil of Aristoteles in the Lyceum.

Theophrastus became an earnest student of Aristoteles' teaching, and his singular grace of expression and knowledge of his mother tongue soon made him a prominent philosopher.

When Aristoteles retired, his pupil became his successor; and as he combined the knowledge of that teacher with the eloquence of Plato, his success was extraordinary. The number of his pupils, on one occasion, is said to have amounted to two thousand who flocked around him from all parts of Greece. He soon began to feel the effects of his well-deserved and useful success upon the envious minds of the men who had caused the retirement of Aristoteles. And this envy and malice were rendered all the more intense because, having been a gallant soldier, and being a great teacher of advanced knowledge, Theophrastus became an authority on all intellectual subjects. A man was put forward by a party in the State, to bring the same charge of impiety against Theophrastus which had succeeded in the instances of Socrates and Aristoteles. But Theophrastus pleaded his own cause before the Areopagus with such convincing eloquence that he was pronounced innocent. On the other hand, his accuser would have fallen a victim to the false charge he had brought, had not his noble-minded antagonist pleaded for his pardon.

After this event the teacher pursued his course of public teaching and private research without any molestation for years. His school increased in reputation, and the most distinguished scholars of the day were members of it. Demetrius Phalereus, ruler of the State, was one of the students in his youth, and he protected Theophrastus and patronized him in every way. Botany was not the strongest subject of this great man, and probably what he knew about it was largely derived from the teaching of Aristoteles; but evidently his work on plants was one of the earliest that was written with anything like scientific precision. Nevertheless, Theophrastus added much original matter, for he had a botanic garden, and he collected plants during his travels in Greece. His military friends kept him supplied with specimens of Asiatic, Egyptian, and Arabian plants, and with descriptions of their natures and peculiarities, some of which were true and others quite imaginary. What was true and what was not true was frequently a puzzle to this philosopher, as it is to modern naturalists. He wrote, " The drug sellers and root cutters tell us some things which may be true, but other things which are merely solemn quackery. Thus they direct us to gather some plants, standing from the wind and with our bodies anointed; some by night, some by day, some before the sun falls on them. So far there may be something in their rules; but others are too fantastical and far-fetched. It is, perhaps, not absurd to use a prayer in plucking a plant; but they go further than this. We are to draw a sword three times round the mandragora, and to cut it looking to the west; again, to dance round it, and to use obscene language, as those who sow cumin should utter blasphemies. Again, we are to draw a line round the black hellebore, standing to the east, and praying; and to avoid an eagle either on the right or on the left; for they say if an eagle be near, the cutter will die in a year."

This was the nonsense, out of which Theophrastus had to extricate the true wisdom of plants, and he tried to put aside fancies, legends, and the opinions of men, and to puzzle out the meaning of the similarities and differences of plants, by first of all learning and describing their construction, habits, methods of growth, and increase.

Only a fragment of the last of ten books on plants written by Theophrastus has come down to us. The writings made such an impression on the students that their general bearing has been transmitted, and the main points are as follows. Theophrastus classified plants by the manner in which they were reproduced, the localities where they were found, their size, as trees or shrubs or herbs, and according to their uses, as furnishing juices, pot-herbs, and seeds that may be eaten. The first book treated of the parts of the plant—the root, stem, leaves, flower, and seed, and the second of the manner in which plants seed, and the proper times for sowing seeds, and how to sow. In this part he mentions that some plants, evidently of the same kind, have seed and others not, or that there are different sexes in plants, the female bearing the seed. That he was a practical observer is proved by his writings on the method of the reproduction in the great palm trees, which are such striking features in the East. Moreover, he studied the way in which figs grew and the seed became fertile, and he compared the reproduction of the fig with that of the palm tree. The third, fourth, and fifth books are devoted to a consideration of trees, their various kinds, the places they come from, and the economical uses to which they may be applied. The sixth book treats of winter shrubs and spring plants; the seventh of pot-herbs; the eighth of plants yielding seeds used for food; and the ninth of those plants that yield useful juices, gums, resins, and other exudations. The love of the marvellous, however, creeps in here and there, and amongst good facts there are very considerable "tough yarns;" but these come from the old soldiers of Alexander the Great.

There is one thing most interesting in the works of this man, and it is the desire he had to make his knowledge useful to mankind. This is especially noticed in another work on the causes of plants, of which six parts remain to the present day. It is really a work on gardening and farming, with a good deal of pure and applied knowledge on botany. It is not everybody, nowadays, that can combine what is scientific, that is to say, exact knowledge, with useful and applied knowledge. Too frequently the scientific botanist does not teach gardening or farming; and certainly, as a rule, the writers on these last subjects are not scientific botanists, and, indeed, they are often of a very different kind of mind. It has been said of the works of Theophrastus that there is much valuable matter in them that deserves the attention of the botanist, and that a very little knowledge of botany will enable the reader to separate the chaff from the wheat.

So noted was the learning of this great man on other subjects, that his good work on plants remained the text-book of centuries; and, in fact, little or no satisfactory knowledge about plants, beyond that given to us by Aristoteles and Theophrastus, was discovered for many centuries.

The fall of Demetrius from power removed the protector of Theophrastus, and the ignorant anti-educationalist party of the day revived their persecutions. In the year 305 B.C. a political noodle managed to frame a law, and to get it passed by the ruling body of the day, which forbade all philosophers under pain of death to give any public instruction without permission of the State.

This curious law was passed in order to prevent the education of the people being advanced, and the result was that Theophrastus and several other teachers left Athens. Good sense, however, seems to have prevailed over ignorance and hostility to learning, and the law was abolished in the following year. Moreover, the proposer of it was fined the great sum of five talents for his folly. Then Theophrastus returned to Athens, and taught there until he died. The whole population followed his body to the grave.

It is a remarkable fact that the writings of Aristoteles and Theophrastus on plants, were not improved upon for many hundreds of years. They were both observers of nature, and their works contained all the knowledge on the subject, of their time. When the Romans obtained the supremacy in Europe, and had possessions in Asia and in Africa, men were not found amongst them who could add to the knowledge of the Greeks about plants; so the books of the two great men who were the fathers of botany were simply copied by their successors, or criticized, and doubtful novelties were added.

There were many Roman writers on agriculture, but few wrote on the nature and structure of plants, and amongst them the most celebrated was Caius Plinius Secundus, commonly called Pliny the Elder.

Where this great man was born is not known, but possibly it was at Como. He was of noble family, entered the army, and became a distinguished soldier. He was appointed Augur at Rome, and subsequently had supreme power in Spain. These were not apparently the positions which were likely to stimulate a young man of wealth to study natural history, and certainly, in later days, the military man and active politician have not proved, as a rule, enthusiastic students of plants and animals. Want of time and inclination are, of course, the usual excuses of such men, and the love of luxury and of intellectual idleness might be added also. Nevertheless there is an instance in the case of the elder Plinius, where a man, greatly and importantly occupied, spent much time in studying nature, in compiling the observations made by his predecessors, and in writing books which have given him a fame which will last with the world. In summer he began his work as soon as it was light; in winter, generally at one in the morning— never later than two, and sometimes earlier. No man, writes his nephew, spent less time in bed, and sometimes he would, without retiring from his books, indulge in a short sleep, and then pursue his studies. Before daybreak he went to the Emperor Vespasian, who chose to transact business at that hour, and when the Emperor had finished, Plinius returned to his studies. After a slender repast at noon, he would in the summer recline in the sun, and during the time some book was read to him, and he made extracts from the author. He used to say that "no book was so bad but something might be learned from it." After this he had a cold bath and took refreshment and rest. Thus reinvigorated, he resumed his studies until supper, when a book was read to him, and he made remarks on it. This, of course, must have been an occasional method of passing the day, for no man could live without some hours of exercise and sleep. Probably he retired to sleep at eight under these circumstances, and had a good sleep in the hot hours of the day. When in the country all his time was devoted to study, except when he slept and bathed. He is said to have used a carriage instead of walking, and, unfortunately, but naturally, he got weak lungs and became corpulent.

Plinius laboured for many years at natural history and the other sciences, and he was a most diligent collector of information. A warrior and a statesman, yet he contrived to write a vast number of works, his books on natural history alone amounting to twenty-seven volumes. He appears to have known all that it was possible to know at his age of the world, and yet there was no great amount of new work put into his books. It has been very properly said that the loftiness of his ideas and the nobleness of his style enhance still more his profound learning. Naturally, as he copied much from other writers, and especially, in one part of botany which relates to medicine, from an author named Dioscorides, he could not examine into the truth of every statement which had been made. Hence Plinius retailed some curious stories now and then, which are more amusing than true; but, on the whole, he established, on solid grounds, the learning of his own and previous ages.

This active-minded man, who lived in luxury and had great responsibilities, is an example to many of the same class who do not care to enjoy the study of the beautiful nature around them. He lost his life whilst endeavouring to sustain the courage of his friends, during the great eruption of Vesuvius, when the cities of Pompeii and Herculaneum were destroyed. He was on shore at the time, and probably was suffocated by noxious fumes.

The name of Dioscorides has been mentioned as that of an author known to Plinius; he was born in Cilicia, at Anazarbus, and flourished during the reign of the Emperor Nero. Nothing is known about his early life, but it appears that he was a soldier, and possibly connected with the surgical and medical art in the army. Certain it is that he travelled over many countries—Greece, Italy, Gaul, and Asia Minor—gathering plants and studying, not so much their structures and mutual resemblances and differences, as their medical or healing powers. He obtained plants from travellers in India, and learned the merits of herbs and drugs from many nations. He wrote on the substances used in medicine in a Materia Medica, and named and briefly described between five and six hundred medicinal plants. Unfortunately Dioscorides wrote in a careless manner, and there is much nonsense mixed up with truth in his writings.

But he was of use; he was not merely a student of the beauties of nature, but of the value of certain plants to man in his pain and trouble, and he founded the science of medical botany.

Aristoteles, Theophrastus, Plinius, and Dioscorides are the men of mark who raised botany and plant-learning out of their infancy and gave them a youthful vigour. They placed the method of learning, on its right basis. Instead of imagining what was true, and then collecting and studying plants to prove the correctness of the imagined notion, they began in the opposite direction. They strove to learn and discover facts,—truths, and then reasoned upon them. Ignorant people, and those men who have the minds of children, always like their opinions and ideas better than facts, and especially if the facts will not fit in with their notions. Such people do not know how hard it is to find out the truth in nature, how difficult it is for finite man to comprehend infinite wisdom. This was as true formerly as it is now, and hence the method of learning, taught by the earlier of those great men, was opposed to the understandings of the majority of their fellow men. They troubled the complacent ignorance of the day, and were therefore persecuted. Like brave men, they did not care for persecution, knowing that they did not deserve the wicked charges brought against them; they persevered, and not only enjoyed life much more than their opponents, but led good and useful lives.

The works of these men were studied by all the

learned, during fifteen hundred years and more; they were the text-books of science during what are called the dark or middle ages, and although now out of date, they were the good seeds of knowledge, sown in difficulty, in those early days.

Aristoteles, Theophrastus, and Plinius were not only botanists, but naturalists in every sense, and the first named is especially celebrated as a student of and writer upon animals; he was a great zoologist. Theophrastus knew much about geology, and so did Plinius.

These men, then, brought the science of botany out of its childhood, and saw it partly on its way through its youth; they had removed it beyond the fanciful ideas and strange notions of the earliest writers on the subject, and had begun to classify plants, and to study the relations of plants to surrounding nature, and to the wants of man. Chemistry and the use of the microscope were unknown, and therefore progress in the necessary direction could not be made at that time of the world.

It must be remembered that botany does not consist in collecting, drying, and drawing plants alone, but it relates to everything about the vegetable kingdom of nature. The growth of the plant from the seed; how it lives, breathes, and its sap circulates; how starch, and sugar, and other products are formed—have to be considered. The manner of unfolding of the flower, the anatomy of its fruits, and of the leaves and stems and root, and the method by which the kind reproduces, and the decay of the plant have to be studied. Then the uses of plants, medicinal and as food, have to be treated. How they can be best grown, and how plants are distributed over the land at different heights, form other subjects; and the arrangement of plants in a classification founded on the similarity of their most important anatomical structures, and constituting what is termed a natural system, is one of the most necessary studies.

CHAPTER II.

THE RISE OF THE SCIENCE OF PLANTS.

John Ray—Joseph de Tournefort—Their lives.

THE world went to sleep for many centuries, so far as natural history and many other things are concerned, after the time of Pliny, and sixteen hundred years elapsed before any advance was made in botanical knowledge. This was the age when the only light on the earth was struggling Christianity, and it was shaded by superstition and violence. At last men began to learn Greek again, and to read the ancient authors carefully, so that nature began to be studied. A few foreign botanists began to attempt to add to the knowledge the ancients had given them, and to classify plants.

But the first man who made a real advance, and whose work has influenced the study of plant life down to the present day, was an Englishman, who was bred in comparative poverty, suffered persecution, and lived a beautiful life.

The name of this distinguished man was John Ray, and he was the son of Roger Ray and Elizabeth his wife, being born in 1628. His father was a blacksmith, of Black Notley, near Braintree, in Essex, and the boy was sent to school at the Grammar School at Braintree. There he found the kindness of Mr. Love, the master, in teaching him, a set-off against the general want of education in the establishment; and he had reason to be thankful, for before he was sixteen years of age he was sent, from the school, to Cambridge. He entered at St. Catherine's Hall, under the tutorship of Mr. Duckfield. But the youth did not like the Hall; he wished to study, and the inmates, he said, chiefly addicted themselves to disputations; so he went to Trinity, where he found the politer arts and sciences were principally minded and cultivated. Ray worked hard, and had an excellent tutor, who was a great Greek scholar, and soon made up for the defective teaching he had had at Braintree. He acquired much Latin and Greek, and some Hebrew, and it soon became evident that the youth could speak well and fluently. His leisure was that of a student; he loved to observe nature, to study the little gems of the garden and country, and all these things brought him speedily before the notice of the authorities of the College. When he had been there three years, he was elected a Minor Fellow, together with his great friend Isaac Barrow, who had been a Charterhouse boy, and subsequently a scholar at Felsted, an Essex school.

They were the favourite pupils of their master. Ray took his degree of Bachelor of Arts, and then that of Master of Arts, becoming then a Major Fellow. In 1651 he was chosen the Greek Lecturer to the College; two years afterwards Mathematical Lecturer, and in 1655 Humanity Reader. Then he was made Junior Dean and College Steward, and he became the tutor to many men of subsequent worth, especially to Mr. Francis Willughby, of Middleton Hall, in Warwickshire. During these years Ray wandered over the country collecting and studying plants. He wrote the story of his journeys in and about England, calling them "Itineraries." His first journey was in 1658, and he rode from Cambridge to Northampton; he passed by Higham Ferrers and saw the outside of a great stone building called a college, and he wrote that Northampton was indifferently handsome, the houses being built of timber, notwithstanding the plenty of stone dug in that county. He saw in a Mr. Bowker's garden "divers physical plants," and he noticed the luxuriance of the lupinus there. Then he went to Warwick by Daventry, and saw Holdenby House. At Shuckborough he did not see the star-stones he had heard of. He visited Warwick, but cared more for Guy's Cliff than for the rib of the dun cow and Guy's sword; and then he went into Derbyshire, and investigated the Pool's-hole, near Buxton, and noticed the wild flowers of the hills. Travelling on to North Wales, he visited the brine-pits of Northwych, and at Chester he noticed the red stone of the cathedral, which he considered had little beauty within or without. He visited Swindon, and got home by Shrewsbury and Gloucester. This was a journey done in the old-fashioned manner, on horseback. It opened Ray's eyes to the immense amount of nonsense that was talked about nature, and especially about any unusual natural phenomenon. He seems especially to have visited the wells and springs, and he expressed his doubts of the wonderful cures, attributing his want of belief to his scientific frame of mind.

At this period, it was usual for young men of ability and learning, though not in orders, to deliver sermons and common-place readings, as they were called, not only in the chapels or halls of their own colleges, but even before the University body at St. Mary's church. In these Ray eminently distinguished himself. He was among the first who ventured to lead the attention of his hearers from the unprofitable subtleties of scholastic divinity and the trammels of the old Greek philosophy to an observation of nature and a practical investigation of truth. The rudiments of many of his subsequent writings originated in these juvenile essays, particularly his celebrated book on the "Wisdom of God manifested in the Works of the Creation," known all over the world by its numerous editions and translations, and universally admired for its rational piety, sound philosophy, and solid instruction. This book is the basis of the labours of all those divines who have made the book of nature a commentary on the book of revelation, a confirmation of truths which nature has not authority of herself to establish. In it the author inculcates the doctrine of a constantly superintending Providence, as well as the advantage, and even the duty, of contemplating the works of God. "This," he says, "is part of the business of a Sabbath-day, as it will be, probably, of our employment through that eternal rest of which the Sabbath is a type." Archbishop Tenison is recorded to have told Dr. Derham that "Mr. Ray was much celebrated in his time at Cambridge for preaching solid and useful divinity, instead of that enthusiastic stuff which the sermons of that time were generally filled with." It would be refreshing to hear a Ray in the nineteenth century. Two of his funeral discourses are mentioned with particular approbation; one, on the death of Dr. Arrowsmith, master of his college; the other, on that of one of his most intimate and beloved colleagues, Mr. John Nid, likewise a Senior Fellow of Trinity, who had a great share in Ray's first botanical publication, the "Catalogus Plantarum circa Cantabrigiam nascentium," printed in 1660 (a catalogue of plants growing around Cambridge). Before this little volume appeared, its author had visited various parts of England and Wales for the purpose of investigating their native plants, as he did several times afterwards. Nor were his observations confined to natural history, but extended to local and general history, antiquities, the arts, and all kinds of useful knowledge. Ray's first botanical tour occupied nearly six weeks, from August 9th to September 18th, 1658. On the 23rd of December, 1660, he was ordained both deacon and priest at the same time by Dr. Sanderson, then Bishop of Lincoln. In 1661 he travelled with Mr. Willughby into Scotland, returning by Cumberland and Westmoreland; and the following year, with the same companion, he accomplished a more particular investigation of Wales. How critically he studied the botany of the countries he visited, is evident from the different editions of his works called "A Catalogue of British Plants," and "A Methodical Synopsis of British Wild Plants." In fact, Ray felt the necessity of being able to recognize plants by their accurate descriptions, and saw that classification was the alphabet of the science.

All this time Mr. Ray continued to enjoy his fellowship and to cultivate his Cambridge connections; but in September, 1662, his tranquillity was disturbed by the too famous Bartholomew Act, by which two thousand conscientious divines were turned out of their livings, and many fellows of colleges deprived of their maintenance and means of literary improvement. Among the latter was the subject of our memoir, with thirteen honest men at Cambridge besides, of whose names he has left us a list. One of them, Dr. Dillingham, was master of Emanuel College; but Ray was the only person of his own college who suffered this deprivation. One of Ray's biographers writes:—"The reader must not suppose that he, or perhaps any other person in this illustrious catalogue, was in the least degree deficient in attachment to the doctrine or discipline of the Church of England, or that they had taken the oath, called the Solemn League and Covenant, which Ray certainly had neither taken nor even approved. They were required to swear to the infamous proposition that the said oath was not binding to those who had taken it, and on this ground they conscientiously gave up their preferment." It is curious to read the apology made for Ray, to Dr. Derham on this subject, by a Mr. Brokesby, "that he was at that time absent from his college, where he might have met with satisfaction to his scruples, and was among some zealous nonconformists who too much influenced him by the addition of new scruples. And we may also ascribe somewhat to the prejudice of education in unhappy times." By this it appears that the "scruples" of nonconformists were most favourable to the sanctity of an oath, and that the "unhappy times" alluded to were more advantageous to principle than the golden days of Charles II., whose ministers doubtless valued the obedience far more than the honesty of any man; nor was this taste by any means peculiar to them or their profligate master.

Mr. Ray (or, as he wrote his name for a while

about this period, Wray), having thus the world before him, made an arrangement with Mr. Willughby for a tour on the Continent; and in this plan two of his pupils were included, Mr. Nathaniel Bacon and Mr., afterwards Sir Philip, Skippon. They sailed for Calais in April, 1663, but being prevented by the state of political affairs from prosecuting their journey through France, they traversed the Low Countries and Germany, proceeding by Venice into Italy, most of whose cities they visited, either by sea or land, as well as Malta and Sicily; and returned by Switzerland, through France, into England in the spring of 1666.

Mr. Willughby, indeed, separated from the rest of the party at Montpellier, and visited Spain. An ample account of their observations was published by Ray in 1673, making a thick octavo volume. The travellers studied politics, literature, natural history, mechanics, and philosophy, as well as antiquities and other curiosities; but in the fine arts they assume no authority, nor display any considerable taste or knowledge. Mr. Willughby's account of Spain makes a part by itself, and a rich critical catalogue of such plants, not, for the most part, natives of England, as were observed in this tour, concludes the volume. There is no doubt that Ray has the credit of having discovered several species of plants in Switzerland not previously known to belong to that country. Ray passed the summer of 1666 partly at Black Notley, and partly in Sussex, studying chiefly the works of Hook,

Boyle, Sydenham, on fevers, and the "Philosophical Transactions," "making few discoveries," says he, "save of mine own errors." The following winter he was employed at Mr. Willughby's, in arranging that gentleman's museum of seeds, dried plants, birds, fishes, shells, and other objects of natural history and coins, and in forming tables of plants and animals for the use of Dr. Wilkins. He began to arrange a catalogue of the English native plants which he had gathered, rather for his own use than with any immediate view of publication at present. He wrote to Dr. Lister, "The world is glutted with bungling;" "I resolve never to put out anything which is not as perfect as is possible for me to make it. I wish you would take a little pains this summer about grasses, that so we might compare notes." The above resolution of our author is no doubt highly commendable, but the world has rather to lament that so many able men have formed the same determination, at least in natural science. If it were universally adhered to, scarcely any work would see the light, for few can be so sensible of the defects of any other person's attempt to illustrate the works of nature, as a man of tolerable judgment must be of his own. This is especially the case with those who, like Ray, direct their aspiring views towards system and philosophical theory. Happily he did not try this arduous path, till he had trained himself by wholesome practical discipline in observation and experience. His first botanical works assumed the humble form of alphabetical catalogues. His and Mr. Willughby's labours in the service of Bishop Wilkins were, indeed, of a systematical description, and accordingly the authors themselves were probably more dissatisfied than any other persons with their performance. They relaxed from these labours in a tour of practical observation through the west of England, as far as the Land's End, in the summer of 1667, and returning by London, Mr. Ray was solicited to become a Fellow of the Royal Society, into which learned body he was admitted November 7th. Being now requested by his friend Wilkins to translate his celebrated work, "An Essay towards a Real Character and a Philosophical Language," into Latin, he undertook, and by degrees accomplished, that arduous performance. The following summer was agreeably spent in visits to various literary friends, and in a a solitary journey to the north. His former companion, Willughby, being just married, stayed at home; but Ray joined him in September, 1668, and remained for most part of the ensuing winter and spring.

The seclusion and leisure of the country, with the converse and assistance of such a friend, were favourable to the prosecution of a new subject of inquiry, which now strongly attracted the attention of our great naturalist—the theory of vegetation. The first step of the two philosophers in this little-explored path was an examination of the motion of the sap in trees; and the result of their inquiries, communicated to the Royal Society, appeared soon after in the " Philosophical Transactions." Their experiments clearly prove the ascent of the sap through the woody part of the tree, which is easily detected by boring the trunks at different depths before their leaves are unfolded; and they observed, also, the mucilaginous nature of the flowing sap, "precipitating a kind of white coagulum or jelly, which," says Ray, in a note preserved by Derham, "may be well conceived to be the part, which every year, between bark and tree turns to wood, and of which the leaves and fruits are made. And it seems to precipitate more when the tree is just ready to put out leaves and begins to cease dropping, than at its first bleeding." The accuracy of the leading facts recorded by these ingenious men is confirmed by subsequent observers, who have further pursued the same subject, which is now sufficiently well understood. The sap originates in the liquid matters which are absorbed by the roots of plants; they enter the minute cells of the ends of the roots and permeate the cellular tissue. This sap ascends in the plant, assisted by the evaporation from the leaves. The sap ascends with considerable rapidity to the leaves, where it is subject to changes, the result of physiological action. It descends from the leaves, having had its chemical constitution altered, and is fit for the nutrition of the plant. The sap ascends through the cellular and woody tissue, especially in the layers of wood not more than two years old. The hard heartwood does not convey sap, but in some trees, like the poplar, sap moves in the very centre.

The elaborated sap returns from the leaves in a slow stream, through the delicate cellular structures of the bark, right down to the root, giving rise to the cambium layer, from the inner surface of which the annual layer of young wood is formed.

At this time Ray began to prepare for the press his "Collection of Proverbs," a curious book in its way, by which he is perhaps better known to the generality of his countrymen, than by any other of his literary labours.

The first edition was published in 1672, but the work was subsequently much enlarged, and the author may almost be said to have exhausted his subject. From its very nature, delicacy and refinement had often to be dispensed with, but this is evidently not the fault or the aim of the writer. His learning and critical acuteness diffuse light over the whole, and make us overlook the coarse vehicle of our instruction. The first edition of the "Catalogue of English Plants," already mentioned, came out in 1670, and the second in 1677. Their great author gave his work to the world with that diffidence for which he alone, perhaps, could perceive any just foundation. It was a wonderful book, considering that there was no recognized authority to help the author, who, seeing that there must be some real method in nature, strove to arrange or classify plants by the similarity or dissimilarity of those structures which were of the greatest importance. About this period the health of Mr. Ray seems to have been considerably impaired. He refused a tempting offer to travel again on the Continent, as tutor to three young noblemen; nor could the powerful attractions of Alpine botany, which was then to be studied, overcome that reluctance to leaving home, which arose from a feeble state of body. Indeed, this very reluctance or listlessness is accounted for by the turn which his disorder took, as it terminated in the jaundice. After this depressing complaint had left him, Ray resumed his botanical travels at home with fresh alacrity, visiting the rich stores of the north of England, with a companion named Thomas Willisel, whose name and discoveries he subsequently gratefully commemorated on many occasions. Nothing forms a more striking feature in Ray's character than the unreserved and abundant commendation which he always gave to his friends and fellow-labourers. Then unfortunately an event occurred which called forth his affectionate feelings. On the 3rd of July, 1672, Mr. Willughby was unexpectedly carried off by an acute disorder, in the thirty-seventh year of his age. The care of his two infant sons was confided by himself to Mr. Ray, who was also appointed one of his five executors, and to whom he left an annuity of sixty pounds for life. The eldest of these youths was created a baronet at the age of ten years, but died before he was twenty. Their sister, Cassandra, afterwards married the Duke of Chandos. Thomas, the younger son, was one of the ten peers created, all on the same day, by Queen Anne, and received the title of Lord Middleton. The care of his pupils, and of the literary concerns of their deceased parent, now interrupted Mr. Ray's botanizing excursions, and caused him also to decline the offer of Dr. Lister, then a physician at York, to settle under his roof. Bishop Wilkins did not long survive Mr. Willughby, and his death made another chasm in the scientific and social circle of our great natural philosopher, who felt these losses as deeply and tenderly as any man. He sought consolation in a domestic attachment, fixing his choice on a young woman of good parentage, whose name was Margaret Oakley, and who resided in the family at Middleton Hall. He was married at the parish church, June 5th, 1673, being then in the forty-fifth year of his age, and his bride about twenty. This lady took a share in the early education of his pupils, as far as concerned their reading English. She is said to have been recommended by her character, as well as by her person, to the regard of her husband. She bore him three daughters who, with their mother, survived him.

The first fruit of our author's leisure and retirement was a book on a new classification of plants, published in 1682. His principles of arrangement are chiefly derived from the fruit. The regularity and irregularity of flowers, which took the lead in the system of contemporary botanists, made no part of that of Ray. It is remarkable that he adopts the ancient primary division of plants into trees, shrubs, and herbs, and that he blamed Rivinus, one of his fellow-labourers, for abolishing it, though his own prefatory remarks tend to overset that principle, as a vulgar and casual one, unworthy of a philosopher. That his system was not merely a commodious artificial aid to practical botany, but a philosophical clue to a correct natural classification, he probably, like his fellow-labourers for many years in this department, believed, yet he was too modest and too learned to think he had brought the new and arduous design to perfection. For whatever he has incidentally or deliberately thrown out respecting the value of his labours, is often marked with more diffidence on the subject of classification than any other. The great service that Ray did to botany was the foreshadowing the so-called natural system of classification, which was to supersede the artificial system of Linnæus, which will be described in a future page. He first applied his system to practical use in a general "History of Plants," of which the first volume, a thick folio, was published in 1686, and the second in 1687. The third volume of the same work, which is supplementary, came out in 1704. This vast and critical compilation is still in use as a book of reference, being particularly valuable as an epitome of the contents of various rare and expensive works, which ordinary libraries cannot possess.

The description of species is faithful and instructive, the remarks original, bounded only by the whole circuit of the botanical learning of that day; nor are generic characters neglected, however vaguely they are assumed. Specific differences do not enter regularly into the author's plan, nor has he followed any uniform rules of nomenclature. So ample a transcript of the practical knowledge of such a botanist cannot but be a treasure; yet it is now much neglected, few persons being learned enough to use it with facility for want of figures and a popular nomenclature; and those who are, seldom requiring its assistance.

But if the fame or the utility of Ray's botanical work has neither of them been commensurate with the expectations that might have been formed, a little octavo volume which he gave to the world in 1690, amply supplied all such defects, and proved the great corner-stone of his reputation in this department of science. This was "A Methodical Synopsis of British Wild Plants." The two editions of his alphabetical catalogue of English plants being sold off, and some pettifogging reasons of his booksellers standing in the way of a third, with any improvements, he remodelled the work, throwing it into a systematic form, revising the whole, supplying generic characters, with numerous additions of species and various emendations and remarks. The uses and medicinal qualities of the plants are removed to the alphabetical index at the end. A second edition of this "Synopsis" was published in 1693, but its author never prepared another. The third, now most in use, was edited twenty-eight years afterward by Dillenius. Of all the systematical and practical floras of any country the second edition of Ray's "Synopsis" was the most perfect of his time, and for many a long year afterwards. "He examined every plant recorded in his work, and even gathered most of them himself. He investigated their different names with consummate accuracy; and if the clearness and precision of other authors had equalled his, he would scarcely have committed an error. It is difficult to find him in a mistake or misconception respecting nature herself, though he sometimes misapprehends the bad figures or lame descriptions he was obliged to consult." Above a hundred species are added in this second edition, and the cryptogamic plants in particular are more amply elucidated. The work led to much disputing, but Ray took no delight in controversy; its inevitable asperities were foreign to his nature. One of the biographers of Ray writes: "We must not omit to notice that in the preface to both editions of his 'Synopsis' the learned author, venerable for his character, his talents, and his profession, as well as by his noble adherence to principle in the most corrupt times, has taken occasion to congratulate his country, and to pour out his grateful effusions to Divine Providence in a style worthy of Milton for the establishment of religion, law, and liberty by the revolution which placed King William on the throne. An honest Englishman, however retired in his habits and pursuits, could not have withheld this tribute at such a time, nor was any loyalty ever more personally disinterested than that of Ray." The year 1690 was the date of the first publication of his noble work on "The Wisdom of God in Creation," of which we have already spoken, and whose sale through many editions was very extensive. In 1700 he printed a book more exclusively within the sphere of his sacred profession, called "A Persuasive to a Holy Life," a rare performance of the kind at that day, being devoid of enthusiasm, mysticism, or cant, as well as of religious bigotry or party spirit, "and employing the plain and solid arguments of reason for the best of purposes." His three "Physico-Theological Discourses concerning the Chaos, Deluge, and Dissolution of the World," of which the original materials had been collected and prepared formerly at Cambridge, came out in 1692, and were reprinted the following year. A third edition, superintended by Derham, was published in 1713. This able editor took up the same subject himself, in a similar performance, the materials of which, like Ray's, were first delivered in sermons at Bow church, he having been appointed reader of Mr. Boyle's lectures.

Ray studied animals as carefully as he did plants, and his influence on zoology will be noticed further on in this book, and he revised a translation of Rauwolff's travels, and gave a catalogue of

Grecian, Syrian, Egyptian, and Cretan plants. Ever wishing for the truth, he was led during a correspondence with Rivinus, a foreign botanist, to revise his system of the classification of plants, and to include that of his friend in it. Ray was impressed with the greater importance of the seeds and fruits of plants in classification than of the leaves and floral envelopes; Rivinus and others believed in the superior importance of the flower as a means of distinguishing and grouping plants. After due consideration, Ray included part of the plan of his friend, but it is certain that plants cannot be safely grouped, in every instance, by the similarity of their flowers.

All this correspondence and alteration of systems was extremely useful, for it led to the foundation of what is called the natural system of classification, in opposition to the artificial style, which was founded by the great man whose life will be noticed in the next chapter.

Ray lived a long, happy, and useful life, and died at Black Notley, in a house of his own building, in 1705, in the seventy-seventh year of his age. A friend wrote of him: "In his dealings, no man more strictly just; in his conversation, no man more humble, courteous, and affable; towards God no man more devout; and towards the poor and distressed no man more compassionate and charitable according to his abilities." He was buried, according to his own wish, at Black Notley; but he would not have his body buried in the chancel of the church, choosing rather to repose with his ancestors in the churchyard. Ray died rich in honours, but not rich in money, as he had to give up his living in the Church for conscience' sake and conform as a layman. He was singularly charitable in his opinions to others; and as his work has lasted until the present day, and has influenced the progress of natural history, England may well be proud of the blacksmith's son.

Joseph Pitton de Tournefort was born at Aix, in France, in 1656. He was of a noble family, and was educated with care, and had all the comforts of life. Living, however, far away from the gay scenes of Paris and in a country town, Tournefort soon began to wander over the fields by himself, and, like most boys, he loved to gather flowers. More than this, he began to study them. But such pleasures were not to be his at once, for his parents destined him to be a priest, and he was obliged to enter the Catholic seminary at Aix. There he began to learn Latin, and in course of time became a great proficient, speaking and writing that language well, which at that time was fairly known by every educated person. His theological studies were rather neglected by him, and whenever he had the opportunity, he got books on natural philosophy, chemistry, medicine, and, above all, on botany. He studied them with great assiduity, and until he was twenty-one years of age. Tournefort's father died in 1677, and the young man then being independent, threw off his cap and gown, said good-bye to the seminary and its priests, and devoted himself forthwith and as long as life lasted to the science of natural history, and especially to botany.

He did not rest satisfied with the books of Plinius and Aristoteles, or of the feeble botanists of his youth, but he intended to study plants as they grew, to discover their uses, and to endeavour to classify and name them. Besides, he got a love for the healing art, for one of his first teachers was a chemist of Aix, who gave him lessons about the common simple plants which were used in medicine. So, after roaming over the country far and wide, month after month, and collecting plants in Provence, on the mountains of Dauphiné and Savoy, he went to Montpellier in 1679 to study anatomy and medicine. The young student was there for two years, and then he seems to have set the example to his fellow-students, for botanical excursions became a favourite method of passing away time. In 1681, in company with several fellow-students, he went to the Pyrenees, and wandered about those difficult mountains, submitting to much fatigue, cold, and hunger. Very robust in health, and vigorous, his fatigues and hard fare seemed to do him good, and at last he obtained a very fine collection of the plants of that region. It is always told that the ardent young botanist and his friends got into trouble, being taken prisoners more than once by *Miguelites* (smugglers); but it is not likely that those people got much out of them.

On his return home he found that his reputation as a practical botanist and as knowing useful plants, had spread about, although he had not written any work at that time. M. Fagon, a distinguished botanist of the age, was physician to Louis XIV., and had had many an excursion to collect plants in Provence, Languedoc, and Auvergne, before he became a great man at court. He got plants from those localities, and had them planted in the botanic gardens, of which the king was fond; and, fortunately for his prospects in life, he discovered the medicinal uses of some natural baths at Barèges, which he recommended to the Duc de Maine. On his return to Paris, M. Fagon was made professor of botany and chemistry to the Jardin des Plantes, and subsequently became physician to the king and princes, and director of the gardens. M. Fagon wanted help, for little was known about the plants of the countries beyond Europe, and he sought the services of a young and wise botanist who had plenty of energy. He destined young Tournefort for a great career, and offered him the professorship of the Botanic garden, intending that the young teacher, after a while, should travel, and collect for the garden. Finding the prospects good, Tournefort accepted the position, and desirous of adding to the collection of plants, visited Spain again, and then Portugal. Subsequently he came over to England, and then collected in Holland. His name was well known as that of a practical botanist, and the Dutch offered him a professorship at Leyden. He was elected to the highest scientific honour in France—to the membership of the Academy of Science. Two years afterwards Tournefort published his first and great work, "The Elements of Botany, or a method of Distinguishing Plants." This work established his reputation all over Europe. It was a very remarkable book. Tournefort travelled in Asia Minor, Circassia, Georgia, Northern Assyria, Candia, and Greece, and was the first man who gave publicity to the truth that the same plants are not found in all countries, and that most countries have many plants peculiar to them. He may be said to have founded the science of the geographical distribution of plants. His descriptions of plants were 10,000 in number; their arrangement in species and genera was excellent. Less praise must be given about the manner of his separating the greater divisions of the plants one from the other. Nevertheless, much of the work of this great traveller has lasted until the present day as good science. Plants are arranged in species, which consist of individuals, having a close structural resemblance without any constant differences of the form of the stem, roots, leaves, flowers, and seeds. A genus is a group of species with a general resemblance, some special character predominating. An order is a number of more or less similar genera, and a class contains orders which have greater resemblance than those of another class.

All this classification relates to accurate observation and description, and then to comparison, and the greater the knowledge of the botanist of species and genera the more useful it is. There is a difficulty in selecting those parts of a plant which should be those on which the classification should depend, and this was the stumbling-block with these early botanists. Ray saw the value of the seed and of the reproductive organs in classification, and Tournefort, although he erred in classifying his "classes" by the coloured part of the flower or corolla, followed nature accurately in his description, and reasoned upon the facts he had discovered.

This botanist, who lived in the days of great luxury, and when war was almost constant, pursued his useful and simple career, and by his collections alone, assisted in laying the foundations of botany as a science. His travels in the East read like romances, for the habits of Eastern nations were then but little known; and, moreover, the diligent student was a scholar, and paid great attention to the splendid antiquities which he constantly saw. Tournefort studied the zoology of the countries he passed through, and was an adept in mineralogy. On his return from his long journey in the East he was made Professor of Medicine to the College de France. For the future his life was destined to be quiet, happy it appears always to have been. Year after year he laboured in arranging, cultivating, and describing the treasure of plants he had brought from the East and elsewhere. Moreover, he taught as professor. His end was sudden, for he met with an accident in the street, and was killed by a passing waggon.

Tournefort's important work was the forming a great amount of good knowledge about the species of plants, and the arranging them in a systematic order. But, as has been mentioned, he was a founder of the science of the distribution of plants. He appears to have laboured independently of Ray, his English fellow-botanist, whose method was the best of the two. There are twenty-two classes in Tournefort's method, chiefly arranged, as has been stated, by the form of the corolla, comparatively an unimportant structure. He distinguishes herbs and under-shrubs on the one hand, from trees and shrubs on the other. His system of classification was much used on the Continent, until it was found to be less easy of application than that of Linnæus.

The life of Ray, by Dr. Derham and Sir J. E. Smith, is to be found in the "Memorials of John Ray," in the publications of the Ray Society, 1846.

CHAPTER III.

THE LIFE OF LINNÆUS.

The science of plants begins to mature, to be reformed, and to be made more exact.

CARL LINNÆUS was born in the month of May, 1707, at Rashult, in the parish of Stenbrohult, in Smaland, a province in the South of Sweden. His father, Nils Linnæus, was assistant minister of the parish, and became, in process of time, its pastor or rector, having married the daughter of his predecessor.*

Our Carl was the first-born child of this marriage. The family of Linnæus had been peasants, and a remarkably lofty linden tree, growing near their native place, is reputed to have given origin to the names of Lindelius, or Tiliander (linden tree man). This origin of surnames taken from natural objects is not uncommon in Sweden.

* The greater part of this memoir is taken from Miss Brightwell's "Life of Linnæus." Van Voorst.

Of his father, Linnæus has given us a few glimpses in his diary, which prepossess us in his favour, and make us wish that we knew more of the worthy pastor. He was brought up by his maternal uncle, Sven Tiliander, himself a clergyman, who educated the lad with his own children, and, being fond of plants and gardening, inspired in his nephew also a love for horticulture; so that this predilection appears to have been, in some degree, hereditary. Young Nils was sent, in due time, to school, and afterwards to the University of Lund, where he had to struggle, for some years, with poverty, and to apply very diligently to his studies, in order that he might qualify himself for the profession of his choice. Returning to his native place, he was admitted to holy orders, and was first curate, and afterwards co-pastor. Soon after he attained to this degree, he was married to the eldest daughter of the pastor, Christina Brodersonia, of whom her son says—" She possessed all the virtues of her sex, and was an excellent economist." No doubt she found ample room for the exercise of this her distinguishing excellence, for her husband's stipend was small, and she brought him a goodly family of two sons and three daughters. We may well believe that thrift and frugality were necessary in the *ménage* of this small household. Linnæus tells us that the young couple welcomed their first-born with joy, and reared him with the tenderest solicitude, " devoting the utmost attention to impressing on his mind the love of virtue, both in precept and example." He has drawn a charming picture of his birthplace; it was situated in a very pleasant valley adjoining the lake Möklen, which formed a bay, in the centre of which stood the parish church of Stenbrohult. On the banks of this fine lake, surrounded by hills and valleys, woods and cultivated grounds, the father of Linnæus dwelt; his garden and his fields yielding him, at the same time, both amusement and profit. The young Carl had no sooner left his cradle than he was constantly in the garden, in which, to use his own expression, he almost lived, delighted with the brilliant hues and fragrance of the beauteous shrubs and flowers which flourished there.

In a letter to Baron Haller, written at the time of his father's death, Linnæus says: "He was an uncommon lover of plants, and had a select garden of numerous rare species." The favourite taste of the father was quickly imbibed by the child, who was his constant companion while he cultivated the choice parterre, and eagerly tried to yield such slight aid as his childish powers permitted. He has recorded the first occasion when this innate passion was decidedly displayed, or rather, perhaps, when it sprung into consciousness. He was hardly four years old when he chanced to accompany his father to a rural fête at Möklen, and in the evening, it being a pleasant season of the year, the guests seated themselves on the flowery turf and listened to the good pastor, who entertained them with remarks on the names and properties of the plants which grew around them, showing them the roots of succisa, tormentilla, orchides, etc. The little Carl attended with the utmost eagerness to all he saw and heard, and "from that time never ceased harassing his father with questions about the name, qualities, and nature of every plant he met with." An unlooked-for result of the evening lecture, and which seems to have cost the worthy man no small trouble, for the child (not unlike other children, for that matter) very often asked more than his father was able to answer; in addition to which he "used immediately to forget all he had learned, and especially the names of plants." To cure him of this mischievous habit of inattention his father refused to answer his questions unless he would promise to remember what was told him, which judicious management wrought a speedy and effectual cure, insomuch that he tells us he ever afterwards retained with ease, whatever he heard. Besides this retentiveness of memory he possessed an "astonishing quickness of sight," an almost necessary qualification for the study of his favourite science.

When the boy was eight years old a separate plot of ground was assigned him by his father, which was called "Carl's garden," and which he soon stored with collections of plants and wild flowers, gathered from the woods and fields around his dwelling. At the same time he introduced a variety of weeds, a treasure which it afterwards cost his father no small pains to eradicate from his flower-beds. The enterprising youngster even tried the experiment of establishing a swarm of wild bees and wasps in the garden, the result of which was a devastating warfare waged against the domestic hives.

At length it was thought desirable that these flowery pursuits should give way to more serious occupations, and he was committed to the charge of a private tutor, whom he calls "a passionate and morose man, better calculated for extinguishing a youth's talents than for improving them." Nor did he fare any better in his next remove, which was to the grammar school at Wexiö, where the masters "pursued the same methods, preferring stripes and punishments to encouragements and admonitions." Probably the boy evinced his distaste for such coercive measures, since we find him soon removed from school to the care of another private teacher, of whose mild and gentle disposition he speaks in terms of approval. Nevertheless, he too failed to inspire in his pupil a love for the studies which were considered necessary as preparatory to admission into holy orders; for Nils Linnæus, desirous that his eldest son should become his assistant and eventually his successor, designed him for the Church. The boy had to work for three years before he was promoted to a higher "form" in the school, called the "circle;" and the principal use he seems to have made of the greater liberty allowed him in this new rank, was to shun the usual exercises and give himself up to the study of his favourite pursuit—the knowledge of flowers. He acknowledges that his time was chiefly spent in wandering about the outskirts of the town, and making himself acquainted with all the plants he could find. According to the system then pursued in Sweden, it was necessary that youths should pass from the schools or private tutors to a superior seminary, called the Gymnasium, where the higher branches of literature were taught; and accordingly, at the age of seventeen, the young Linnæus was removed thither. But the original predilections of his mind were then still more strikingly evinced and matured. He showed the strongest distaste for theological studies. In the metaphysics, ethics, Greek and Hebrew, and theology his companions far outstripped him; but in mathematics, and particularly physics, he as much excelled them. His favourite science, botany, which at that time was wholly neglected, still continued to be his most engrossing pursuit, and he soon contrived to form a small library of books in that branch. Among others he mentions the "Chloris Gothica" of Bromelius, and Rudbeck's "Hortus Upsaliensis," which he confesses his inability then to comprehend clearly. Nevertheless he says he "continued to read them day and night, and committed them to memory." His own copies of these books, "used with the utmost care and neatness," were preserved among his library, and after his death were sold with his collection. The zeal and eagerness he evinced in these studies procured him, both among masters and scholars, the name of "the Little Botanist."

At the end of two years his father went to Wexiö, "hoping to hear from the preceptors the most flattering account of his beloved son's progress in his studies and morals." But he was sorely disappointed at learning that, unexceptionable as the general behaviour of the youth had been, he was evidently quite unfit for a divine; and, indeed, in the opinion of the authorities, it was a pity to incur any further expense towards giving him a learned education, some manual employment being far more suitable for him. The youth, they thought, would be well placed as apprentice to some tailor or shoemaker!

Grieved at having thus lost his labour, and supported his son at school for twelve years (an expense he could very ill afford) to no purpose, the venerable clergyman went his way, pondering what course to pursue. It chanced that he was suffering from a complaint which required medical advice, and he betook himself to the house of Dr. Rothmann, the provincial physician, also a lecturer in physics, to whom, in the course of conversation, he mentioned his perplexity with reference to his son Carl. Rothmann suggested that, though the opinions of his colleagues might be correct as to the boy's inaptitude for theological studies, there was good reason to believe he might distinguish himself in the profession of medicine, and possibly that he might accomplish great things in the pursuit of natural history. At the same time he liberally offered, in case the father's circumstances did not permit him to maintain his son in a course of studies, to take him into his own house, and provide for him during the year he must remain at the gymnasium.

This generous proposal was gratefully accepted, and the result was most satisfactory. Linnæus received from his benefactor a course of private instructions in physiology with so much success, that the youth was able to give a most accurate report of all he had been taught. At the same time, this worthy teacher put him into the right method of studying botany, showing the necessity of proceeding in a scientific manner, and directing his attention to the system of Tournefort. The very imperfections he found in this work stimulated his desire for something more perfect, and were, in this way, of use to the future naturalist.

The year following (1727) Linnæus proceeded to the University at Lund, furnished, as he has himself recorded, with a "not very creditable certificate." This curiosity, after its kind, was to the effect that youth at school may be compared to plants, which sometimes baffle all the skill of the gardener, but, being transplanted to a different soil, occasionally turn out well. With this view, and no other, the bearer was sent to the University, which, possibly, might prove propitious to his progress !

Happily, the young man had a friend at the

University, in his former preceptor—he of the mild and gentle disposition—who kept back the doubtful recommendation, and procured his matriculation as one of his private pupils.

At Lund, Linnæus lodged in the house of Dr. Stobæus, professor of medicine, and physician to the king. This eminent man, perceiving the industry of his lodger, and his acquirements in natural science, allowed him free access to his excellent museum of minerals, shells, and dried plants; and, highly delighted with the idea of a *hortus siccus*, Linnæus immediately began to collect all the plants which grew in the vicinity, and to "glue them upon paper." Still, he was denied the privilege of access to the doctor's library; but, as it fell out, he managed to obtain that also. He formed an acquaintance with a fellow-lodger, a young German student, who enjoyed the advantage he coveted, and, in return for teaching him the principles of physiology, he obtained of this youth books from Stobæus's library. He passed whole nights in reading the volumes thus clandestinely procured; but it happened that the mother of Stobæus, who was infirm and ailing, lay awake several nights in succession, and seeing a light constantly burning in Linnæus's room, fearful of fire, desired her son to chide the young Smalander for his carelessness.

Two nights after, at midnight, the lad was surprised by a visit from his host, who found him, to his astonishment, diligently poring over his books.

Being asked why he did not go to bed, and whence he had procured the books, he was compelled to confess everything. Stobæus ordered him immediately to go to bed; and the next morning, calling for him, gave him permission to make what use he pleased of his library. From that time this excellent man admitted the youth to the utmost familiarity, received him at his own table, and treated him even as a son.

While botanizing in the country, in the following spring, Linnæus was bitten in the right arm by a venomous reptile, and so serious were the consequences that his life was endangered. As soon as he was partially recovered, he returned to his father's house, in order to recruit his health during the summer vacation, and while staying in Smaland he was persuaded by his kind friend and benefactor, Dr. Rothmann, to quit Lund for Upsala, as a superior school of medicine, and affording besides, many other advantages of which he could easily avail himself.

In this University—the first and most ancient seat of Swedish learning, and the scene, in after-years, of his greatness—our young student underwent a severe process of training. Poor and unknown, he had no means of adding to the scanty pittance his parents were able to allow him. Scarcely could they afford to give the small sum of 200 silver ducats (about £8) towards the expenses of his education there. In a short time he found his pockets quite empty; and having no chance of obtaining private pupils, he vainly looked for any other source of maintenance. In a few words, he thus touchingly records the tale of his suffering, and the first beam of hope that shone across his path. As Petronius says, poverty is the attendant of a good mind; and Linnæus was not without it in this university, . . . he was obliged to trust to chance for a meal, and in the article of dress was reduced to such shifts that he was obliged, when his shoes required mending, to patch them with folded paper instead of sending them to the cobbler.

Years afterwards, the most distinguished zoologist France ever produced, M. de Lamarck, stated to a friend, " I was poor, indeed, but I had not, like Linnæus, to gather up my fellow-students' old shoes to wear."

He repented of his journey to Upsala, and of his departure from the roof of Stobæus; but to return to Lund was a tiresome and expensive undertaking. Stobæus, too, had taken it very ill, that a pupil whom he loved so sincerely had left that University without consulting him.

At this time Linnæus, in spite of his great industry and simple manner of living, naturally had considerable anxieties about his success in life.

It chanced one day, in the autumn of the year 1728, whilst Linnæus was very intently examining some plants in the academical garden, there entered a venerable old clergyman, who asked him what he was about, whether he was acquainted with plants, whence he came, and how long he had been prosecuting his studies? To all these questions he returned satisfactory answers, and was then invited to accompany his interrogator to his house, which proved to be that of Dr. Olaus Celsius.

This estimable and learned man, to whom Scandinavia owes so much in regard to natural history, had just returned from Stockholm, where he had been engaged in preparing his celebrated work upon the plants mentioned in the Holy Scriptures, which he published in 1745, having travelled to the East on purpose to make it more complete. Little did Celsius imagine that the youth, whom he first met, by chance, in the academical garden at Upsala, was destined, in after years, by his genius, to immortalize its fame. He, however, soon discerned the merits of Linnæus, took him under his protection, offering him board and lodging in his own house, and allowing him the full use of his library, which was very rich in botanical books. Among all his patrons, Linnæus appears to have dearly cherished the memory of this venerable man, never referring to him but in terms of reverence and gratitude. The friendship and patronage of one so distinguished, did not fail to procure for the youth the advantages he so much needed. Before long, the son of Professor Rudbeck, and other young men, became his private pupils, and by this means his pecuniary wants were supplied.

Nothing, however, seems to have given Linnæus

so much satisfaction in reviewing the events of this period of his early history, as the intimate friendship he now contracted with a fellow-student, named Artedi, who afterwards distinguished himself by his knowledge of fishes and umbelliferous plants. To the picture he has drawn of his friend, Linnæus has added a slight sketch of himself. There was a great difference in the personal appearance, as well as in the temperament and disposition of the two youths. Artedi was of a tall and handsome figure, more serious, and of a deliberate judgment; whereas his friend was short in stature and stout, hasty in temper, and of a sanguine turn. The two companions pursued their favourite studies with an honourable spirit of emulation. They divided the kingdoms and provinces of nature between them, and while Linnæus yielded the palm to Artedi in ichthyology (the science of fish), the latter acknowledged Linnæus to be his superior in entomology, or that of insects. Each kept his discoveries to himself, though for no great length of time, since not a day passed without one surprising the other by narrating some new fact, so that emulation produced mutual industry of research, and stimulated each to new exertions.

Linnæus was now in his twenty-second year, about which time he met with a review of Le Vaillant's treatise, "Sur la Structure des Fleurs" ("On the Structure of Flowers"), by which his curiosity was excited to a close examination of the stamens and pistils (the central and reproductive structures), and, perceiving the essential importance of these parts of the plant, he formed the design of a new method of arrangement, founded upon these organs. This was the first dawning idea of that great system upon which his subsequent fame was based.

A flower of a complete kind consists of the parts of the plant which reproduce or form the seed, enclosed within two particular envelopes. The envelopes of the flower are the beautifully coloured parts called petals, which form the corolla, or inner envelope, and the duller-coloured or green sepals outside the corolla, and which form the calyx.

Protected by these coverings, are the central parts or organs. Quite in the middle of the flower is the ovary, made up of one or several portions—the pistils, which contain the future seeds or ovules. The top of the whole, which projects in the middle of the flower, is the stigma, and the prolonged part beneath it is the style, and this surmounts the seed-case or ovary. Outside this central part, and between it and the corolla, are the stamens, each of which—for their number varies—may consist of a stalk or filament, bearing an anther, which is coloured, and contains the pollen, or dust, which fertilizes the ovule, by falling on to the stigma.

These central parts are the reproductive organs, and are those which, above all others, are the most important, for without them a plant cannot increase and multiply, and would become extinct. The floral envelopes, beautiful as they are, are not so essential, and are of secondary importance in classification. Now, in some kinds of plants the stigma and the ovary exist in one individual and the stamens in another. The plant which bears the ovary is called the female, and that which has the pollen-making part is termed the male. Hence it is said that plants have sexes. But in a vast number of plants these organs are combined in the same individual. Linnæus considered the stamen to be of primary importance, and established eleven classes of plants distinguished by the numbers of the stamens, and these all relate to plants in which the male and female organs are combined in the same individual. Thus the red valerian has one stamen only, and it was classed in *monandria*, the first part of the word meaning "one" and the last "male." The lilac has two stamens, and was classed in the *diandria*—"two male;" and other plants were classified up to those which have ten stamens, the pink, for instance, as *decandria*. An eleventh class included all plants which bear flowers containing from twelve to nineteen stamens, such as mignonette. Then two more classes were invented to comprise—1, plants with twenty or more stamens placed on the calyx, as the cherry; 2, others with twenty or more stamens which are placed on stalks rising from below the ovary, as in the buttercup. Other classes were formed according to the relative length of the stamens, as in the foxglove and wallflower, and also from the grouping of the stamens in bundles. Then there were three very important classes in which the sexes are in separate flowers. Finally, the flowerless plants, such as the ferns, lichens, and fungi, were united as cryptogamia, having their organs of reproduction more or less concealed.

The next part of the classification refers to orders which are sub-divisions of classes. The orders of the first thirteen classes, mentioned above, are founded on the number of styles (or of stigmas if these are absent), and the names given, relate to the number and the term gynia, or female.

Thus the order monogynia includes plants of all the thirteen classes that have only one style to each flower, such as the primrose; and so on, until polygonia, or "many female"—plants of such an order, having more than twelve styles, like the rose and clematis.

One class has a very important division into two orders, one of which has naked and the other covered seeds; another has orders from the shape of the fruit or pod. Linnæus divided the cryptogamia into six orders—the ferns, mosses, liverworts, lichens, fungi, and seaweeds. There is no doubt that this classification enables the name of a plant to be discovered, if it has been properly described and named, very easily, and it added to the facilities of classificatory botany. But it did not bring plants having many other and very important characters together, and it separated many which are closely allied by similar structures. It was and is called the artificial system. It was not a natural classification like that foreshadowed by Ray. The careful distinction of the sexes of plants was, of course, the foundation of the system, and to that Linnæus paid great attention. Writing a little treatise on the subject, he showed it to Celsius, who communicated it to Dr. Rudbeck. This man, free from the usual jealousy of the age, took Linnæus as his assistant, and asked him to lecture in the botanical garden. Thus the young man became a teacher in the very place where he had applied the year before for the humble situation of gardener. Dr. Rudbeck, moreover, took him into his house as tutor to his children, and thus he had access to a fine collection of books and drawings on natural history subjects. His mornings were then occupied in giving instruction to the students, and his evenings in composing the new system and meditating a general reformation in botanical science. He had no time to waste at Upsala. It will have been noticed how kindly Linnæus was treated by a few true lovers of science, and it was greatly to the honour of the good simple people of science-loving Scandinavia.

People imagine that the progress and prosperity of scientific men depend upon themselves alone; but many a promising career has been arrested by petty jealousy and the expression of ill will on the part of those who are second-rate men of science. On the other hand, truly distinguished scientific men are mostly only too glad to assist earnest, hard-working, and meritorious students. Linnæus found that he was no exception to the rule that appears to determine that a prosperous poor man shall have enemies. He was opposed by a Dr. Rosen on his return from foreign travel, but Linnæus stood his ground. But when his father suggested a voyage into Lapland to collect plants, Linnæus gladly seized the opportunity, and after arrangements had been made, he went to stay awhile at home.

Early in 1732 Linnæus left his father's house, to set out on his arduous undertaking. On his way to Upsala he paid a visit to his former friend and preceptor, Stobæus, at Lund, and studied his collection of minerals, the only branch of natural history with which (he tells us) he was unacquainted. He shortly after proceeded to Upsala, from which place he set out on his journey alone, May 12th, 1732, "being at that time within half a day of twenty-five years of age."

During this journey Linnæus travelled over the greater part of Lapland, skirting the boundaries of Norway, and returned to Upsala by the eastern side of the Bothnian Gulf, having performed a journey of near four thousand English miles, mostly on foot, in five months. He necessarily endured many hardships and vast fatigue, and his life was several times imperilled. Bogs and forests intercepted his way, and food, even of the coarsest description, was occasionally not easily procured; yet, amid all difficulties, his spirit was unflagging, and obstacles only seemed to quicken his zeal. The natural curiosities of the country, the manners of the people, and the general features of the various regions he traversed, all were observed and written down for future use. He collected above a hundred plants, entirely undescribed and unknown before, and upon his return arranged all the flora of Lapland according to his own favourite system, and delivered an account of his journey publicly.

The result of his botanical observations was not published for several years afterwards, during his residence in Holland. This expedition was the first and most difficult of all the six journeys of Linnæus. He spoke of it afterwards in one of his academical addresses in these words: "My journey through Lapland was particularly toilsome, and I own that I was obliged to sustain more hardships and dangers in that sole peregrination through the frontier of our northern world, than in all the other travels I undertook in other parts. But having once sustained the toils of travelling, I buried in the oblivion of Lethe all the dangers and difficulties I endured, the invaluable fruits I reaped having compensated for every toil." Writing to a friend on the same subject, he says: "All my food in these fatiguing excursions consisted, for the most part, of fish and reindeer's milk. Bread, salt, and what is found everywhere else, did but seldom recreate my palate. One of the greatest nuisances which I met with in Lapland was the immense number of flies. I used to keep them off, by drawing a crape over my face." The youthful traveller started on his adventurous journey "without encumbrances of any kind, and carried all his baggage on his back," by which means alone he was enabled to prosecute the objects he had in view. Leaving Upsala by the northern gate, he travelled for a considerable distance through fertile corn-fields, bounded by hills, and the view terminated by extensive forests. With respect to situation and variety of prospects, the young Swede was of opinion that scarcely any city could stand a comparison with this. At a short distance from the gates he left, on the right, Old Upsala, the place renowned for the worship of the primeval gods of Sweden, and for the inauguration and residence of her earliest king. Here, in days of high antiquity, human sacrifices were offered at the shrines of the pagan deities, and here our traveller noticed the three large sepulchral mounds which tradition has assigned to the bodies of Odin, Frigga, and Thor.

"Cheered with the song of the charming lark," which attended his steps through the lowland, his approach to the forest was welcomed by the redwing, "whose amorous warblings from the tops of the spruce firs" appeared to him to rival the nightingale itself. As the summer was advancing, he thought it not desirable to lose time by the way, nor to stray far from the high road in the early part of the tour; but attentively observing what presented itself to him as he passed along, he noted the various plants, animals, and insects, together with the general features of the country.

Arrived in the province of Medelpad, he ascended its highest mountain, leaving his horse "tied to an ancient Runic monumental stone." He found several uncommon plants here; and from the summit, gazed on the country spread out below, varied with plains and cultivated fields, villages, lakes, and rivers—a most picturesque and romantic region. The descent was very difficult, and even dangerous. Leaving this mountain, he took his route along the sea-shore, which was spread with the wrecks of vessels, telling to the feeling heart of the young traveller a sad tale of woe. "How many prayers, sighs, tears, vows, and lamentations—all, alas! in vain—rose to my imagination at this melancholy spectacle!" he exclaims. The sight reminded him of a student who, going by sea from Stockholm to Abo, experienced so severely the terrors of the ocean, that he chose to walk back round the head of the Bothnian Gulf, rather than adventure himself again upon the deep. This youth, afterwards a Professor at Abo, assumed the surname of Tillands, expressive of his attachment to *terra firma*, and Linnæus named in honour of him, a plant which cannot bear wet.

In five or six days, Linnæus reached Hernosand, the principal town of Angermania, on the Bothnian Gulf, and visited a tremendously steep and lofty mountain called Skula, where was a cavern, which he desired to explore. Here he was within a hair's breadth of a fatal accident, for one of the peasants who accompanied him, in climbing up, loosened a large stone, which was hurled down the track Linnæus had just left, and fell exactly on the spot he had occupied. "If I had not (he says) providentially changed my route, nobody would ever have heard of me more; I was surrounded by fire and smoke, and should certainly, but for the protecting hand of Providence, have been crushed to pieces." From this point of the journey a change came over the face of nature. The country was covered over with snow, in some places inches deep; the pretty spring flowers disappeared, and in their place nothing but wintry plants were seen peeping through the snow. At length, on the 23rd of May, he reached Umœa, in West Bothnia, where he turned out of the main road to the left, designing to visit Lycksele, Lapmark; by which means he lost the advantage of the regular post horses, and found the ways so narrow and intricate, that at every step he stumbled. "In this dreary wilderness I began to feel very solitary, and to long earnestly for a companion (he says); the few inhabitants I met had a foreign accent, and always concluded their sentences with an adjective."

As the night shut in, the way-worn traveller began also to long for a good meal, and has thus recorded the result of his application, on arriving at a village where he passed the night :—" On my inquiring what I could have for supper, they set before me the breast of a cock of the woods, which had been shot and dressed some time the preceding year. Its aspect was not very inviting; but the taste proved delicious, and I found, with pleasure, that these poor Laplanders know better than some of their more opulent neighbours, how to employ the good things which God has bestowed upon them."

The bird is prepared by a process of salting and drying, and will keep even for three years, if necessary. Linnæus next proceeded up the river of Umœa as far as Lycksele, where he was hospitably received by the worthy pastor of the place; and the next day, being Whit-Sunday, he stayed there, and would fain have remained longer; but, for fear of the floods impeding his journey, he hastened his departure on the morrow, and on the 1st of June entered the territories of the native Laplanders, passing through wild forests, with no traces of roads. A more desolate picture of wretchedness than this region presented, could hardly be imagined. It was flooded by the rivers, and the bogs were utterly impassable. At every step the water was above the knees, and the feet felt the ice at the bottom. "We pursued our journey (continues the diary) with considerable labour and difficulty all night long, if that might be called night which was as light as the day, the sun disappearing for half an hour only, and the temperature of the air being rather cold." The poor inhabitants had themselves, at this season, nothing to eat but a scanty supply of fish; for they had not begun to kill their reindeer, nor to milk them. In addition to these evils, the villainous bites of the gnats and other insects tortured the unhappy travellers, till at length he exclaims—"I had now my fill of travelling!"

Gladly would he have returned by the way he came, but he could find no road back; and even the hardy Laplanders themselves, "born to labour, as the birds to fly," could not help complaining, and declared they had never been in such extremity before. It is evident that even the robust frame of Linnæus was beginning to yield to the combined effects of fatigue, exhaustion, and hunger. He at length obtained some food which he was able to eat, and after incredible exertions succeeded in retracing his steps to the river, on which he again embarked, and returned to Umœa; having, as he ingenuously acknowledged, "with the thoughtlessness of youth, undertaken more than he was able to perform."

From Umœa, Linnæus proceeded to Pithœa, which he reached after two days' journey, "the night being as pleasant for travelling as the day." He notices the beauty of the fresh shoots of the spruce fir, which constitute one of the greatest ornaments of the forests which adorn this part of Sweden.

Being anxious to proceed with all haste, in order if possible to reach the Alps of Lulean Lapland, "in time to see the sun above the horizon at midnight, which is beheld then to the best advantage," the traveller made no longer stay at Lulea than was needful for the purposes of exploring the neighbouring coast and islands. He has noted the various entomological and other specimens he observed, and, after admiring the beauty of some of them, exclaims, in a sort of rapture—" The observer of nature sees with admiration that the whole world is full of the glory of God."

During this voyage, Swanberg, who has taken great delight in Linnæus's conversation, offered to instruct him in the art of assaying within a very short time, if he would agree to visit Calix, on his way homeward. At Quickjock, the wife of the curate provided our traveller with stores sufficient for eight days, and procured him a Laplander, whose assistance as interpreter and servant was highly necessary.

"On my first ascending these wild Alps (he says), I felt as if in a new world. Here were no forests to be seen, but mountains upon mountains, larger and larger, as I advanced, all covered with snow; no road, no tracks, nor any sign of inhabitants were visible. The declining sun never disappeared sufficiently to allow any cooling shade, and by climbing to the more elevated parts of these lofty mountains, I could see it at midnight, above the horizon. This spectacle I considered as not one of the least of nature's miracles, for what inhabitant of other countries would not wish to behold it? O Lord, how wonderful are thy works!"

In this frozen region there were no traces of verdure, save in the deep valleys between the mountains. Very few birds were visible, except some ptarmigans, those hardy inhabitants of the bleak mountain tops. A pretty little incident, recorded by Linnæus, shows so kind a heart that it must not be omitted here. "The little Alpine variety of the ptarmigan was now accompanied by its young. I caught one of these, upon which the hen ran so close to me that I could easily have taken her also. She kept continually jumping round and round me, but I thought it a pity to deprive the tender brood of their mother; neither would my compassion for the mother allow me long to detain her offspring, which I returned to her in safety."

After a long and wearisome journey along these mountain passes, the traveller reached one of the cottages of the country. Here the inhabitants, sixteen in number, received him kindly, and gave him two reindeer skins to sleep between. In the morning some hundreds of reindeer came home to be milked, and it amazed the stranger to perceive that, although to his eyes they were all perfectly alike, yet each of the herd had its appropriate name, and was readily distinguished by the owners.

Steering his course south-west, Linnæus proceeded to the lofty ice mountains, or "main ridge of the country," which he had no sooner reached, than a storm overtook him, accompanied by a shower of thin pieces of ice, which soon encrusted his garments. The cold was intense, and the whole country was one dazzling waste. No sooner, however, had he crossed the summit of the ridge than a change was perceptible, and soon, from the lofty heights, he beheld the ample forests of Norway lying far beneath. The whole appearance of the country was perfectly green, and, notwithstanding its vast extent, looked like a garden in miniature. The descent was slow and long protracted, but at length he reached the plains, of which he had enjoyed so glorious a prospect. "Nothing (he exclaims) could be more delightful to my feelings than this transition from all the severity of winter, to the warmth and beauty of summer. Oh! how most lovely of all is summer! The verdant herbage, the sweet-scented clover, the tall grass reaching up to my arms, the grateful flavour of the wild fruits, and the fine weather that welcomed me at the foot of these Alps, seemed to refresh me both in mind and body."

Here Linnæus found himself close to the seacoast, and he went to sea in a boat to search for the natural productions of that element. He would fain have approached the celebrated whirlpool, called the Maelstrom, but he found no one willing to venture it. On the 13th of July, he arrived at the parsonage house of Rorstadt, from the occupant of which, himself a traveller and a naturalist, Linnæus received a cordial welcome. A rather significant entry in Linnæus' diary tells us that here, "in this far distant nook of the wide peopled earth," the young enthusiast found an object of surpassing interest. "The pastor (he says) has a handsome daughter, named Sarah Rask, eighteen years of age; she seemed to me uncommonly beautiful." The next morning, Linnæus took his leave of this elysium, and proceeded on his way. Climbing the mountains again, he found a work of "no small fatigue and exhaustion," and he has given us a most painful account of the subsequent route he pursued towards the Alps of Tornea. "What I endured," he concludes, "is hardly to be described; how many weary steps I had to set, the precipices that came in my way, and my excessive fatigue. Water was our only drink during the journey, and it never appeared so refreshing as when we sucked it out of the melting snow." At length, tired of advancing further into this inhospitable country, he determined to return to Quickjock. In the course of his journey thither his life was twice endangered, but at length he reached the place of his destination, "having been four weeks without tasting bread." After resting some days at Quickjock, Linnæus descended the river again to Lulea, where he "learned the art of assaying from the minemaster, Swanberg, at Calix, in two days and a night," and thence his journey was continued through Tornea. He had intended to visit the mountains, but before he could get thither the winter set in, and he was obliged to return along the coast on the eastern side of the Bothnian Gulf. The last entry in his journal is dated October 10th, and is as follows: "About one o'clock, P.M., I arrived safe at Upsala. To the Maker and Preserver of all things be praise, honour, and glory for ever!"

At first, indeed, he seemed to reap but a humble reward for his toils. On his arrival at home, he presented to the Academy of Sciences an account of his expedition, which obtained their approbation, and they gave him 112 silver dollars (not more than £10) — his travelling expenses. In the following spring, he began a private course of lectures on the art of assaying (which he had learned so cleverly from his chance companion during the Lapland journey). This art had never been taught at Upsala before; and the novelty of the subject, the skilful manner in which he communicated instructions, and the reasonable terms he exacted, secured Linnæus a considerable number of pupils.

CHAPTER IV.

THE LIFE OF LINNÆUS (*Continued*).

The publication and reception of the artificial system of classifying plants.

LINNÆUS had many difficulties to contend with, however. He found his old rival, Rosen, at work; and Linnæus accuses this man of the meanness of obtaining, partly by entreaty, partly by threats, his manuscript lectures on botany, which he valued more than anything he possessed, and which he afterwards detected his rival in copying. This formidable enemy next proceeded to prevent Linnæus from obtaining the means of subsistence. There was no room for the young botanist at Upsala, and, indeed, botany appeared to be a bad profession. So he turned again to mineralogy, and got up a students' expedition to Fahlun and Dale-carlia. He settled down at Fahlun for a while as a teacher, and found himself as it were in a new world, where everybody loved and assisted him. He earned money by his medical knowledge. The

Bishop of Abo asked Linnæus to give him some instruction in botany and mineralogy, and became much attached to the young man. The bishop advised Linnæus to go abroad and get his doctor's degree, and also to marry. The last was as difficult as the first, but being more to his taste at the time, he wooed the daughter of Dr. John Morœa, a man of considerable property. The young student made his proposals with considerable trepidation, and had he not been satisfied that the lady was willing, he would have let the matter alone. The worthy doctor thought well of Linnæus, but not of his prospects in life, but he decided that after a lapse of three years he would give his reply. Thus, at the age of twenty-nine, Linnæus found himself with a betrothed, no occupation, and a great deal of knowledge and perseverance. He had to live, and so he determined to stick to physic, and to get a doctor's degree. He contrived to scrape together £15, and went on his way to the University of Harderwyk. First, like a good son, he went to see his father, and to console him on the loss of the mother—a loss greatly felt by the young man at this critical period of his life. Then Linnæus journeyed to the south, and arrived at Hamburg, where his whole time was employed in viewing the fine garden, and everything else worthy of attention. The public library he examined, and also the principal cabinets of natural history, and he read there for the first time the botanical works of Ray, whom he esteemed as one of the most penetrating observers of the natural affinity of plants. Amsterdam was the next place, and then Harderwyk, where, after being examined, and publishing a paper on the cure of intermittent fever, he was dubbed M.D. He left for Leyden, and met Dr. Gronovius, to whom he showed his classification. Gronovius was so delighted with it that he had it published at his own expense in eight large sheets. He called on the celebrated Boerhaave, and after eight days' waiting obtained an audience. Boerhaave took a liking to the young man, and recommended him to Dr. Burmann, of Amsterdam, in whose house he remained for many months. During that time Linnæus printed his "Fundamenta Botanica," of which a great writer has said, "it contains the very essence of botanical philosophy, and has never been superseded nor refuted." He commended his book to his friend Artedi, who had just finished a work on Fishes. Death put an end to this friendship with Artedi, who was accidentally drowned.

This stay at Amsterdam determined the future career of Linnæus, for he was introduced there to an English banker, Mr. Clifford, whose garden at Hartecoup was one of the finest in the world. Linnæus removed to Mr. Clifford's house, where he said he lived like a prince, had one of the finest gardens in the world under his inspection, permission to procure all the plants that were wanted in the garden and such books as were not to be found in the library, and of course enjoyed all the advantages he could wish for, in his botanical studies, to which he devoted himself day and night. He got his description of the plants of Lapland printed, and everybody recognized the charms of the descriptions in the book.

In the year 1736, Linnæus paid a visit to England. He did so by the request, and at the expense, of Mr. Clifford, who was desirous to procure various plants for his collection, and that he should communicate with the most celebrated botanists and horticulturists of the day. He carried with him a letter from Boerhaave to Sir Hans Sloane, who was a mere rich collector in natural history, and afterwards founder of the British Museum. This letter is still preserved among the archives of that institution, and it is written in the strongest language of recommendation. Notwithstanding such an honourable introduction, however, the old baronet, who was a sort of highly cultivated curiosity-shop keeper and not a scientific man, was indisposed to do justice to the merits of a young man whose innovations on established systems he viewed with suspicion and dislike. He therefore treated the stranger with coldness, and dismissed him without any marks of regard. One of the principal objects of interest to Linnæus, in this country, was the botanical garden at Chelsea; and from the keeper of that collection, Philip Miller, an excellent botanist, he experienced much attention, and was supplied with many rare plants. The garden at Chelsea was the first in

Great Britain that was subsequently arranged according to the Linnæan system. Dr. Shaw, the Oriental traveller, Professor Martyn, Peter Collinson, and many other men of true science, received Linnæus consistently with his testimonials, and admiring his genius, forwarded his objects by all the means in their power, and, on his return to the Continent, continued to correspond with him on subjects of mutual interest in science.

From London our traveller proceeded to Oxford, where he paid his respects to the celebrated Dillenius, justly considered one of the first botanists of the time. This learned man was not by any means disposed to regard Linnæus favourably. He had received from Gronovius a sheet of the "Genera Plantarum," and conceiving it to be written in opposition to him, was irate, and, pointing to the young Swede, said to a gentleman who chanced to be in his company at the moment of Linnæus's entry, "See, this is the young man who confounds all botany!" Linnæus did not understand English, but the word "confound," so similar to the Latin *confundere*, let him into the secret of the professor's words. He, however, showed no sign of comprehending him.

Linnæus almost despaired of gaining the friendship of this learned man, and obtaining from him the plants he wanted. At length, on the third day of his visit to Oxford, he went to take leave of Dillenius, and, in parting, said, "I have but one request to make of you; will you tell me why you called me, the other day, the person who confounds all botany?" Unable to evade so direct a question, Dillenius took him to his library, and showed him the sheet of his genera which he had obtained. It was marked in sundry places with notes of query. "What signify these marks?" said Linnæus. "They signify all the false genera of plants in your book," answered the other. This challenge led to an explanation, in which Linnæus proved his accuracy in every instance. The result was an entire change on the part of Dillenius, who afterwards detained Linnæus with him a month, and found so much satisfaction in his company that he kept him always in close converse, scarce leaving him an hour to himself. At last he parted from him with tears in his eyes, after making him the offer to stay and share his salary, which would have sufficed for them both.

Linnæus never learned any language, not even Dutch, although he lived three years in Holland. "Nevertheless," he says, "I found my way everywhere well and happily." Despite this great obstacle, Linnæus appears to have counted among his friends and correspondents some of the fair sex, in several countries. Lady Ann Monson in London, and Mrs. Blackburne at Oxford, were among this number; and he had a most enthusiastic admirer in Miss Jane Colden, of America, who was introduced to his notice by one of his correspondents, as the only lady known to be scientifically acquainted with the Linnæan system.

She had drawn and described four hundred plants, according to his method, using English terms.

Pleased with the favour and interest thus manifested, Linnæus acknowledged his sense of them, by preserving the names of these ladies in the vegetable kingdom, and, among others, he named two genera of beautiful plants, Monsonia and Coldenia. The study of botany was so greatly promoted and facilitated by the easy and pleasant method introduced by Linnæus, that it is no wonder the ladies acknowledged, with gratitude, their obligation to the naturalist who first originated a method by which this delightful study could be brought within the attainment of all who loved it.

Linnæus wished to visit Paris, and travelled by way of Leyden, where he enjoyed the society of Lieberkühn, a professor possessed of "incomparable microscopes." He stopped there until the spring of 1738, and not long before his departure, he had an affecting interview with the great Boerhaave, then on his death-bed. This illustrious man, who had proved himself so generous a friend to the young naturalist, took a sorrowful and affectionate leave of him. His parting words were: "I have lived out my time, and done what I could; may God preserve thee, from whom the world expects much more. Farewell, dear Linnæus!" Linnæus fell ill, and was attended by his fellow-labourer, Von Swieten, and on his recovery Mr. Clifford sent him for a tour into Brabant. Thence he went to Paris, saw the Jussieus and Réaumur, and was admitted a coresponding member of the Academy of Science. Leaving Paris, he went northwards to see his father, and then to his love. The course of true love had run very crookedly, for a mutual friend, who had been the medium of the correspondence of the lovers, fell in love with the lady himself. She was true, however, and they were finally betrothed. It was strange that the greatest botanist of the day could not get a living out of his science, and it is not to the credit of his native country. Again Linnæus had to take to physic, and settling at Stockholm, found that the people would not trust him with the cure of their dogs, much less with that of themselves. Abroad he had been honoured everywhere, and in his own country he was a nobody. All of a sudden things changed, he cured somebody, and everybody went to him to be cured. Then his star began to shine, the people of Upsala began to remember him. Count Tessin, who had been tutor to the King of Sweden, and who was a lover of natural history, procured him a salary of two hundred ducats a year, on condition that he would give public lectures on botany and mineralogy. Linnæus wrote of this good friend: " He received me, a stranger, on my return; he obtained me a salary from the States, the appointment of physician to the Admiralty, the professorship of Botany at Upsala, the title of Dean of the College of Physicians, the favour of two kings, and recommended me by a medal, to posterity." Having a good income at last, Linnæus entreated that his marriage might not longer be delayed. He married Sara Elizabeth Moræa, at her father's home near Fahlun.

One of Linnæus's biographers says, "He was fonder, on the whole, of meddling with plants than with patients;" and in the true spirit of science, Linnæus gave up his lucrative practice to settle down as Professor of Botany to the University of Upsala. It was the summit of his wishes, and in 1741 he began to reside at Upsala, which was to be his future home.

His zeal, talents, and widespread renown soon produced the desired effect, and in a few years the garden at Upsala ranked equal, if not superior, to similar institutions in Europe. Contributions to its stores continually poured in from all quarters, and the most celebrated botanists vied with each other in presenting the treasures of every region and climate of the globe to its distinguished superintendent. Six years after the establishment of this garden, the new professor published its description. The numbers of the foreign species of plants in it at that time, amounted to one thousand one hundred. He was filled with delight when he beheld these fruits of his labours. As a teacher and lecturer, Linnæus distinguished himself in a particular manner. His old students always spoke well of his teaching, and he trained some of the most distinguished botanists in Europe.

The names of Kalm, Thunberg, Sparrman, Solander, and Fabricius, for instance, are well known in the scientific world; and there is perhaps nothing more truly honourable to the memory of their great master, than the fact that he was the founder of such a school of able and enterprising men.

Linnæus impressed upon his students, and took care to remember in his own writings, that it was absolutely necessary to be exact in botanical descriptions—that the genus should be properly named, and that it should represent an idea into which certain species could enter.

To the poor, and even to the rich, foreign students who resided at Upsala entirely on his account, he was most generous, refusing the perquisites which he should have received for his lectures. To the former he remitted the money from purely benevolent motives, while he declined it from the others, that he might convince them how truly proud he was of his science, so that he would fain make it free of cost to those who sought after it. One of them having repeatedly urged Linnæus to accept a Swedish bank-note as an acknowledgment for the pains he had taken to teach him, he said, "Tell me candidly, are you rich, and can you afford it? Can you well spare this money on your return to Germany? If you can, then give the note to my wife; but, if you be poor, so help me Heaven, I will take not a single farthing from you." "You are the only Swiss that visits me, and I feel a pleasure in telling you all I know, gratis," was his answer to another, who importuned him in the same manner. It was evident that he was never so much at home, so entirely happy, as in his garden, and while searching into the secrets and hidden properties and workings of nature. Hence he reckoned it among the choicest favours vouchsafed him by Providence, that he had been "inspired with an inclination for science so passionate, as to become the source of highest delight to him." His diligence and minute observation were continually adding to his knowledge, and imparting some fresh light in the study he loved. Indeed, after mentioning with evident satisfaction the honours showed him, Linnæus somewhat significantly, and very curtly, adds, "Thus was he obliged to be a courtier, contrary to his inclination." From his own account of his personal appearance we learn that he was a little below the standard height, and of a strong and compact figure. He rather stooped in walking, having contracted this habit from the frequent examination of plants and other objects. His head was large, and a good deal raised behind, and there was a wart on the side of his cheek. His hair was of a dark brown, till silvered by age, when his brow became much furrowed and wrinkled. His eyes were brown, bright and piercing, and his sight exceedingly keen. His ear, too, was very acute, and quick in catching every sound, except that of music, in which he took no delight.

His natural temperament, he tells us, was vivacious; prompt to joy, sorrow, and anger, but the latter was speedily appeased, and he was so averse to disputes that he never would answer any of his numerous assailants. In his early days he was full of energy and spirit, and through life his movements were rapid and agile. In his habits he observed the strictest temperance and method. He never delayed anything he had to do, and noted down immediately what he wished to remember. He has recorded that he never neglected a lecture; and by rigid economy of time, and a regular and exact distribution of the hours, he completed those extraordinary labours which remain lasting proofs of his talents, acuteness, and industry.

Of his wife, Linnæus makes honourable mention, and numbers her as among the choice gifts bestowed on him. "She was," he says, "the wife for whom he most wished, and who managed his household affairs while he was engaged in laborious studies."

The year 1764 was marked by several events of domestic interest in the life of Linnæus. Early in the spring he was attacked by a violent pleurisy, which threatened to cut short his existence. He relates how, with great difficulty, and through the kind assistance and consummate skill of Rosen, his present friend and old enemy, he was brought safely through the crisis. It is truly pleasing to read in his private memoranda, the gratitude he felt to his old rival, and the expressions of intimate regard which thenceforward prevailed between them. Recovered from this illness, Linnæus retired to Hammarby, to enjoy the fresh invigorating air of the country, and to celebrate his "Silfer Bröllop," a Swedish custom of commemorating the twenty-fifth return of the wedding day. One of his most celebrated pupils, Professor Fabricius, has given some interesting particulars respecting his eminent master at this period of his life.

"For two whole years," he says, "I was so fortunate as to enjoy his instruction, guidance, and confidential friendship. When I became acquainted with the Chevalier von Linné, although he had not attained his sixtieth year, increasing age had already furrowed his brow with wrinkles. His countenance was open, almost constantly serene, and bore great resemblance to his portrait in the book called Species Plantarum. But his eyes, of all the eyes I ever saw, were the most beautiful. They certainly were but small, but they shone with a brilliancy, and had a degree of penetration, such as I never observed in another man. His mind was noble and elevated, though I well know some persons have accused him of several faults. But his greatest excellence consisted in the systematic order of his thoughts. Whatever he did or said was faithful to order, truth, and regularity. His passions were strong and violent, his heart open to every impression of joy, and he loved jocularity, conviviality, and good living, An excellent companion, he was pleasant in conversation, and full of entertaining stories; at the same time, suddenly roused to anger, he was boisterous and violent, but immediately his displeasure subsided, and he was all good-humour again. His friendship was sure and invariable, science being generally its basis; and every one who knew him must be aware what concern he always manifested for his pupils, and with how much zeal they returned his friendship. In summer we followed him into the country. Our life was then much happier. Our dwelling was about a quarter of a league distant from his house at Hammarby, in a farm. He rose very early in summer, mostly about four o'clock. At six he came to us, because his house was then building, breakfasted with us, and gave lectures upon the natural orders of plants as long as he pleased, and generally till about ten o'clock. We then wandered about among the neighbouring rocks, the productions of which afforded us plenty of entertainment. In the afternoon we went to his garden, and in the evening mostly played at the Swedish game of trissett, in company with the ladies. Occasionally, the whole family came to spend the day with us, and then we sent for a peasant, who played on an instrument resembling a violin, to which we danced in the barn of our farm-house; and though the company was but small, and the dances superlatively rustic, we passed the time merrily. While we danced, Linnæus sat looking on, and smoking his pipe; sometimes, though very rarely, he danced a Polish dance, in which he excelled every one of us young men. He was exceedingly delighted when he saw us in high glee, nay, even if we became noisy. His only anxiety was, that we might be well entertained. Those days, those hours, will never be erased from my memory, and every remembrance of them is grateful to my heart!"

He seems, before sending it, to have added at the close a sort of summary of his deeds, his merits, his honours, and his obligations. With the scrupulous care, and love of truth and justice, which always characterized him, he reckoned up, under the latter head, the various aids afforded him by his pupils and friends; and, conscious of his higher obligations, he enumerated the favours he had received from the Divine hand which he acknowledged had led and prospered him. He had permitted him to visit His secret council chambers, and to see more of the creation than any mortal before him, and given him greater knowledge of natural history than any one had hitherto acquired. Even beneath the pressure of increasing infirmities, the fondness of Linnæus for his beloved studies continued undiminished, and his desire of adding to his knowledge was keen as ever. Some of his letters at this period are full of vivacity, and strikingly express the ardour of his zeal. An idea of their spirit may be gained from a short extract taken from one, dated August 8th, 1771. "I received an hour ago," he writes, "yours of the 16th July, nor did I ever get a more welcome letter, as it contains the happy tidings of my dear Solander's safe return. Thanks and glory to God, who has protected him through the dangers of such a voyage. If I were not bound fast here, by sixty-four years of age and a worn-out body, I would this very day set out for London, to see this great hero in botany. Moses was not permitted to enter Palestine, but only to view it from a distance ; so I conceive an idea in my mind of the acquisitions and treasures of those who have visited every part of the globe."

In the spring of 1774, while lecturing in the Botanic Garden, he suffered an attack of apoplexy, the debilitating effects of which obliged him to relinquish all active professional duties, and to close his literary occupations. In 1776 a second seizure supervened, which rendered him paralytic on the right side, and impaired his mental powers so much that he became a distressing spectacle. Yet, even then, with the natural flow of cheerfulness so peculiar to him, he thus described his own situation :— "Linnæus limps, can hardly walk, speaks unintelligibly, and is scarce able to write." Nature remained, to the last, his sole comfort and relief. He used to be carried to his museum, where he gazed on the treasures he had collected with so much care and labour, and as long as possible he continued to manifest peculiar delight in examining the rarities and new productions which had been latterly added to them by some of his pupils.

It is scarcely possible to find a more striking illustration of the "ruling passion strong in death," than is afforded in the instance of Linnæus. Lingering and painful were the last twelve months of his existence; but at length, on the 10th January, 1778, he gently expired in his sleep, in the seventy-first year of his age. The death of Linnæus was regarded, in Sweden, as a national calamity. The whole University went into mourning, and all the professors, doctors, and students then at Upsala, attended his funeral. The king, in his speech to the States in the same year, publicly lamented his death, and ordered a medal to be struck in his honour; and in 1798 a monument was erected to him in the cathedral at Upsala, where he was interred.

Such a life needs but little comment. It speaks for itself to the youth leaving school and knowing not what to do, to the young man struggling for existence and position, to the middle-aged man in his wealth and influence, and to the old man who cares to leave a good name behind him.

CHAPTER V.

THE CONSOLIDATION OF THE SCIENCE OF PLANTS.

The life of De Candolle—The Natural System.

THERE is a name which is very familiar to young and old botanists nowadays, and which is always mentioned with feelings of great respect. It is that of M. de Candolle, one of the founders of the modern system of the classification of plants which is used by everybody now in preference to the celebrated artificial method taught by Linnæus.

Augustin Pyramus de Candolle was born at Geneva, in February, 1778, and his father, M. Augustine de Candolle, was descended from one of the oldest families of Provence. One of his ancestors, M. Pyramus de Candolle, became a Protestant, and left France for the freer air of Switzerland, and settled at Geneva in 1591. This gentleman became a citizen of the town, a member of the legislature, and took up the business of a printer. His presses gave forth translations of the works of Tacitus and Xenophon.

They were stirring times, and this energetic man once, in travelling through Grenoble into Switzerland, learned that the Duke of Savoy intended to take Geneva by surprise, with his army. When the attempt was made, Pyramus de Candolle fought as a citizen of his adopted town. Subsequently he went to Yverdun and established manufactories, but the jealousy of the Bernese ruined him, and he died broken-hearted. The family returned to Geneva to live on small means, and the father of De Candolle became a banker, and was much employed by the State during troublous political times.

An industrious, simple, loving, clever man was the father, and he married Mademoiselle Brière. De Candolle wrote of his mother: "She was an educated woman, good, fond of fun, and clever; she was gifted with all the graces and virtues of the mind, and she contributed by her amiable conversations and teachings to give me a taste for science and literature. She had only one fault, and it strangely enough influenced my character. She was proud of her family, which she considered was superior in station to that of my father, because her mother was a distant relation of La.Fort, the minister of Peter the Great of Russia. She took every opportunity of making my father feel this pretended superiority, so that when he became forty-eight years of age, he thought that he would make himself known to his relatives and take up his nobility in Provence, and show his wife that his descent was better than hers. But my father took every opportunity of teaching me that ability alone was the real distinction amongst men, and that nobility by itself was nothing, and was a matter of accident. So that my mother's exaggerated family notions, and my father's wise precepts, coming as they did to me, during times of political change, developed in me a sincere love for freedom, and a contempt for all success except that which was deserved." De Candolle was born when his father was in active office, and the earliest recollections of the future naturalist were about his father's military command, and the endeavours of this good citizen to pacify the populace and the ruling powers, who were always in opposition. The little fellow was always ill, and lost much of the outdoor play of his companions; but there was compensation, for he learned to read fairly soon, and at five years of age he used to read and pretend to act plays; and his heart was in his studies, for when M. de Florian, an author, came to see the family, the child told him that he was going to write comedies, and had acted them. At seven years of age he was far in advance, and then came illness—scarlet fever, ear-ache, and threatening brain disease. He used to say in after years that he well remembered seeing everything looking double. His recovery was very slow, and he was taken to the country to a brisk air, and then he began to be robust, and for fifty years after he never spent a day in bed. But his father did not send him to the public school; he employed a tutor, and the child learned nothing during three years. Then came a little country life, and the friendship of a man, a distinguished naturalist, Mr. Charles Bonnet. His first start in science was homely enough. His mother used to collect the herbs and fruit out of the garden, and the boy used to arrange what she gathered, keeping the different kinds separate with an exactitude that made everybody amazed. He said that he ought to arrange the fruit according to their natures.

When eleven years of age, De Candolle was sent to the college at Geneva, and was placed in the fourth class, under a master of only moderate powers of teaching. No great progress was made in study, and the boy was rarely seen in the upper part of the class. One day his father came to the college to inquire how the boy was getting on, and being a Government official was, of course, well received. A little arrangement by the master, which excited the contempt of the boy, placed him at the head of the class, and so unfair did this seem that the little fellow told his father that he had no right to be there. However, he was removed to the third class, and fortunately came under a better master. Young De Candolle played hard and got more healthy, and his studies were not onerous. In fact, his mother did more for him than the school. She taught him his native language, and gave him a love for poetry. But this was almost crushed out by the foolish method of teaching in the school. If a boy wanted a holiday he had to write to the rector of the college for it in Latin verse, and of course children of twelve years of age could not compose sufficiently well. So they copied, and the result was that, year after year, the rector received a collection of Latin letters which resembled those of the year before, and this had gone on for several generations. However, the boy wrote to the rector in French verse, and in original verse. This was considered something out of the common, and the boy was praised, and his peculiar gift was fostered. He became very intimate with a school-fellow named Gaudy, who had the same tastes, and they used to spend much of their time in turning Latin prose and poetry into very bad French verse. Soon after his old fondness for acting returned, and he was successful in private theatricals. The boy worked hard at this amusement, and learned many of the great French tragedies and comedies, and although the time was apparently wasted, yet De Candolle used to say that it did his memory good, gave him a good style, and took away nervousness. Then his father gave him a good private tutor, and the boy entered the first class. There he found a master who insisted on regular and profitable study, besides Latin verse, and the result was that De Candolle began to distinguish himself and took prizes. One prize which he gained, made him think very deeply afterwards. It was an essay relating to the existence of God. De Candolle wrote his essay in four hours, and it consisted of from fifteen to twenty pages; it included all he had learned of his catechism, what he remembered of many sermons, and a host of quotations from the Bible. But although the youth got the prize, and was much applauded, he felt that he was a complete stranger to the spirit of the truths he had written, and that his heart had little to do with the sentences which came from his pen. He learned religion just as he learned Greek and Latin. In 1792 De Candolle left the college and began to study literature, and, released from the troublesome discipline of the class, worked as if he were a man. But things did not go on smoothly, for the political troubles of that age soon affected Geneva. A French army occupied Savoy and encamped near Geneva. The Government prepared to defend the town, and the fathers of families began to send their wives and children into the interior of Switzerland. De Candolle was in despair when his father told him and his brother to accompany their mother; he longed to fight for his country, but he had to leave, and they went to Champagne, a small village near Grandison, where the father, foreseeing the trouble, had bought an estate. There the summer and autumn were passed peaceably, and in superintending the vines, the gathering of the grapes, and managing the property with his mother. Montesquieu, the French general, did not care about crushing the little town of Geneva, and other matters called him away. So the immediate danger passed and the family returned to Geneva.

The youth returned to his studies amidst popular

discontent within the town. A revolution occurred, and a provisional committee occupied the position of the former Government. Strangely enough this occurred whilst De Candolle's father was chief magistrate, and the Government fell whilst he was in office. Of course the man who had done so much for the town was obliged to go into exile, and he left for his little estate at Champagne, leaving his son behind to pursue his studies. The youth was left under the charge of his tutor, a young married man, and much good work was done, and in 1793 he rejoined his father. During the next year M. Vaucher gave some lectures on botany in the very modest little Botanical Garden of Geneva. He was a clergyman and Professor of Theology, but his amusements led him to study plants, and especially those which live in fresh water. His manner of teaching and the subject, attracted De Candolle, and indeed so much so that he felt that botany would be his special study through life. What he learned from M. Vaucher was about the principal organs of plants, and he began to get books describing plants and to endeavour to describe for himself. Singularly enough, the methodical courses of study which De Candolle had undergone assisted him; for although he obtained some botanical works of a very indifferent kind, which would have satisfied most youths, he began to see their errors of method. Knowing nothing of the labours of the great botanists, the youth managed to see his way to the most reasonable plan of describing plants, and he noticed the organs, one after the other, in the proper manner. Teaching himself the rudiments of the study of plants, and giving much time also to literature, young De Candolle remained much at home, for Geneva was in a horrible state of political revolution. Robespierre managed to send emissaries there, and most of the better class of citizens were imprisoned. De Candolle's father was sentenced to death, but being away from the town the sentence had no effect. This state of things lasted for some time, until the good sense of the majority annulled the sentence and restored order. Many Genevese emigrated to America, and when De Candolle returned to his studies he found the town sad, and nearly all his old friends exiled or gone in disgust. He had no amusements and therefore his studies were prosecuted with vigour, and he began a course of natural philosophy. In 1796 he left his studies and spent the summer with his father, reading good botanical works on the natural philosophy of trees, the uses of leaves; and, what was of more importance, he wandered far and wide over the Jura Mountains, collecting plants to describe and study. He got Linnæus's European Botany, and soon began to learn many plants by their proper names. But he used Linnæus's book as a simple dictionary, for he saw that although the names of plants could be easily found out by it, there were plants grouped together in it that had no close resemblance in their most important parts. At this time his interest in his study was intensified by a terrible instance which he witnessed of the hidden powers of simple-looking plants. He saw three little children die who had eaten belladonna berries.

When eighteen years of age, De Candolle went to Paris and lived in the same house as Dolomieu, a very distinguished mineralogist, a wise and moderate man whose simplicity charmed the young man. This wise friend did not press his special study on De Candolle, but advised him to follow his fondness for botany, giving him, however, some little insight into the nature of crystals and their laws of form. De Candolle then learned that there was a philosophy in stones, and he always stated in after life that this instruction made him think about the philosophy which linked plants together in the scheme of creation. He had an instructive conversation with a well-known botanist, about the structure of the stems of palms and grapes—which differ so much from those of the oak, plane, willow—and of ordinary shrubs; and this distinction of two great groups of plants gave him an insight into some of the grand distinctions between plants, and which enabled hundreds of species or genera to be grouped and separated. Unfortunately, at the time of his arrival at Paris, the botanical courses at the college were not being given, so he began to attend the lectures on chemistry, physics, and mineralogy. He often went to hear Cuvier, the great comparative anatomist, whose great ability and dignity of manner impressed everybody, and he made the acquaintance of the still greater Lamarck in a very curious manner. De Candolle had seen M. de Lamarck at the French Academy of Sciences, but he did not know anybody who could introduce him to the great man. However, he found out that Lamarck used to dine at the same little restaurant which he patronized. So a little plan was adopted to draw the celebrated zoologist and botanist into conversation. De Candolle asked his friend Pictet, who afterwards became a professor at Geneva and a great man, to come by chance as it were and sit beside him at the same table as Lamarck, and they began a conversation about botany. De Candolle especially stated how useful he had found a book called the "Description of the French Plants" in his studies. This was overheard by Lamarck, who was the author of it, and he joined in the conversation. Lamarck asked the young man to come and see him, and a friendship commenced; and although they did not have at that time much to say to one another about botany, still the distinguished French naturalist gave good advice, and, when De Candolle left Paris, presented him with a letter and a book to give to M. Sénebier, of Geneva, whose friendship probably decided the future career of the rising young botanist. Certainly the acquaintance of Lamarck stimulated De Candolle to study the physiology of plants—how they grow, breathe, how the sap circulates, how the colours are produced, and how the young seeds are formed. The happy circumstances which surrounded the young man at Paris enabled him to see the great comedies of the day and to admire the splendid acting at the theatres. But he was a philosopher then, and he could not but be struck with the furious gaiety of society and the great frivolity of the day, and with that careless method of living and thinking which followed as a kind of revulsion on the awful scenes of the Revolution and the Reign of Terror. In the spring of 1797, De Candolle returned to Geneva. There he studied the physiology of plants with M. Sénebier, going to his father's house in the holidays, which were spent in botanical excursions. In one of these, on the Jura Mountains, De Candolle discovered a new fungus of a beautiful red colour, and his adventure in obtaining the specimen was very characteristic of the man. On the sides of those hills are many very precipitous trough-like paths, down which the wood-cutters pass the fir trees they cut high up on the mountains, to the valleys. They are rugged at the sides, and have really been worn out of the hills by running water and the rushing downwards of the trees. Active people can slide down these "couloirs" by sitting on a stick placed between one's legs, and down went young De Candolle in that fashion. As he rushed along, he saw a beautiful red plant on a branch of a tree overhanging the couloir, and as he slid down he managed to cut the branch and obtain his prize—his first new plant to describe.

But it was done at the expense of his clothes, which got torn off from him in many parts, by the rocks, so that he had to slink home to avoid being seen. Working hard at botany, the young enthusiast had very agreeable hours of relaxation. He was in the midst of a charming homely society; and there is no doubt that his purity of character and thorough honesty of disposition were fostered and intensified, by his having the friendship of several young married and single women of good education and position. They made him a polished gentleman, and he used to say that that was the happy time of his life; he had no cares or anxieties, everything smiled on him, yet he was conscious that it must end, and that he must prepare for work and the struggle of life.

Politics were always the trouble of the De Candolle family, and they settled the future career of the young botanist. Geneva was about to become a portion of the French Republic, the father of De Candolle lost one-half of his fortune, and the young man went to Paris to learn how to earn his bread after preliminary study. He had a sad parting from the father who had been so good to him, and who loved him so well, and arrived at Paris, being received by an uncle, in March, 1798. After a few days of quietude, which he spent in calling on his former friends, he determined to go into lodgings near the Jardin des Plantes, and to work, leaving pleasure behind him, and to be sought for when he could afford it. He began to study medicine, and led the odd life of a medical student, attended to by old crones in their second childhood, and witnessing all the sad sights of the hospitals. Whenever he could, he made his way to the Botanical Garden, and yet he did not attend the lectures on botany. He found them not consistent with what he knew. But he was ever studying, describing, and observing plants, and, knowing nobody at the gardens, sought out Lamarck, who offered him some articles in his Encyclopædia to write. The articles were written, and mistakes were naturally made, and in after years they were readily acknowledged and set right. But the work did not advance the young botanist in his studies, although it confirmed him in the necessity of examining all the parts of a plant in classifying it, and in paying especial attention to those organs which are the most important to the life and reproduction of the kind. Leaving his lodgings to board with a friend, De Candolle was robbed, as was usual in those days, by his housekeepers; but he got into a worse scrape by being inveigled into a gambling-house, where he lost nearly all the money he had earned. It cured him of that folly. At work he began to make experiments on the action of different gases on the roots of plants, and obtained some curious results; and M. Desfontaines, the Professor of Botany, gave him hints about the correct method of describing plants, so as to enable him to write the letterpress to the plates of a work on those succulent plants called Crassulaceæ, of which the houseleek and stonecrops are familiar examples. Medicine was quite given up; and, in fact, it was hateful to De Candolle, who used to say, "If I make a mistake in naming a plant, I can set it right, but if I had made mistakes as a medical man, who knows how many dear little children I might not have killed?" He became a friend of the Delessert family, and met at their house all those rising naturalists who were forming the great French school, and this society was of great importance to him. Botanical excursions to Fontainebleau were made by him, with Brongniart, Cuvier, and Dumeril, all great men in their day, and then he went botanizing into Normandy, and nearly got drowned collecting seaweeds. Returning to Paris, he was fortunate enough to be again kindly looked after by some good families, and he became attached to Mdlle. Fanny Torras, one of a bright circle of ladies who liked the brilliant conversation and good manners of the rising young man. Going to Holland for a trip, De Candolle was struck with the curious vegetation of the hills or dunes of sand near the coast, and this appears to have attracted his attention to the geographical distribution of plants. Nevertheless, and in spite of all those attractions, he studied human anatomy and zoology. In course of time he went home to Champagne, and his future marriage was agreed upon. On his return to Paris, he was received as the future husband of Mdlle. Torras.

He studied the "sleep of plants," the classification of the Vetches, was presented at the Institute, and elected a member of the Société Philomathique, where he met and became the associate of his old botanical companions at Fontainebleau.

There is no doubt that a singular political position which was thrust upon this young man of twenty-two years of age, decided his future career, for it brought him under the eye of Napoleon Bonaparte, the First Consul of France. Geneva nominated him as a "notable" to whom the consul might apply for information about the requirements of the town. De Candolle wrote in his memoirs: "I was not much of a partisan. Born a republican, a friend of peace, I saw with anxiety Napoleon's evident love of war and desire for monarchy, but I was obliged to look favourably on him, for he had destroyed anarchy, and possessed great abilities." Napoleon and the young man had two interviews, one a peaceable one, which did good to the town of Geneva, and a second and stormy one, during which the simple student of the truth stood up, like a man, against the angry despot, and quailed not beneath that eye which most men feared. He was not forgotten, however, and after a while he was nominated on a commission to investigate the teaching given in the schools of Paris, under the charge of laymen. This commission was necessary, for the Roman Catholic authorities were anxious to put down lay teaching. De Candolle, a firm Protestant, took great care in making his report, and he decided that although there was much to be desired, still the lay schools were doing their duty.

Pursuing his studies, De Candolle began to form an herbarium, and his time was divided between science and philanthropy—for he was a visitor at the hospitals and prisons of Paris—and his Fanny, whom he married in 1802. Immediately afterwards he began to write his description of the plants of France, and Cuvier asked him to lecture for him during a term. The subject chosen was the physiology of plants; it was well managed, and it tempted De Candolle to head his new book with some chapters on it. Grief came in due time; De Candolle and his wife lost their firstborn, a pretty little girl, and a long absence from Paris was necessary. On their return, De Candolle recommenced his work on his book, and after its completion he began a series of excursions in different parts of France, studying the botany and geology. After a while a son was born, and De Candolle was offered the professorship of Botany at Montpellier.

He visited the city to see how he liked it, and he took this opportunity, also, to go to the Pyrenees for a botanical trip, collecting at the time many interesting plants. A difficulty existed about the acceptance of the position, for there was much teaching required, and there would not be much time for these excursions about France, which were absolutely necessary for the knowledge of the different local assemblages of plants or floras. De Candolle had a salary of about £160 a year, which enabled him to start from Paris and to botanize. If he went to Montpellier, all his original work might cease, and he could not earn this money and teach at the same time. So, loving real work, he determined not to accept the position. A great endeavour was being made, however, to restore the teaching of natural history at Montpellier, and the friends of the young man called on the then Minister of the Interior, M. Cretet, and urged him to see the rising botanist. At the interview Mr. Cretet, who had no botanical tastes, was wonderfully amused at a man's giving up a good place for the sake of running about France picking up plants, and said, in a good-humoured manner, "Now, young man, if you don't take both the situations you shan't have either." The professorship at Montpellier was accepted, and the necessary journeys were to be allowed. This M. Cretet seems to have been a man of great sense, and quite upset M. de Laplace, the great mathematician, about De Candolle. Laplace wanted to pay a compliment to the minister, and also to bring the young botanist before his notice, so he said, "Sir, you have done us a doubtful service in sending M. de Candolle to Montpellier, for we expected soon to have him as a member of the Institute." M. Cretet turned on him with an angry air and said, "Your institute! Do you know what I should like to do with your institute?" "What?" said Laplace, rather astonished at the tone of voice. "I should like to fire a cannon well into the middle of it." M. de Laplace seemed as if he would sink. "Yes," continued the minister, "I would fire a cannon at you all, and disperse you all over France. It is frightful to concentrate all the lights of the age in Paris, and to leave the departments in ignorance and idleness! I have sent M. de Candolle to Montpellier to stimulate others to activity." Considering that the members of the Institute of France have always considered themselves the very cream of the cream of science, this was very shocking.

The new professor started with his wife, little boy, his library and herbarium, and with many a regret at leaving such friends as those who enlightened Paris as anatomists and botanists. It was a great position for a man of thirty years of age, however, and it gave him sufficient to live upon; and this was welcome, for hitherto he had been poor.

When he was settled in his new establishment his father, then seventy-two years of age, came to see him, and, after a short sojourn, took his leave, accompanied by his daughter-in-law and grandson. Whilst they all went to Geneva, De Candolle prepared for and went on an excursion into Italy. During the visit to Italy, in 1808, politics came in the way of botany, and nothing was heard of De Candolle for a month, his letters having gone astray; but he turned up at Geneva, well, and in good spirits, for he heard that he had a chance of being made a member of the Institute. But he found that even great scientific men have their little foibles and favourites, and he did not get elected. In fact, he never was elected a member, although he was the most distinguished botanist of the age. Years afterwards, when he was in Geneva, he was made one of the eight foreign members, and that has always been considered a great honour. Nevertheless, politics, social position, and agreement with the authorities of the day, on all subjects, are of very considerable moment in these elections.

The return to Montpellier was sad, but the fine sunshine of the south, and cheerful society, soon made De Candolle forget his disappointment. After a botanical trip in Savoy, De Candolle wrote an important volume on geographical botany and agriculture. The first of these subjects infers a thorough knowledge of the names and kinds of plants, and it is of great importance in associating certain plants with soils, rocks, and climates.

By November, 1811, De Candolle had nearly completed his botanical tours, and he then considered that he was settled at Montpellier for a long time, and that his work would be more that of a teacher than investigator. He found that travelling and collecting had enlarged his mind, and he never regretted the six years of wandering about. About this time the young professor commenced a great work on the statistics of French vegetation. It did not deal with descriptions of species, or of the special localities where they could be found; but, first, with the general distribution of wild plants in France, and then with the relation of the plants of France to the different wants of mankind. This last part was eminently practical, and it dealt with food plants, medicinal plants, dye plants, and those which are used for clothing. It was a prodigious attempt, and it never came to a conclusion; only fragments of it were in his possession fourteen years afterwards, and he attributed much of the difficulty thrown in his way, to the alterations which occurred in the boundaries of France after the fall of Napoleon. Moreover, he had to complete his description of the plants of France, and that was not done until 1815.

De Candolle was always fond of society, and, after his labours of the day, was glad to go into or receive company. Being a Protestant, and a man of mark in his native town, he was well received by most of the families of Montpellier, and his wife also. Society consisted of good Protestant families of old, so-called nobles, and some who thought themselves nobles. It was split up like the society of most small towns, into cliques, but De Candolle escaped, for a long time, any discomforts or social antagonisms. They came at last, however.

De Candolle, like many active-minded men, was not popular with the officials who had "places" in their gift. He was intrigued against, and lost the rectorship of the University, but he had the pleasure of exposing the intrigue in 1813.

Napoleon had fought his last fight, and had gone to Elba, and the Bourbons had been restored.

Disgusted with the military spirit of the Empire, De Candolle rejoiced at the restoration of the Bourbons, and even became a volunteer to keep the town in order. He began to change his mind soon, however, for the Count d'Artois, one of the royal family, received the professor with great haughtiness, and, by way of making amends, paid particular attention to a rascal of the first water who had returned from the galleys, where he had been sent for stealing, and not for devotion to the Bourbons, as he told the duke. Going to Geneva on a visit, to place his eldest son at school, De Candolle found the city just being received into the Confederation of the Swiss Republic. He returned to Montpellier, which was full of rejoicing at Napoleon's exile, but shortly afterwards all was disorder during the hundred days in which Napoleon was, for the last time, ruler of France. Beyond the reach of direct politics, the professors of Montpellier had their little evenings, and even got up private theatricals. In the midst of a scene in one of these came the news that Napoleon had landed at Cannes, and was on his way to Paris. That was the last quiet hour that De Candolle had in the town. An unfriendly man, who was a royalist, began to set people against the professor, who resented their interference. He began to limit his circle of friends, left literature alone more and more, and plunged more deeply into science. He determined to leave Montpellier and its littlenesses. His principal care was to enlarge and utilize the botanic garden of the place, and then he devoted much time to teaching, and with great success. Civil war was imminent, and the defeat at Waterloo produced outbreaks at Montpellier. De Candolle had been elected Rector of the University during the Hundred Days, and was ordered to give up the title. This he did, and prepared to leave the place. He had sent his family to Geneva, and in travelling himself to join them, by way of Nimes, he saw traces of the horrible treatment the Protestants had received. Subsequently the family went to Paris, passing through the towns occupied by the allied troops. Having time, De Candolle visited England, and became the guest of Dr. Marcet, and was introduced to the best of the scientific world. He met and enjoyed the reticent Robert Brown, and went to a sitting of the Royal Society, which he said was dull. He was introduced to Hooker and Sir James Smith, the proprietor of the Herbarium of Linnæus, which he very properly said was the basis of botanical nomenclature. In 1816 De Candolle found himself settling down in his native town of Geneva, where he was well received, and became Professor of Natural History, and taught students of both sexes, and began to establish a botanic garden of some importance. There he was obliged to go into local politics, and for years was a representative of the town, doing good work for the poor, for liberty by receiving and protecting political fugitives and by insisting on the freedom of the press, which was considerably hated in France under the restored Bourbons. Nevertheless, year after year he taught well, and most of the great botanists of later years were either his students or his visitors and friends. As age crept on, De Candolle continued his researches, and got through the description and classification of a considerable number of known plants. These were published in a book which will always be his masterpiece. Honours crowded on him, the gifts of learned societies of all nations, and he visited most of the great cities of the Continent. In 1832 he published the second part of his work. He had great happiness with his wife, and his parents lived to great ages, content with the prosperity of their son, who was ever good and loving to them, and got his reward. He had a little estate, out of Geneva, at Saint Seine, and enjoyed it much; but, as years rolled on, the death of a son there, affected his tender heart, and he sold the place and bought another, called La Barrière, near Geneva. His eldest son, Alphonse, followed well in the father's steps. Finally, when old age troubled De Candolle, he gave up his professorship.

Ill health succeeded, but the man worked on at his great book, and even entered the political arena once again at a time of emergency. The winter of 1840–41 was one of illness, and he could no longer work. His friends were dying off, month after month, and when death came to him, he was content. He had been a good son, an excellent father, a loving friend, a true patriot, deserving everything that elevated mankind; and it is admitted by all botanists that he consolidated the science, and gave it a definite natural classification.

De Candolle early in life grasped the truth that plants grow, reproduce, and arrive at maturity, not by accident, but according to natural law, and he soon saw that some parts of plants were of more importance to their well-being and multiplication than others. He was thus a follower of Ray, and he became impressed with the belief that in arranging plants, the resemblances of the most important parts and organs, should be considered before those of the less important. This manner of proceeding he called the natural method. It was founded upon the knowledge of the anatomy of the plants and upon their physiology, and the method required care and research. The artificial method of Linnæus enabled botanists to distinguish plants readily, by examining the most readily examined, and often unimportant, parts of the plant's flower. It was not a scientific plan, but a ready method. It did not bring one plant into relation with another, showing the common method of growth and reproduction, but simply enabled one plant to be separated and distinguished from another, and this is the least part of botany.

The works of Whewell on the inductive sciences, the article on botany in the "Encyclopædia Britannica," Pulteney's "Life of Linnæus," and that written by Miss Brightwell, of Norwich, and De Candolle's "Mémoires et souvenirs écrits par lui même" have been freely and largely quoted in these chapters.

CHAPTER VI.

HEROES OF ZOOLOGY.

The nature of the science of zoology—Great zoologists usually botanists also—Aristoteles as a zoologist—Plinius—The long age of no progress—The life of Conrad Gesner—The zoology of Ray and Willughby—Swammerdam — Réaumur — The zoology of Linnæus.

ZOOLOGY does for animals what botany does for plants. It is the science which treats of the resemblances and differences of animals, their shapes, and habits, and which explains their position on the earth in different countries, and classifies them. It is inseparably linked on to the study of comparative anatomy and to physiology which treats of the internal structures and the influence which the outside world has upon the living thing. Like botany, the science arose in a simple manner, and men first of all learned to distinguish one animal from another, giving them names. Then their habits were noticed, and some attempt was made to arrange animals by their greater or less resemblances of oysters. He examined, one by one, all the species he could procure, and then classed together as a subordinate generic group all those, which resembling each other in the more important parts of their structure, differed only in size or colour, or in other points of little importance.

Aristoteles founded the natural history of his age, and no one came near to him. He left nobody behind to follow his work.

In after years, Plinius wrote on beasts, fishes, birds, and insects, and on human and comparative anatomy, but he made no great advance on Aristoteles. Then there occurred as great a gap in the study of zoology as happened in botany, and many hundreds of years elapsed before progress was made.

Conrad Gesner, a Swiss, made the first great step in zoology after the ancients, and his life was a most remarkable one. A writer says of him, that he was a shining example of the truth of the remark, that those who have most to do, and are willing to work, find the most time. He was a great scholar, and a profound naturalist. He began life in extreme poverty, soon became an orphan, laboured whilst ill, and sacrificed himself for the sake of others. A son of a poor skinner and worker of hides, he was born in 1516, at Zurich, and had to suffer pinching poverty, with his numerous brothers and sisters. An uncle was kind to the boy, and began to educate him, but death stepped in and he lost his kind relation. When only thirteen years of age, Gesner was cast upon the world, his father having died fighting in the battle of Zug. The lad was seriously ill and dropsical, and his sole fortune was a little knowledge of classics, which he had picked up. Probably one of the professors at Zurich, Ammian by name, and who had instructed him, gave him introductions, for we find the lad at Strasbourg when fifteen years of age. His thoughts were to go into the Lutheran Church, and it is certain that the Lutheran Wolfgang Fabricius Capito gave him some employment, and enabled him to begin the study of Hebrew. Returning again to Zurich, the university there gave him a little pension, to enable him to travel, and he went into France to Bourges. There he taught at a school, and occupied his spare time in learning Greek and Latin. Then he went to Strasbourg again, hoping for employment, and finding none, was asked to return to Zurich, and to teach in the university. At the age of twenty he married, and, of course, much against the wishes of his friends, who do not appear to have done anything for him, except to have given gratuitous advice. Although the Church was to be the career of Gesner, he took much interest in the healing art, and resigning his position at Zurich, he went, having a small pension, to Basle as a medical student. Anxious to know the wisdom of the Greek physicians, he paid unusual attention to that language, and edited an edition of a dictionary of it. This study brought strange results, for he was offered a professorship of Greek at Lausanne, and he accepted the position. He was very young, and yet learned men found his friendship valuable. Going, subsequently, to Montpellier, he became acquainted with a naturalist named Rondelet, and he gradually began to earn enough money to be independent. So he returned to Basle, and in 1541, being twenty-five years old, took his degree in medicine. He settled in practice at Zurich, and occupied his spare time in studying zoology and botany, and soon became wealthy. Occasionally he travelled, and during one of these trips he became acquainted with the leading men at Venice and Augsburg, and at their instance began a great work, a kind of universal catalogue of Greek, Hebrew, and Latin works. All this time he was slowly and surely studying animals and plants, and in 1551 the first part of his "History of Animals" appeared, to be followed by others in 1554, 1555, and 1556. The volumes contained descriptions of viviparous quadrupeds, that is to say, four-footed beasts, whose young are born in active movement; of oviparous quadrupeds, or those which lay eggs; of birds and of fishes, and other aquatic animals. He wrote also upon insects. All agree that this book is a miracle of industry, having for its object no less than a general history of animated nature. It contains a careful criticism of the works of previous authors, and, besides much valuable and solid knowledge on zoology, many interesting remarks on the habits and medicinal uses of animals. He followed the method of Aristoteles, and the notion of the genus was, of course, not satisfactorily established; but the book was the source of much of modern zoology, from which succeeding writers drew largely.

Gesner's botanical works were as great as those relating to animals, and he designed and painted fifteen hundred figures of plants, which were of great use to his successors. As if he had not enough to do, he translated the Greek works of Aelian, on animals, in 1556. Scientific and industrious, he had much to contend with, and was short-sighted. He was the first person who used concaved glasses to remedy this defect in his sight. As years rolled on, Gesner was much liked and honoured in his native town; he was very amiable, a great peacemaker, and a liberal citizen. He established a botanic garden, and gave employment to artists. Whilst in the full vigour of life, and in active practice as a physician, the plague attacked Zurich, and Gesner successfully combated the contagious disorder in many cases. He exposed himself without fear, after the fashion of most medical men, and unfortunately caught the disease. When the worst symptoms came, he knew his hour was at hand, and asked to be carried into his library and museum, where all the treasures he had collected and described, to the delight of his students and friends, were deposited. There he breathed his last, in the arms of his affectionate wife, for whose love contagion had no terrors. He died with the calmness of a Christian philosopher, on the fifth day of his attack, at the early age of forty-nine. His remains rest, much honoured, in the cloister of the Greek church at Zurich. Not only did Gesner consolidate the knowledge of the animal and vegetable kingdom of his day, but he also influenced other authors to do good work, and to avoid unkind criticism. His calm, candid, and equable temper enabled him to soothe the angry feelings of others, under their real and imaginary wrongs. He laid aside his own labour to assist others, and he devoted much time to the supervision and publication of a work which was left incomplete, by a deceased friend, so as to provide for the family.

Gesner's life is a very good proof that where there is a will there is a way, and that poverty does not impede the path of a thoroughly industrious and earnest man. The poor skinner's son's name is respected at the present day, and will be so, as long as science lasts.

The interesting life of Ray has already been given amongst those of the heroes of botany; he was, however, a zoologist of the first class, and his devotion to that part of natural history was part of his great friendship for Mr. Willughby. This promising young man studied under Ray, at Cambridge, and whilst the master took plants under his care and study, the pupil began to work at animals. They made a tour together, visiting France, Spain, Italy, Germany, and the Low Countries. Ichthyology, or the study of fishes, and ornithology, or the study of birds, occupied the attention of Willughby. Having collected a vast number of specimens and observations, they returned to England, and Willughby immediately commenced working with a view to the publication of a great work on the animal kingdom. He even contemplated a visit to America; but health failed, and he died in the prime of life, on July 3rd, 1672. The education of his two infant sons was confided to Mr. Ray, who was one of his executors. Willughby thought his works too imperfect for publication, but Ray felt otherwise, and urged it upon him for three reasons: first, the glory of God; secondly, the assistance of others in the same studies; thirdly, the honour of his native land. Upon these grounds he gave his consent, and Ray became their editor. A book on birds, "The Ornithologia," was the result, and it contains a large amount of original observation, and is a full and exact description of the habits and maladies of birds, and the best means of domesticating them. Excellent anatomical descriptions are added. Subsequently, a book on the fishes of the Mediterranean appeared.

The merits of Willughby as a natural historian still continue to be recognized. He was a most accomplished zoologist, and he gave Ray and Linnæus the method of classification of animals which is usually associated with their names. Ray acknowledged this, and he says that he found among his friend's manuscripts the histories of beasts and insects, no less than of birds and fishes, "digested with a method of his own." He was not a simple wealthy and intelligent amateur, for he was master to one of the greatest naturalists. Ray, in editing Willughby's "Book on Birds," gives a most touching preface to the memory of his friend. He says, "He was from childhood addicted to study, and ever since he came to the use of reason, so great a husbander of his time, as not willingly to lose, or let slip unoccupied, the least fragment of it; detesting no vice more than idleness, which he looked on as the parent and source of all others. Of his skill in natural philosophy, chiefly the history of animals, I shall say no more at present, but that it hath not yet been my hap to meet with any man, whether in England or beyond seas, of so general and comprehensive knowledge therein."

A very different career, but one which has had a greater general influence on natural history, was that of John Swammerdam, who was born at Amsterdam, in 1637, his father being an apothecary. His grandfather, Jacob Dirkz, was born in the village of Swammerdam, near Leyden, and his father, a well-to-do apothecary, lived there and took his name from the village. He married Berendina Corvera and settled at Amsterdam. The family lived in comfort, and the little one was destined, like many other naturalists, to the Church. His education consisted of sound Latin and Greek, and when he became old enough, he began to feel that there were responsibilities about his future office as a clergyman, which he did not think he could fulfil. Holland at that time was in a religious ferment, and sects of all kinds existed, religion being more talked about than practised. The lad, as he grew up, desired to follow in his father's footsteps, and to learn the healing art; but his genius led him to the study of nature. Before he was fifteen years of age, he began to make collections of natural history objects, and whenever he could get away from home, and spare time from his medical studies, he pursued his favourite employment, searching the woods and fields, the sand-hills and muddy shores, the lakes, rivers, and canals, for insects, worms, and molluscs, until he acquired, even as a youth, a more extensive knowledge of the lower animals than all the naturalists who had preceded him. In 1661 he went to Leyden and studied surgery and anatomy. In this last he excelled, and became celebrated for his methods of preserving dissections. Then he went to Saumur, in France, and to Paris, where he gained the friendship of Thévenot the traveller, who was his patron subsequently, and assisted him when in Amsterdam in after years, by obtaining permission for him to dissect human bodies. His fellow-pupil was Nicholas Steno, of whom more will be said under the title of "Heroes of Geology." On his return to Leyden, Swammerdam discovered the method of injecting arteries with coloured wax, and of keeping the internal organs in a dry condition for purposes of study, and investigated the nature of the lymphatics. He graduated soon after, and after receiving his diploma, returned to his old love, nature, and occupied nearly all his time in the anatomy and physiology of insects.

Swammerdam worked so incessantly, that he got into bad health, and was obliged to relinquish the medical profession for a time. He followed up his researches into the minute construction of insects, and really never ceased them until death. The Grand Duke of Tuscany visited Amsterdam at this time, and examined Swammerdam's collections. Greatly impressed with their value, and with the splendid dissections, he offered a home to the young naturalist in his palace, and twelve thousand florins for the collection. Swammerdam, however, did not care to wear a collar; and loving freedom of thought, which he did not think he would have in Italy, declined the offer. He knew that he would be expected to change his religious tenets, and said that he would not sell his soul for money. He published a "General History of Insects," in 1669, and soon afterwards broke down, entirely, in health, so that he had to go into the country to rest and do nothing. But this was impossible; and he began to study bees, and their natural history. Probably it was this constant weak health, and the solitude necessary for the peculiar nature of his work and observations, that had a very remarkable influence on the mind and emotions of this great investigator. Always religious, he longed more and more for communion with his Maker and the author of all the wonders he was constantly studying. When in better health he was happy in his thoughts, and considered that it was his duty to study nature; but when ill, from the effects of overwork, he began to think that his labours were leading him astray, and that to seek the good opinion of his fellow-creatures and to become famous, was a sin. Sometimes he gave up science, to begin again with fresh zeal, and then he would neglect it, giving up his whole time to religion. Unfortunately he was unreasonable in his method of working. Boerhaave, the great physician, thus wrote of Swammerdam: "He laboured so assiduously at this work as to destroy his constitution, nor did he ever recover a shadow of his former strength. The labour, in fact, was beyond the power of ordinary men—all day he was employed in examining objects, and at night described and delineated what he had seen by day. At six in the morning, in summer, he began to receive sufficient light from the sun to enable him to trace the objects of his examination. He continued dissecting until twelve, with his hat removed lest it should impede the light, and in the full blaze of the sun, the heat of which caused his head to be constantly covered with profuse perspiration. His eyes being constantly exposed to a strong light, the effect of which was increased by the microscope, they were so affected by it, that after midday he could no longer trace the minute bodies which he examined, although he had then as bright a light as in the forenoon."

Swammerdam investigated the nature of the changes of outside form and internal structure which accompany insect life. Some of his drawings of the escape of the ephemera fly from its sheath of delicate skin on the surface of the water, and out of the wingless or nymph condition, are very beautiful. But his accuracy regarding the minute internal changes of the tissues and organs in the larva, pupa, and perfect insect is being more and more acknowledged. He taught that these changes were not sudden, but that a continuous growth of organs and tissues culminated at certain times of the life of the insect. The larva, or caterpillar, admirably adapted for its course of life, was a stage of the life cycle of a more perfect form, the imago or flying insect. Swammerdam stated that all the organs of the perfect insect—a butterfly, for instance—were in a visible yet only slightly developed condition in the caterpillar. And late researches are leading to prove that he was right, for the wings of the future fly are to be detected in the body of the tiny crawling thing that escapes from the egg.

Happy in this toil when he was well, for it was all about what was entirely new and previously unknown, he often laboured on, when he was ill, with "sighs and tears." Naturally sensitive, pious, and very amiable, he at one time quite gave up his work under the influence of a remarkable woman, Antoinette Bourignon. She was a wealthy, well-educated person, extremely plain, and who believed that a mission had been given her to preach according to her own fancies, and not in accordance with the general doctrines of the age. She seems to have stimulated Swammerdam to lead a purely religious life, and to give up his studies. It was the age of sects and of intolerance; and possibly the disagreeable reception which this certainly very good woman met with, made the man care more about her peculiar tenets. He began, seriously, to try and sell his collections, made catalogues of his possessions, and corresponded with Antoinette. While various negotiations were pending, Swammerdam published the results of his ten years' labour and the "Anatomy of the Day Fly," a great work, and his best. Then he went on a journey into Denmark to use his influence with the king in order to get Antoinette a home in that kingdom, the Lutherans of Holland having ordered her to leave their country. He was not successful; and probably this affair made a great commotion at home. On Swammerdam's return, his father, enraged at him for his utter carelessness about earning money and his want of application to business, determined to allow him only a small sum of money to live upon. He was in utter despair, for this prevented his following his wish to lead, for the future, a life of meditation and religion. The father died soon afterwards, and a lawsuit was commenced by the family to prevent Swammerdam having his share of the property. This trouble brought on illness, and severe ague followed, and, although recovery took place, the sensitive, able man sank soon afterwards. Swammerdam made an epoch in zoology by showing the value of the microscope, and by his extreme exactitude in descriptions, drawings, and dissections. His contributions to human anatomy alone will always render his name illustrious.

Although everybody must regret that Swammerdam had not good means, and that his work was so sadly brought to a close by poverty and trouble, yet it must be remembered that wealth is not a great incentive to distinction in subjects that require great self-denial, and which are not much valued by what is called public opinion. The temptations incident to, and the real duties of wealth, are as great antagonists of successful scientific research, as poverty. And certainly the frivolity and vice of the wealthier classes of Europe, during the earlier part of the eighteenth century, were not likely to inspire any of their members with a desire for natural science. But some very remarkable instances occurred, in which the genius and determination of some great men prevailed over the intolerance and habits of the age, and enabled them to become men of great mark in zoology and other subjects.

The first to be noticed is René Antoine Ferchault

de Réaumur, who was born at Rochelle, in western France, in 1683. Well born, and having wealthy parents, he was well educated, and destined for the law. He did not follow the propensities of the age, but began to study the arts and manufactures of France with great care, and to spend his spare time in natural history researches. From what is known of his career, it is very evident that he had learned chemistry and mineralogy, and that his education had been a most careful and liberal one. His fortune was considerable, and it not being necessary for him to work for his bread, he determined to follow the bent of his inclinations. When twenty years of age, Réaumur went to Paris, and his first essay was in the form of some geometrical work which was read before the Academy of Sciences. At the early age of twenty-four he was admitted a member of that learned and somewhat emotional body, and was a very constant contributor to its publications for fifty years. At first his desire was to improve the arts and manufactures of his native land, and in 1711 he made experiments upon the manufacture of ropes, and he showed that the strength of a cord is less than the sum of the strength of the threads of which it consists, whence it follows that the less a rope is twisted after a certain point, the stronger it is. In 1715 he began to study the process of colouring artificial pearls, and probably it was during these researches that his attention was attracted towards natural history. He found out the nature of the substance which gives the pearly progressive development of the minute young to the full-grown creature. Réaumur was sufficiently wealthy to form a large collection of animals, and a very able man, M. Brisson, was employed by him as its curator, and was allowed to describe the quadrupeds and birds. Réaumur did not care so much about classifying insects, as describing their habits and anatomy; but his six great volumes are still most valuable memorials of his conscientious care. He says that the number of observations necessary for a tolerably complete history of so many minute animals is prodigious. When one reflects on all that an accomplished botanist ought to know, it is enough to frighten him. His memory is loaded with the names of twelve or thirteen thousand plants, and he is expected to recall, on occasion, the image of any one of them. There is perhaps not one of those plants but has insects peculiar to itself; and some trees, such as the oak, give sustenance to several hundred different species. And after all, how many are there that do not live on plants? How many species that devour others? How many that live at the expense of other animals? How many species are there, some of which pass the greater part of their time in water, while others pass it entirely there? The immensity of nature's works is nowhere more apparent than in the prodigious multitudes of these little animals. This being the case, he deems it impossible for any one man to acquire a knowledge of all the insects of even a limited district;

therefore, instead of burthening the memory with the characteristic distinctions of these creatures, to the neglect of matters of greater importance, he recommends attention to particular *genera*, and especially to those which are of most frequent occurrence, that a knowledge of their peculiarities, food, and propagation, and the different forms they assume, may be accurately obtained.

In the first two volumes, Réaumur treats of caterpillars, their changes of form into the chrysalis, and this into the butterfly; about their different kinds and habits, and concerning the other insects which attack them, and live within them, in their early stage.

The third volume includes the description of the habits of the clothes moths, and the plant-lice, or aphides; the fourth treats of gall insects and two-winged flies; the fifth contains the history of bees, and the sixth of wasps and hornets. The natural history of the grasshoppers, crickets, and beetles was to have been written in a seventh volume, but it was never completed. The published volumes contain much very valuable information, and their great merit consists in the wonderful care Réaumur took, in investigating facts and in recording them carefully and systematically. He especially studied the instincts of insects, and thus brought their nervous system into prominent notice, and also the evident connection between the surrounding conditions and the peculiar lives of animals.

Years rolled on and the worthy man became

old, but still persisted in his simplicity of life and desire for study. He was so superior in intellect to the class to which he belonged, that he lived free from jealousy and intrigue. Probably few men have led a happier life than Réaumur, and certainly his useful works will last as long as mankind. At the age of seventy-four he met with an accident whilst riding, and died October 18th, 1757. He had no personal vanity, and, being influenced by the true scientific spirit, sought truth and not personal distinction and reward.

Linnæus, whose life has been given under the title of a hero in botanical science, was almost as great a zoologist as botanist and mineralogist. His classification of animals produced as great a change in the direction and possibility of studying zoology, as that of plants did in the case of botany. It led the way, through an artificial system, by which animals could be readily known, to a natural system which united animals not only by their common general shape, but also by the nature, position, and use of their internal organs. His system of naming animals was equal to that of plants, and the reasonable generic and the applicable specific names, going together, stamped the animal with a kind of individuality. Classification, description, and proper naming were the important parts of Linnæus's zoology.

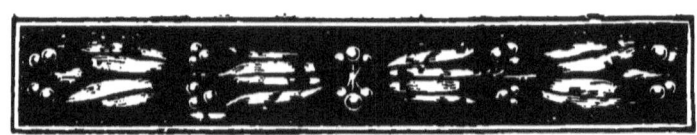

CHAPTER VII.

THE LIVES OF BUFFON, PENNANT, AND LAMARCK.

The popular writings of Buffon, and his life—Pennant's life—Lamarck and his life—The rise of popular natural history, and of exact descriptions and philosophical zoology.

IF natural history had never been studied in an easy manner, and had not the results of those studies been given to educated men desirous of knowing something about animals in popular yet correct works, very few men would have cared to become zoologists. It is the good, easy, popular, but not necessarily jocular book on natural history that, as a rule, excites the attention of the young, and stimulates the youth to obtain further knowledge. Such books were written at a very interesting time of the world, and just when they were wanted; and the writer was a very remarkable man—a man born to wealth and station, but who, like many others, preferred hard work and the study of nature to sloth and luxurious idleness, and even to the profession of arms, so much in vogue in the early part of the eighteenth century.

George Louis Leclerc de Buffon was born on September 7th, 1707, at Montbard, in Burgundy. He came of good family, and his father was councillor of the Burgundian parliament. His mother, Anne Christine Mazlin, appears to have possessed considerable natural gifts. She was also of good family, and was remarkable, in those days, for the elevation of her mind and strength of character. She was a better parent than the father who, although he was looked upon as a wonder in his province, in consequence of his wasteful living and devotion to feasts, balls, and concerts, was really only a person of average merit. The mother was tenderly loved by her son, but the father gave him some trouble in after years, on account of his follies. Nevertheless, it adds to the interest and good example of Buffon's character to learn that he did not care to follow the agreeable life of his father, but that he broke away from it and took to wisdom, although having great property, he always lived and behaved like a nobleman of wealth and mental distinction.

Buffon was the oldest of five children, and the rest were devoted by the parents to the priesthood, or to nunneries; so it would appear that the father not only followed the rule of the day, to keep the property in the hands of the eldest son, but to provide for the others in the cheapest possible manner. The young noble was in due course sent to a school at Dijon kept by Jesuit fathers, the best instructors in those days; and report says that the boy was fond of arithmetic and had a character for decision and perseverance. After a while Buffon was entered at the academy of Angers, it being decided that the boy should follow his father as a magistrate and public man. There his love of study became evident, and his application was considerable. One of his associates was a young English nobleman, Lord Kingston, and they became great friends, and probably this friendship was caused and fostered by his lordship's German tutor, Hinckman, who was a man of considerable learning. When he was nineteen years of age the three friends started for a tour in Italy. Returning to Angers to resume his studies, Buffon became a little wild, and got into a quarrel with a young Englishman at play. Buffon wounded his antagonist and had to leave the town. He went to Paris, but not to waste time; on the contrary, his former love of figures, and his later studies in mathematics, inspired him to translate Newton's "Fluxions" into French, and also Hale's "Vegetable Statics," which subsequently he presented to the Academy of Sciences. Still keeping up his friendship with Lord Kingston, Buffon visited Italy again; and there is no doubt that Hinckman instilled the love of nature into the young man's mind. They were all at Rome in 1732, when Buffon heard of the death of his mother, who was greatly mourned by him. He was then twenty-five years of age, and became very wealthy, as he was his mother's heir. Journeying in Switzerland he began to know other English people of distinction. All these friendships led him at last to England, and he went to Thoresby, the seat of Lord Kingston, and remained in the country for some months.

Buffon had a very fine person, liked a little "show," and the rather solemn and stilted manners of the British nobility pleased him. It was this stay in England, and his friendships, that gave Buffon some of the manners of the aristocracy of the day, so that Hume said of him that he resembled a marshal of France more than a man of letters. These habits, amongst which courtesy and true gentility—that is to say, treating other people as we would they should treat us in society—were predominant, clung to Buffon; and even when at home, and at his very hard and incessant labour in natural history, he kept up his state, and was the great French noble as well as the humble student of nature.

It is a curious fact, but one very readily explained, that Buffon, like nearly all the great zoologists, began his scientific life as a botanist. Plants are ever at hand, and their classification, good or bad, is readily learned. One of his first works, presented after receiving the honour of election to the Academy of Sciences at Paris, was on a question of the influence of barking trees; and others were on agriculture. He gave a proof that he was acquainted with the human frame, for he wrote on the causes of squinting.

Scientific men of nobility were rare in France in those days, and Buffon was appointed keeper to the Jardin du Roi and the Royal Museum. Anxious to continue his studies about trees, he prevailed on the king to let him experiment on a grand scale in one of the royal forests. But this was only a part of his work, for he commenced that great book on natural history which was always after to be associated with his name. It was not to be a simple book on animals, but on the history of the earth as well; and, in fact, he intended it to be an encyclopædia of all natural knowledge except mathematics and figures. It was a great conception and it was carried out year after year during success, domestic happiness and trouble. The perseverance and patience of the man were wonderful; and fortunately he had the means of collecting what was required, of buying books and of having secretaries to do the very troublesome and mechanical part of writing. He was short-sighted and wrote badly. It was not vanity, nor the desire of being great, that made Buffon work; certainly it was not amusement. But he was happy in his work, and he stated that genius is a gift which comes not from man; and the great man is an instrument in the Divine hand; he has a mission which may be for light or to ruin, and neither the environment of pleasure or glory or the troubles of fortune, ill-health, or misery should deter him from his ends. Genius, Buffon also termed, a very great aptitude for patience.

Daubenton assisted Buffon in his first three volumes of natural history, and they came out in

1749, and the other volumes came out year by year until his death.

Buffon lived carefully, and kept up the curious state of the French gentlemen of his day in his house. After he was dressed, he dictated letters and regulated his domestic affairs, and at six o'clock he retired to his studies in a building called the tower of St. Louis. This was in the garden, and far away from the house, and the only furniture in it was a wooden writing-table, with its cupboards and drawers, and an armchair. Neither pictures nor books relieved the naked appearance of the apartment, or distracted the thoughts of the learned professor. The entrance was by green folding doors, the walls were painted green, and the interior had the appearance of a chapel in consequence of the elevation of the roof. Within this garden was another building, where Buffon resided during the greater part of the year, as it was warmer than the other place, and here he composed most of his works. It was a small square building, situated on the side of a terrace, and was ornamented with drawings of birds and beasts. At nine o'clock Buffon usually took an hour's rest and his breakfast, which consisted of a piece of bread and two glasses of wine. When he had written for two hours after breakfast, he returned to the house. At dinner he spent a considerable time in conversation, and relaxed his mind from work entirely, enjoying the wit and gaiety of his friends. He usually slept for an hour after dinner in his room and took a solitary walk, and during the rest of the evening he either conversed with his family or his guests, or sat at his desk examining papers which were submitted to his judgment. At nine o'clock he went to bed. In 1762, when fifty-five years of age, Buffon married a lady who was in every way suited to him, and who, moreover, took a deep interest in his studies. He was greatly attached to her, and her companionship made the country life all the more pleasant. Four years afterwards Louis XIV. ennobled Buffon and invited him to Fontainebleau to offer him the post of Administrator of the Forests of France, but Buffon declined the office. This great man was not above a little vanity: he liked to read the most interesting parts of his works to his friends, and to draw forth their admiration. He was, moreover, fond of dress and grandeur, but that was part of the society of his day. He had a fine countenance and figure, and it was his delight to display them to the best advantage. He dressed in the extreme of fashion, and amidst his studies found time to submit his head (perhaps it was only his wig) to the hairdresser, two or three times a day. On Sundays the peasantry of Montbard assembled to gaze at the Count after the service of the church, when he passed through their ranks magnificently dressed, with his son and his retainers.

The natural history was translated into English, German, Italian, Spanish, and Dutch, and its charming pages brought a knowledge of nature to many a home. Like most naturalists of eminence,

Buffon interested himself about the ancient history of the earth. His writings were not original in that part of his subject, but what he did write contained much common sense. Nevertheless, the Faculty of Theology at Paris found fault with the geology, and informed him that no less than fourteen propositions in his works were reprehensible and contrary to the creed of the Church. Buffon was invited to recant, which he very foolishly did; and it must be mentioned that the "improper statements" are now believed in, by every educated man. It has been written of the great naturalists of the past, that Aristoteles has shown the profound combination of the laws of nature, Plinius her inexhaustible riches, Linnæus her wonderful details, and Buffon her majesty and power. Certainly his great work contains such pictures of nature as were never given before, and rarely since, by any naturalist. Buffon therefore had the happiness of bringing the cultivation of the science more generally into fashion than it had been previously. He was deficient in the orderly method of science, however; his work, supremely interesting and popular, was soon found to be inconsistent with the severely scientific study of nature. This want of order and classification led to the establishment of a new school of zoology.

Buffon's social position was of great value and importance to him as a naturalist and to the state also, for he became the object of personal regard to many distinguished foreign princes, who did not hesitate to make presents of specimens to the national museums, through him. His wealth also enabled him to help the state, for he often purchased minerals and specimens of animals for which no public money had been granted. Frederick the Great of Prussia and his son Henry, the Emperor Joseph II. of Austria, Catherine of Russia, and the kings of Norway and Sweden, all knew Buffon, admired his works, and sent presents in order to complete his museum, which was devoted and given by him to the public. The Jardin du Roi was greatly enlarged at Buffon's expense, and public opinion spoke well of the amiable and benevolent owner of Montbard.

But, as with other and less happily placed men, Buffon had to suffer, and the loss of his child, followed by the death of the wife he tenderly loved, in the prime of her life, were great shocks to him. He never was the same man afterwards, and sought to find forgetfulness in increased work and literary toil. Moreover, the ingratitude of the ruling power affected Buffon, who behaved, however, excellently, and took up the position which every man of his social condition should have maintained.

In February, 1771, Buffon was alarmingly ill, and, unknown to him, the king, Louis XV., nominated a Count d'Angiviller, to succeed in the administration of the Museums and Jardin de Roi. Buffon recovered, and found out this little job, and was naturally annoyed at the indecent haste of putting a man in his place at such a crisis; but he was most indignant when he knew who the man was—an ignoramus and court favourite, a perfectly incompetent man. It is said that Louis XV. on this occasion, to compensate Buffon for his annoyance, raised the Montbard property to the holding of a count. Certainly he ordered the sculptor, Pajon, to erect a full-sized statue of Buffon in the garden during his absence, and to put the inflated inscription on it, "His genius equals the majesty of nature." Buffon resented this, and he wrote to the President de Ruffey: "I thank you for the part you have taken in procuring this statue, which I neither required nor solicited, and which would have done me greater honour if it had been erected after my death. I have always thought that a wise man should rather fear envy then value glory; all this has been done without consulting me."

Some years afterwards an architect, who was employed in embellishing some of the buildings in the Jardin du Roi, wished to compliment Buffon, but this simple-minded, scientific man stated, "I cannot agree to any expenditure which will contribute to my personal glory, and I had nothing to do with the statue they erected to me." In writing to Madame Necker, he showed how exactly he understood the French court, and appreciated its praises : "I passed the whole of yesterday and the day before in making observations and notes on a most important project presented to the king, relating to the planting of 100,000 fir trees for the masts of the navy. I would not grudge the time if my advice were likely to be useful and valued and taken; but in the high circle where you have not cared about remaining, they do sometimes consult competent men, and end, invariably, by following the advice of the ignorant."

Buffon lived for many years after these troubles, and gained fresh laurels. Those which will last the longest were the results of his charming descriptions of the habits of animals. At last, at the age of eighty-one years, he died, full of honours, his last words addressed to his son being, "My son, never leave the path of virtue and honour; it is the true road to happiness."

About a year before the death of George I., a son was born to a family of good old name and renown at Downing, in Flintshire. The child was christened Thomas, and his other name was Pennant, and these names are constantly coming before naturalists who particularly study zoology at the present time. Little is known about the early years of this ardent student, except that he was educated at Wrexham school. Like most boys he took notice of birds and their habits, and if one may judge from the results, he must have really begun to study the different kinds of birds, carefully, when he was about twelve years of age. He owed his opening career as a zoologist to Ray and Willughby, for it was a present made to him of the book of birds of this last author, that drew his attention to the study of nature which he never subsequently neglected.

After leaving school, Pennant was sent to Oxford, where his studies do not appear to have been of any importance, so far as the subjects which were taught were concerned. He did not take his degree, and yet it is evident that he studied the nature of things visible to him, and that he was well read in the science of the day. His mind was rather influenced by the writings of Linnæus, and in consequence he took an interest in mineralogy as well as about natural history. Immediately after leaving Oxford, Pennant began to travel about his own country, and visited Cornwall. He examined many of the mines, and studied the natural history of the districts, but he did not publish anything, being apparently an earnest student of what was already known. When twenty-four years of age an earthquake occurred at Downing, and Pennant wrote a description of it, which was read before the Royal Society and published in the "Philosophical Transactions." This was a great honour for so young a man. Animals, however, and their shapes, habits, and similarities were his special study, and he laboured hard, year after year, in describing them. He got much practical knowledge of those of our own country, and finally, at the age of thirty-five, in 1761, he commenced the publication of his first great work, the "British Zoology," which was printed in large folio, and when complete contained one hundred and thirty-two plates. He was well known before this magnificent work appeared, and Linnæus had urged the University of Upsala to elect him a member of their Royal Society. His great book appeared afterwards in smaller editions, and one in quarto is often used.

The "British Zoology" included the description of the species of animals at that time known to inhabit Great Britain, except the insects. So good was the work and so accurate were the descriptions, that it was translated into Latin and German, and had a large circulation abroad. Anxious to compare his work with those of foreign naturalists, and to see the specimens of similar animals in the great continental museums, Pennant travelled abroad in 1765, and made the acquaintance of the most important zoologists of the day. He visited Buffon at Montbard, and their friendship led to a correspondence, which lasted for years. Then he went on to Switzerland, and met Haller at Berne. Coming home by way of Germany and Holland, he met a distinguished traveller and naturalist, Pallas by name. Pennant wrote about him: "Our conversation related chiefly to natural history, and as we were both enthusiastic admirers of our great Ray, I proposed his undertaking a history of quadrupeds on the system of our countryman, a little reformed. He assented to my plan, and wrote me a long letter in which he sent me an outline of his design, and his resolution to pursue it with all the expedition consistent with his other engagements." Pallas went to Russia, and never accomplished his object, but Pennant followed out the idea himself, and in 1771 published a work with the title of

"A Synopsis of Quadrupeds," illustrated with about thirty plates. This was intended as a kind of index to the species of animals described by Buffon in his great work on natural history. He gradually, however, extended its limits, and included in it the description of many animals which he had observed in collections or which had been discovered by travellers, and which had been unknown to Buffon. Years afterwards the great Cuvier said of this work, "that it is still indispensable to those who wish to study the history of quadrupeds."

Struck with the interesting nature of the animals of India, which were then beginning to be studied, Pennant commenced a work about them, and twelve plates were completed. But it was a work far beyond the powers and pocket of a naturalist of that date, and it was not completed. A more congenial work was undertaken by him when he rambled about Scotland noticing the habits of the people and the birds. He seems to have observed much that was interesting, and to have published his remarks. Then he began a work on the genera of birds, on the plan of his books on quadrupeds, and this was not completed. He wrote a book on "Arctic Zoology," which was of course a compilation from the works of travellers and foreign zoologists who had visited the countries within the arctic circle. He also received stuffed specimens from different foreign museums. It was a capital book, and it acquired a considerable reputation amongst naturalists, from its containing figures and descriptions of animals hitherto but little known. It is read at the present day, and is a proof of Pennant's exactitude. Ever anxious to go on working, he even in his sixty-seventh year planned an extensive work which was to consider the natural history and antiquities of every country in the world. He absolutely did produce two great volumes of this work, taking Hindostan as his subject.

The great merit of Pennant was that he observed so much and was a capital practical zoologist. Moreover, his great knowledge of other things and his general accomplishments enabled him to sift the good from the bad zoology of his day. He appears to have lived the life of a student and naturalist when the kingdom was always in a whirlwind of politics, and when foreign troubles prevailed. Unlike most of his class, for he was a little country squire, living on his own estate at Downing, he devoted himself to nature, and for many years his books gave great enjoyment to thousands of his countrymen. They are most readable books, full of anecdotes, and it is evident that he was a master of his mother tongue, a great antiquary, besides a naturalist of the first order. He was one of the few men who followed the science of zoology without having the previous education of a medical man, and, like all good zoologists, he was an excellent botanist.

Some of Pennant's tours through England, Wales, and Scotland are exceedingly instructive in the antiquities of places, but the most interesting remarks are upon natural history subjects, some of which are scientific and others not at all so. When in Lincolnshire he noticed the fens near Revesby Abbey, eight miles beyond Horncastle, which he says are of vast extent, but serve for little other purpose than the rearing of great numbers of geese, which are the wealth of the fenmen. "During the breeding season these birds are lodged in the same houses with the inhabitants and even in their very bed-chambers. In every apartment there are three rows of coarse wicker pens, placed one above another; each bird has its separate lodge divided from the other, which it keeps possession of during its time of setting. A person called a gozzard attends the flock, and twice a day drives the whole to water; then brings them back to their habitations, helping those that live in the upper stories to their nests, without even misplacing a single bird. The geese are plucked five times in the year. The first plucking is at Lady Day, for feathers and quills, and the same is renewed, for feathers only, four times between this and Michaelmas. The old geese submit very quietly to the operation, but the young ones are very noisy and unruly. I once saw this performed, and observed that the goslings of six weeks old were not spared, for their tails were plucked, as I was told to habituate them early to what they were to come to. If the season proves cold, numbers of geese die from this barbarous custom. Vast numbers are driven annually to London to supply the markets ; among them all the superannuated geese and ganders (here called cagmags) which serve to fatigue the jaws of the good citizens who are so unfortunate as to meet with them." He proceeds, "It is observable that once in seven or eight years, immense shoals of sticklebacks appear in the Welland below Spalding, and attempt coming up the river in a vast column. They are supposed to be the collected multitudes washed out of the fens by the floods of several years, and carried into some deep hole. When, overcharged with numbers, they are obliged to attempt a change of place, they move up the river in such quantities as to enable a man who was employed in taking them, to earn, for a considerable time, four shillings a day by selling them at a halfpenny per bushel. They were used to manure land, and attempts have been made to get oil from them."

"The birds which inhabit the different fens are very numerous ; I never met with a finer field for the zoologist to range in. Besides the common wild duck, wild geese, gorganies, pochards, shovellers, and teals breed here. I have seen in the east fen a small flock of the tufted ducks ; but they seemed only to make it a baiting place. The pewits, gulls, and black terns abound ; the last in vast flocks almost deafen one with their clamour, and a few of the great terns are seen amongst them. I saw several of the great crested grebes on the east fen, called there gaunts, and met with one of their floating nests with eggs in it. The lesser crested grebe, the black and dusky grebe, and the little grebe are also inhabitants of the fens, together with the coots, water-hens, spotted water-hens, water-rails, ruffs, redshanks, lapwings or wipes, red crested godwits and whimbrels." "But the greatest curiosity in those parts is the vast heronry at Cressi Hall, six miles from Spalding. The herons resort there in February to repair their nests, settle there in the spring to breed, and quit the place during the winter. They are as numerous as rooks, and their nests are so crowded together that myself and the company that was with me, counted not less than eighty on one spreading oak. I found that the crested heron was only the male of the other, and it made a most beautiful appearance with its snowy neck and long crest streaming with the wind." Visiting Scarborough, and giving much information about the different kinds of fish caught, he states: "At a distance of four or five leagues from shore, during the months of July and August, it is remarked that at the depth of six or seven fathoms from the surface, the water appears to be saturated like a thick jelly, filled with the ova of fish, which reaches ten or twelve fathoms deeper; this is known by its adhering to the ropes, the cables, and anchor when they are fishing." "Landing at a small island further north, we found the female eider ducks at that time sitting; the lower part of their nests was made of sea plants, the upper part was formed of the down which they pulled off their own breasts, in which the eggs were surrounded and warmly bedded. In some nests were three and in others five eggs of large size and pale olive colour, as smooth and glossy as if varnished over. The nests are built on the beach among the loose pebbles, not far from the water. The ducks sit very close, nor will they rise until you almost tread upon them. We robbed the nests of some down, and found that the down of one only weighs three quarters of an ounce, but was so elastic as to fill the crown of a hat."

Pennant deserved good health and had it, for, except when old age came on, he was a singularly healthy man. He died in 1798, at the age of seventy-two years.

Jean Baptiste Antoine de Monet, also called the Chevalier de Lamarck, was born at Bazantin, a village of Picardy, on April 1st, 1744. He was the eleventh child of Pierre de Monet, the principal person of the neighbourhood, whose small estate was disproportionate to his huge family. But the Church was a resource for such families, and occasionally its great prizes were taken by the younger members of noble houses. So M. de Monet determined to prepare his son, at an early age, for this hopeful future, and sent him to the Jesuit College at Amiens. However, the inclinations of the child were not those which made it probable that he would succeed in the direction which his father had chosen for him. Everything around the boy, at home, was quite opposed to a clerical career. For centuries his ancestors had carried arms, and his eldest brother was killed at the siege of Bergen-op-Zoom. Two brothers were in the army, and at that time France was in dire trouble, and required every man who could fight, it was therefore not probable that young Lamarck would stay at home. Nevertheless, his father resisted his desire to enter the army, and the young man had to study year after year, until he was sixteen years of age. Then in 1760 the father died, and the youth was left to his own resources. He set forth for the army, mounted on a sorry horse, and accompanied by a poor boy out of the village, to journey across France into Germany to join the French army. He had a letter of introduction from one of his neighbours, Madame Lameth, to M. de Lartié, colonel of the regiment of Beaujolais, who did not receive him very gladly, for the wretchedness of the boy made him look more helpless than he really was. Nevertheless, he sent Lamarck to his barracks and had him to do duty. It was at a most critical moment that the brave, self-reliant boy joined the army. It was about July 14th, 1761, and M. de Broglie had just united his force with that of the Prince du Sorbise, preparatory to attacking, on the next day, the allied army, commanded by Frederick of Brunswick. At break of day M. de Lartié inspected his regiment, and the first person he saw was the newly-arrived volunteer, who, without orders, had placed himself in the first rank of the grenadier company. The battle, which was fought at Fissingshausen, between Ham and Leppstadt, was lost by the

French, and during the fight, the company, in which was M. de Lamarck, was placed in a locality on which the whole of the allied artillery was concentrated, and it was forgotten to be moved during the confusion of the retreat. All the officers and sub-officers were killed, and only sixteen men remained, when the oldest grenadier, seeing that they were left behind by their army, proposed to the young volunteer that they should retreat. Lamarck said, "They have posted us here, and we ought not to move until we are relieved," and insisted on remaining. By-and-by the colonel, missing the company, sent them an order to retreat by safe ways, and under the shelter of what they could get. This act of great courage was told to the Marshal de Broglie, and he made Lamarck an officer on the spot. Then he was made lieutenant. But such a brilliant commencement was not to have a military termination, and a miserable accident gave a new direction to his life. When Lamarck, after the war, was in garrison at Monaco, one of his fellow-officers lifted him up by the head, and the result was to injure his neck. He nearly died from the effects of this folly, and was saved by a distinguished surgeon at Paris, M. Tenon, whose operation left Lamarck with life, and a fearfully scarred neck, and unable to follow his profession. The treatment occupied a whole year, and he was so poor, that one of his biographers states, rather cruelly, that his necessary solitude gave him plenty of time for meditation. It is remarkable that although Lamarck cared more for the army than for his studies at college he really worked there, and what he learned was of great use to him in his future career. His hours of weary suffering were sometimes employed in studying the clouds, and in noticing their different shapes and appearances. He got by this means some vague ideas of meteorology. He had already been attracted, during his stay at Monaco, by the curious vegetation of that rocky country, and had taken a fancy for botany from reading a treatise on common plants, which happened to fall in his way. He therefore began to see that the profession of arms was not the only one worth living for, or in which distinction might be earned; and he took the bold resolution of applying himself to the study of medicine. This, considering the smallness of his resources, was hardly less hazardous than his former determination to join the army. Unable to defray the expense attending the studies to which he now applied himself, he was forced to seek employment as a banker's clerk, and thus to work for the means of pursuing his purpose. He studied medicine four years, and at the end of that time, not finding it accord with his taste, he relinquished it, in order to attach himself the more closely to botany. In this science he laboured most perseveringly, and after a preparation of ten years he suddenly revealed himself and his views to the learned world in a work as remarkable for the novelty of the plan, as for the mode of execution. "For a long time," says Cuvier, "while collecting plants, and visiting the Jardin du Roi, Lamarck gave way to discussions with other botanists on the imperfections of all the systems of classification then known, and on the ease with which a new system might be created, capable of determining plants with greater quickness and certainty. Wishing to prove what he had so often affirmed he set to work, and after six months of incessant labour he produced his "Flore Française." This work was merely an epitome of plants indigenous to France, to which Lamarck had not ventured to add one new species; but it was a convenient and sure guide to the name of every plant, and was peculiarly acceptable at a time when the writings of Rousseau had rendered botany popular. By Lamarck's arrangement, the most easily reconciled portions of the systems then in vogue, namely, those of Tournefort, Linnæus, and Jussieu, were selected to form a new method of classification. This method was admired by the Academy of Sciences, and was also recommended by Buffon, who had sufficient interest to get it published at the expense of the government, for the benefit of the author who much needed such aid. Lamarck was promoted to a vacant place in the Académie des Sciences, and during 1781-82 he went as tutor and botanist to Buffon's son through Holland, Germany, and Hungary, visiting public establishments and learned men. On his return to France, he applied himself zealously to his former studies, and produced the botanical portion of the "Encyclopédie Methodique." Lamarck laboured diligently at his work, and even with too much precipitation, for haste was injurious to correctness. He also drew a series of plates to illustrate the different genera of plants. These appeared, arranged according to the Linnæan system, though contrary to the wish of the author. Lamarck went on with the work until the breaking out of the Revolution arrested the publication of the Encyclopédie.

In 1788 Lamarck was associated with Daubenton as botanist of the Cabinet du Jardin du Roi, and charged with the preservation and arrangement of the herbariums. Here, amidst his peaceful occupations and studies, he remained unmolested amidst all the troubles of the Revolution. But Lamarck was miserably poor; his pension for his services in the army, was less than one shilling a day, and he wrote for bad pay. Buffon could not give him a position worth anything; and it was not until the successor of that great man came in office that Lamarck had a little salary given to him as one of the assistants in the herbarium. Even this miserable appointment was not assured to him, for the National Assembly was desirous of suppressing the establishment, and finally did so. Lamarck had married, and had a family, and weary indeed must have been his life had he not been devoted to science. He took no part in the French revolution, and whilst poverty at home and danger out of doors were constant, he persisted in studying nature. Years passed away, and the best part of a life was spent, and still Lamarck was not a zoologist. The eternal fame which he attained began to be earned after the fiftieth year of his age, when circumstances over which he had no control gave him the opportunity of distinguishing himself, and of adding materially to the truths of science as well as to its theories. The Jardin et Cabinet du Roi were rearranged in their purpose and name in 1793, and were called the Museum of Natural History; and all the old officials were made professors, and had to teach the subjects best known or chosen by them. Lamarck, as the last comer, had to take what the others left and would not undertake to teach. It was the professorship which related to the class of animals, called by Linnæus, worms and insects, and which had hitherto been almost overlooked, on account of the supposed unimportance of the subject.

Until that time Lamarck had never studied animals, and of course knew nothing of the branch of zoology which was now entrusted to him. He had taken an interest in shells, and had made a small collection, but this was all. But he did not shrink from the task before him. He set to work with inexhaustible courage, availing himself of the advice of his friends, and applying to the new study all that sagacity and perseverance which had already been so invaluable to him in his botanical works. By his indefatigable zeal in this new sphere of inquiry Lamarck was soon enabled to discover and to demonstrate that the animals whose history had been left to him through contempt, were quite as interesting as others, if not more so, on account of their vast numbers, the important part they perform in nature, the infinite variety of their forms, and the wonders of their organization. His extraordinary labours in this department have contributed much more to his fame than his botanical writings, and are certainly more valuable. He seems to have exercised his abilities to the utmost in these researches; and if, since that time, it has been necessary in some instances to alter, to amend, or to extend the limits of his work, yet it remains a lasting memento of his talents, and it will be long ere any one will be found sufficiently profound in knowledge to undertake a general revision and alteration of his works.

At the present day, when any student begins to learn the zoology of the lower animals, he will find a very great number of genera with the name of Lamarck placed after them, indicating that he first of all described and published them. As the student becomes accomplished he will appreciate Lamarck more and more, and will come to the conclusion that no one has done such good and solid work as that distinguished Frenchman, amongst the vast assemblage of animals which he first of all called invertebrata, or animals without backbones. This term he used in preference to the old one of white or colourless-blooded animals, as he soon saw that some had red blood. Lamarck worked very hard in describing and grouping the genera, and gradually modified the zoology of those lower forms of life. First of all he classified them by their anatomy, and then, after about fifteen years' labour, remodelled his classification, and published a system of invertebrata, containing the classes, orders, and genera of the animals, mentioning their most important anatomical characters. In this book he, for the first time amongst zoologists, began with the most simple and least highly organized animals, the converse having been the method previously. There was a reason in this that will be noticed further on. Out of the confusion of old he made the great groups appear clear and well defined. Thus from amongst the insects he separated the crustacea or crab tribe, and he introduced that of the arachnida or spiders. Then he described and limited a class of worms called by him annelida; moreover, he placed the microscopic infusoria in a class by themselves, and removed them from the jumble of the polypes. His work extended into the mollusca, both bivalve and univalve; he named many genera and species of corals, and in every group showed a master mind. The fossil shells found in such abundance at this time, in the neighbourhood of Paris, attracted his attention, and he laboured on their description and explanation. In fact, the enormous labours of Lamarck consolidated the zoology of the lower animals, and his writings became the text-books of all his successors, and will be referred to, as long as science lasts. He had a most singular capacity for distinguishing animals into kinds or species, and a more important one of observing the alliances or common characters of different species. All his descriptive work was of a standard and solid nature. His great work appeared from 1815 to 1822, and it was founded on that just mentioned; some of it was edited by his daughter, and M. Latreille wrote the parts on insects, and much of those of the mollusca was due to M. Valenciennes. Five volumes were by Lamarck himself.

It is a very unusual occurrence for a man to take up a new subject after he is fifty years of age, and to become a master in it. But Lamarck did this. It is true that his previous training as a botanist had prepared him, and it is also true that his years of solitude and poverty had given him a singularly placid and meditative mind, and this was strengthened by his natural courage. Had Lamarck been a descriptive zoologist only, he would have been great; but the very method which made him great originated in some remarkable speculations which had hardly been expressed, seriously, by any man before. Not only did he place the animal kingdom with the lowest first, but he considered the will, instinct, and apparent reason of animals, and classified them accordingly with those which are apathetic, sensible, and intelligent. The idea of lowness of organization or of structure and lowness of nervous power amongst the simplest animals struck him to be of primary importance. Hitherto, quite as many people believed that the highest and most intelligent animals were created first, and that the lower ones had degenerated from them. Lamarck conceived that nature, acting by law, commenced with the simplest things, and that one species formed others, so that the present animals and plants are the outcome of those of the past history of the earth. He believed in incessant change in nature, and that when our knowledge is complete the apparently well separated and defined species will be found to be united by intermediate forms, and cease to be species.

Hitherto naturalists had considered kinds of animals and plants, or species as they are more properly called, to have been specially created as they are seen by us, and that they were unalterable and invariable. No one with any great knowledge of animals and plants had speculated about the origin of species, and the causes of the differences of kinds, or had endeavoured to place all the great classes of the animal kingdom in a series, maintaining that they were related by descent. Right or wrong in his speculations, Lamarck made an epoch in zoology, by writing on the philosophy of zoology, and dealing with the possible causes of the different kinds of animals. He considered that during all the geological ages, down to the present time, animals and plants had been exposed to great changes in their external conditions; changes of climate, and of physical geography had happened, and that whilst some species had become extinct many had been changed, little by little, into others. Lamarck, and M. Geoffrey St. Hilaire declared it to be their opinion that there had been an uninterrupted succession in the animal kingdom, effected by means of birth and offspring from parents, from the earliest ages of the world to the present day, and that the ancient animals, whose remains have been preserved in strata, however different, may nevertheless have been the ancestors of those now in being.

If the reader will turn to the short notice of Aristoteles, he will find the ordinary idea of what a species means given. But Lamarck added something: "A species consists of a collection of individuals resembling each other, and reproducing their like by generation, so long as the surrounding conditions do not alter to such an extent as to cause their habits, characters, and forms to vary." He stated what is only known to those naturalists who have had experience; the more we advance in the knowledge of the different organized bodies which cover the surface of the globe, the more our embarrassment increases to determine what ought to be regarded as a species, and still more how to limit and distinguish genera. In proportion as our collections are enriched, we see almost every void filled up, and all our lines of separation effaced; we are reduced to arbitrary determinations, and are sometimes fain to seize upon the slight differences of mere varieties in order to form characters for what we choose to call a species, and sometimes we are induced to pronounce individuals, but slightly differing, and which others regard as true species, to be varieties. The greater the abundance of natural objects assembled together, the more do we discover proofs that everything passes by invariable shades into something else; that even the more remarkable differences are evanescent, and that nature has, for the most part, left us nothing at our disposal for establishing distinctions save trifling, and in some instances puerile, peculiarities. We find that many genera amongst animals and plants are of such an extent, in consequence of the number of species referred to them, that the study and determination of these last has become almost impracticable. From a great number of facts we learn, wrote Lamarck, that in proportion as the individuals of one of our known species change their situation, climate, and manner of living, they change also little by little, the consistence and proportions of their parts, their form, their faculties, and even their organization, in such a manner that everything in them comes at last to participate in the mutations to which they have been exposed. Even in the same climate, a great difference of situation and exposure causes individuals to vary; but if these individuals continue to live, and to be reproduced under the same difference of circumstances, distinctions are brought about in them which become in some degree essential to their existence; and, in a word, at the end of many successive generations, these individuals which originally belonged to another species are transformed into a new and distinct species.

All this came from the study of a man who had an enormous experience, and if he had not gone on any further it would have been better. Lamarck's views already stated may be accepted by everybody, and the grand changes in living forms under law are doubtless true. But he introduced the notion that "wants" exercised an influence and produced new organs, and wrote about effects of internal sentiment, and the influence of subtle fluids. Thus he argued that otters, beavers, waterfowl, turtles, and frogs, were not made web-footed in order that they might swim; but their wants having attracted them to the water in search of prey, they stretched out the toes of their feet to strike the water and move more rapidly along its surface. By the repeated stretching of their toes, the skin that united them at the base acquired the habit of extension, until, in the course of time, the broad membranes which now connect their extremities were formed.

Lamarck taught that the first animals and plants which appeared on the globe were the simplest, and that the more complex are of comparatively late date. He insisted that nature was an order of things constituted by the Supreme Being, and subject to laws which are the expressions of His will. There is no doubt that these views of Lamarck were the result of many a pleasant hour of thought when things were dark enough around him. He was always poor, he married four times, had a large family, and a very small income. His genius led him to investigate other branches of natural science for which his education had not very well prepared him, and he got into disgrace with Napoleon for paying attention to meteorology. His patrimony and savings were lost in some wild speculation, and his thorough independence of thought and behaviour did not make him friends with the great and wealthy. His sight failed, and age grew apace, and he may be said to have simply existed for some years. Strangers and scientific men saw his state and poverty with surprise and regret ; and their sympathy with Lamarck was redoubled when they observed the fortitude with which the illustrious old man supported the vicissitudes of fortune, and the failing of his natural powers. They also admired the devotion with which he had been able to inspire those of his children who remained under his roof. His eldest daughter consecrated her time to the duties of filial love for many years, never quitting her father for an instant, lending herself to every study which could in any way supply the defect of his vision, writing under his dictation part of his last works, accompanying him, and supporting him when he was able to take any exercise, and enduring sacrifices greater than could be expressed for his sake. When the father could no longer leave his chamber, the daughter no longer quitted the house. So long was she deprived of fresh air, that when she again faced the open breeze it was more than she could bear. If such conduct as this is rare, so is the power of inspiring such devoted affection; therefore we add to the renown of Lamarck, when it is told what his children endured for his sake. Lamarck died on the 18th December, 1829, aged eighty-five, and left two sons and two daughters behind him. Full of ability and perseverance, he has left such monuments of industry and solid learning behind him, that his favourite theory, containing indeed the germs of truth, may be well pardoned. People who know nothing of his good work, laugh at his memory; but every true student of nature constantly recognizes his obligations to the founder of philosophical zoology.

CHAPTER VIII.

THE LIFE OF CUVIER.

The union of zoology and comparative anatomy, and the examination and study of fossil remains.

GEORGE Léopold Chretien Frédéric Dagobert Cuvier was born at Montbéliard, in the Department du Doubs, a town which was subsequently united to France, although at the time of Cuvier's birth it belonged to the kingdom of Wurtemberg. He was born on August 23rd, 1769. His family originally came from a village in the Jura mountains, which still bears the name of Cuvier; but, becoming the victims of religious persecution, they were obliged to leave and to go to reside at Montbéliard at the time of the Reformation. Cuvier's grandfather had two sons, one celebrated for his learning, and the other belonging to a Swiss regiment in the French service. The soldier, after forty years' service, retired on a small pension to Montbéliard, where he was appointed commandant of the artillery of the town. He was made Chevalier de l'Ordre Merite Militaire, which, among Protestants, was equal to the Catholic order of the Croix de St. Louis. The old soldier married, late in life, a young and highly accomplished lady, by whom he had three sons. The eldest died a short time before the birth of the second, who is the subject of this biography, and who was extremely delicate. The mother, sad at the death of her firstborn, took the curious fancy of calling her little weak second child by the name of George, which was that of her firstborn also. Cuvier was not baptized with that name, although he ever used it in deference to his mother; but in after years, when legal difficulties presented themselves, he took the necessary measures to have a right to use the name. Feeble in constitution, the child required all the attention of his mother, and he never forgot her loving care. She taught him carefully and well during his early years, and the child grew strong and able. He could read fluently at the age of four years, and when the time came for him to be placed at school, the mother went over his exercises at night, and by her good knowledge of Latin enabled him to be better prepared than any other boy in the school, for his daily tasks. She taught him drawing, and this necessary art was subsequently taught Cuvier by an architect in the town. At the age of ten years he was placed at a school of a higher description of teaching, called the Gymnase, where he remained until he was fourteen. Cuvier made rapid progress at this school, and he was constantly at the head of his classes, and he became a fair classic. It was at that time that the future great zoologist began to like natural history, and he began by studying animals. One of his relations had a complete copy of Buffon's works, and the boy's study of it was constant. He copied the plates of animals and birds, and coloured them according to the printed descriptions, and when he could not use water-colours, employed pieces of coloured silk to denote the tints of the wings. When he was able to borrow the book, a volume was his constant attendant, and he read the work over and over again. About this time, Cuvier, being the leading spirit in the school, began to collect his schoolfellows and to get them to discuss the merits of books on natural history, philosophy, and travels, etc., taking the chair as president. The assembly must have been amusing in the extreme, and these little "prigs" doubtless expressed their opinions very decidedly. Cuvier managed to teach himself to speak in public, however, and was not a bad hand at declamation. So, on the anniversary fête of the Duke of Wurtemberg, he composed an oration in verse on the prosperous state of the principality, and delivered it, fresh from his pen, in a manly tone which astonished the audience. Nevertheless, Cuvier was snubbed by his master, who put him down to the third place, giving the palm to two other boys. It is said that there was some favouritism in this affair; but it was a blow to the boy, whose future career depended on the place he might take at the school on the occasion. Nevertheless, as things turned out, Cuvier had every reason to be very thankful. The fame of the young student, and his disappointment, reached the ears of Duke Charles by means of the princess, his sister-in-law, and when he visited Montbéliard he saw Cuvier, and asked him questions and looked at his drawings. The duke, satisfied that he had a good subject before him, agreed to send him to Stuttgard to the university, where the youth would be well educated, free of expense, in the duke's own academy. At this academy the pupils were instructed in every branch of knowledge that was actually useful to men destined to govern and direct the affairs of communities, and many who were educated there, became members of the various courts of Germany and Russia. The school had a military character, the scholars wearing uniforms and being under the orders of a colonel and major; but the education was not military, and such men as Schiller were taught there.

At the age of fourteen Cuvier quitted his home to go to this school, and under circumstances enough to frighten any school-boy. He travelled with the chamberlain and secretary of the duke, sitting between them without understanding a word they said, as they spoke German the whole time. He always remembered this journey and its miseries. The youth quickly made himself comfortable at the academy, and his really good training soon placed him high amongst his fellows. For four years he studied all that was taught in the higher classes, mathematics, law, administration, tactics, and commerce, and obtaining various prizes, was made, with five or six others out of the four hundred, to belong to a class bearing the order of "Chevalerie." These youths were under the immediate patronage of the duke, and had privileges besides that of dining at a separate table. Nine months after his arrival at Stuttgart, Cuvier gained the prize in German. But all this time Cuvier led a second life. Out in the fields and in the museum he was supremely happy. Collecting, observing, drawing, and describing were his occupations in his leisure hours, and his drawings of birds, insects, and plants were very excellent and correct. All the books he could get on natural history he read, and the works of Linnæus were especially learned with zeal. At the end of his academical career Cuvier was promised a place in the administration of the country, and if he had got it probably he would have become a kind of civil service clerk, and have never been heard of. But trouble came, and that of the bitterest kind for a rising young man. Circumstances against which he could not bear up necessitated his seeking a totally different kind of employment. The unsettled state of money and finance in France caused Cuvier's father's pension to be withheld, and the young man, very properly desiring to be no burthen to his parents, gave up all hopes of political distinction, and accepted the modest position of tutor to a French family, that of M. d'Hericy, at Caen, in Normandy. He was to educate the only son; and so, without bewailing his lot, which was thought a very sad one by his companions and admirers, Cuvier settled down to work and found that he was in the very position for using those remarkable powers as a naturalist, which determined his future career. The sea was close by, and Cuvier began to study the marine animals. After some time some fossils were discovered at Fécamp, and Cuvier began to compare them with the living things which most resembled them. Then the accidental discovery of a calamary led him to study the higher mollusca, or shell-fish. Cuvier also began to study the huge class of vermes, or worms, in which Linnæus had included a vast number of lower animals, and which Lamark subsequently investigated. Cuvier examined the anatomy of the groups, and arranged them according to their resemblances in structure. This was an excellent piece of work, and it was done for the purposes of self-instruction, and not for fame. Nevertheless, the manuscript was full of good observations and of new truths. Whilst Cuvier was thus employed, and the time was that of the reign of terror, a society was formed at Valmont, in his neighbourhood, for the encouragement of agriculture. L'Abbé Teissier had sought at the place a refuge from the persecutions of the revolutionists of Paris, and under the disguise of a surgeon attended the meetings. On one occasion Cuvier was struck with the manner of speaking of the worthy old man, and thought that it resembled the writings of the well-known Abbé. Inadvertently Cuvier addressed him as L'Abbé, and this gave at first great alarm. He found in Cuvier, however, a great admirer and a generous friend, and was so pleased with his talents and industry, that he afterwards wrote to the celebrated botanist, Jussieu, as follows: "At the sight of this young man, I experienced the delight of the philosopher who was thrown on an unknown shore, and saw traced there the figures of geometry. M. Cuvier is a violet which was concealed among common herbs. He knows much, and draws figures for your work. I doubt your finding a more able person for comparative anatomy, for he demonstrates with much method and clearness. It is a pearl worthy of being gathered by you. I contributed to draw M. Delarbre from his retreat, help me to draw M. Cuvier from his; he is made for science and the world."

Cuvier was, in consequence, asked to read some of his essays to the Society of Natural History at Paris, and these gave such satisfaction that he was invited to take a position at the Jardin des Plantes. This occurred in 1795, and Cuvier was then twenty-six years of age. He was thus settled for life in the very position he desired, for although called the garden of plants, a grand museum of the comparative anatomy of animals was to rise there under the superintendence of the young man. He was soon made professor at the central school of the Pantheon, and began to write capital manuals of his subject for the students. The next year the National Institute was formed, and Cuvier was one of its first members. At this time his knowledge of zoology was very great, and he had more than the usual amount of information about the internal anatomy of the different great groups of animals. He published an elementary title or scheme of the natural history of animals, and gradually the collection of skeletons began to be great in his establishment. Cuvier paid great attention to the relative shapes, and different developments of the same kind of bones in various animals, and especially to the nature of their teeth. So great did his experience and correct knowledge become, that he rarely failed in naming an animal from part of its skeleton. This power impressed Cuvier with the idea of a philosophy in nature, and with the evidence of creative design and purpose, of means for ends. But this kind of study led to some very remarkable results. Had it influenced Cuvier as it previously had zoologists, he would have still become the most accomplished and important naturalist of this century. It would have been said, as it may well be, that he established the study of animals on a firm basis, and that his natural classification has lasted, because he considered not only the outsides of animals, but also the importance of their most peculiar organs, in arranging them into groups, or separating them from others. But Cuvier had seen and studied the bones and skulls of animals which had been dug out of the earth in a mineralized condition. The strata at Montmartre, near Paris, had yielded a great number of bones, which presented some resemblances to those of animals still living but which were clearly not the bones of any existing genera or species. Comparative anatomy was made to connect the past and present animals, and to indicate the possibility of all the past and present creation being placed in one great classification. As Cuvier progressed in this study, he endeavoured to restore, and with considerable success, the extinct animal's shape, to discover its habits and method of life, and to find out its nearest modern ally. Palæontology, or the study of extinct animals, is under the greatest obligations to this great Frenchman, and it may be called the zoology of the past ages of the earth. He did not, however, forget his one great desire, which was to form a perfect book on comparative anatomy, and one in which all animals would find a place, called "La Regne Animal." (The animal kingdom.)

As soon as Cuvier found himself well established as assistant to M. Mertrud, the professor of comparative anatomy to the Jardin des Plantes, he sent for his old father, then eighty years of age, and for his brother, M. F. Cuvier, to live with him. The first thing he did was to collect all the available specimens of bones and preparations of animals, and he found many hidden away in vaults and which had been collected by Daubenton and Buffon. Other specimens were obtained, and thus the great collection was commenced. In 1796, Cuvier discovered the curious fact that there is naturally red blood in leeches, and in the following year he read a famous paper on the nutrition of insects. Refusing to go to Egypt, as he had his proper work to do at home, for his pupils Dumeril and Duvernoy were working hard for and with him, dissecting and describing, the result was the publication of the first volume of the lessons on comparative anatomy already alluded to. This led to Cuvier being made professor of natural history to the College of France. Of the young professor's ability there could be no doubt, and everybody was struck with the excellent method of his lectures and books. His mind was essentially an orderly and very contemplative and reasoning one, and his fame soon reached the ears of Napoleon, then first consul. He made Cuvier one of the six inspectors general of education who were to found public schools in some thirty towns in France and what are now called Royal Colleges. Cuvier founded those of Bordeaux, Nice, and Marseilles. In this last-mentioned place he continued his work on marine animals. Whilst Cuvier was performing these very important duties for the state, with great benefit to the towns and credit to himself, he was chosen to be one of the perpetual secretaries to the National Institute, and had a salary given to him for it of two hundred guineas a year. Although this sum was to be well earned, and the secretary had to receive distinguished foreigners at table, a fuss was made about it. Cuvier, however, knew his own value, and insisted on retaining it. The labourer is worthy of his hire, and the sum was less than the salary of a first-class clerk. A great Italian politician once said keep the professors poor. Why? Because he knew that the diffusion of liberal knowledge would be fatal to civil and military tyranny. However, Cuvier gave up his school inspectorship and laboured on at his favourite studies. He lost his father and his brother's wife died leaving a child, so that Cuvier and his brother were alone. Marriage became a necessity for the rising man, and he was attracted by a lady of great merit, who had suffered both poverty and misfortune. Madame Duvancel was the widow of an official who perished on the scaffold in 1794, and she had some children of her own. Cuvier had a great affection for her and she made him happy, was a great companion, and when he rose to his greatness, she was an admirable helpmate. In 1808, as secretary to the National Institute, Cuvier had to write a report on the progress of the natural sciences from the year 1789. A mere report was required, but Cuvier was too thorough, and his essay was an admirable and most lucid treatise. Napoleon, then emperor, was greatly struck with it, and presented the paper to the council of state. Some of the sentences should be written in letters of gold in every senate and learned by heart by all politicians. " The true object of science is to lead the mind of man towards its noble destination—a knowledge of truth—to spread sound and useful ideas among the lowest classes of the people, to draw human beings from the effects of prejudices and passions, to make reason the arbitrator and supreme guide of public opinion." Napoleon, who nearly always chose the best men for a place, made Cuvier a counsellor of the new Imperial University, and the two men thus came frequently in contact. Repeated personal interviews preceded Cuvier's appointment to organize new universities in the foreign states more or less under the sway of France. He undertook the reorganization of the old Italian universities of Piedmont, Genoa, and Tuscany. His reports of these missions speak of the enlightenment of his mind and his truly reasonable and very liberal spirit. Speaking of the universities of Tuscany, he deprecates a too hasty and rash interference with institutions which had been founded and maintained by so many distinguished men of old and in which he found so much to praise and to retain. He made good use of his time in Tuscany by taking drawings of and collecting fossil bones, and in 1811 his great work on the fossil remains of animals appeared. He examined into the condition of the universities of Holland, and finally those of lower Germany. These journeys were doubly useful, for they established his health and gave him plenty of opportunity of visiting museums. While at Hamburg, Napoleon gave him the title of chevalier, which was confirmed to him and his heirs. But such honours were not destined to descend, for Cuvier lost his son in his seventh year. It was a great grief, and it saddened and subdued the man. This trial happened when Cuvier was at Rome, trying to arrange the universities there. Being a Protestant, the mission was one requiring peculiar forbearance and firmness. Yet the enlightened tolerance of Cuvier, and his mild and benignant manners, gained for him the esteem and respect of all parties. Risen from the ranks, having been poor and often anxious to know how to learn, Cuvier was a capital man for his position. He paid particular attention not only to the higher branches of education, but also to popular or elementary education. His principle was that instruction would lead to civilization, and civilization to morality, and therefore that primary or elementary instruction should give to the people every means of fully exercising their industry, without disgusting them with their condition. That secondary instruction should expand the mind, without rendering it false or presumptuous; and that special or scientific instruction should give to France magistrates, advocates, generals, clergy, professors and other men of learning. He taught—"give schools before political rights; make citizens comprehend the duties that the state of society imposes on them; teach them what are political rights before you offer them for their enjoyment, and then all amelioration will be made without causing a shock. Imitate nature, which in the development of beings acts by gradation, and gives time to every member to arrive at perfection."

Napoleon had great confidence in Cuvier, and wished to make him tutor to his son, and ordered him to draw up a list of books as a preliminary step. In 1814 he made him a councillor of state, and Louis XVIII. confirmed him in the appointment subsequently.

Cuvier wrote in early life, on living and fossil elephants, the different species of rhinoceros, the structure of ascidians, and the anatomy of bivalve molluscs. Later on he described the crocodilians of the old and new world and the fossil tapirs of France. Subsequently to 1801 he read memoirs on the teeth of fish, on the worms, the anatomy of the mollusca, the comparative anatomy and classification of fishes, the fossil mammals and reptiles, and the bony structures of these last two groups. Most of these works were the joint productions of other very distinguished men and himself. Thus the work on fishes, which contained descriptions of no less than five thousand kinds, was by Cuvier and Valenciennes. Year after year Cuvier added to the store of knowledge he was so anxious to give to the history of the earth, and his descriptions, monuments of exactitude, of the fossil kinds of rhinoceros, hyænæ, and of some of the great sloths, were the result of his careful examination of the living species of the genera or families which were found fossil. We owe to Cuvier the truth that ancient forms of life, the bones and teeth of which alone remain, and which were buried by nature formerly, can be "restored." That is to say, by taking the existing or modern example, and by reasoning upon the nature of the teeth, claws, hoofs, and horns present or absent, the nature, shape and destiny of the ancient animal can be given to the world at the present time.

After the abdication of Napoleon and the defeat at Waterloo, it became necessary, in the ideas of Louis XVIII., that the universities should be remodelled, and a committee of public instruction was created to exercise the powers formerly belonging to the grand master, the council, and the treasurer of the University. Cuvier was one of the committee, and was made chancellor of the University, a position which he retained until his death under most trying circumstances. No man did greater or better and more lasting work for state education than Cuvier. His heart was in the work of education; he had nothing but mental progress to desire; and it was a much more satisfactory thing for France to have a renowned, scientific man at the head of a great university, who, moreover, really controlled the education of the country, than to have had such important offices held by mere politicians and soldiers.

In 1817 Cuvier published a second edition of his

"Fossil Bones," and the great book, the "Règne Animal" (the "Animal Kingdom"), was re-issued. In this last work Cuvier immortalized himself; and his classification has been of the greatest possible value to his successors. He reduced the six classes of animals which had been suggested by the ancients and Linnæus, namely, quadrupeds, birds, reptiles, fishes, insects, and worms, to four, or vertebrated animals (animals with backbones), molluscous animals (such as snails and oysters), articulated animals (insects and crabs), and radiated animals (such as corals and sea anemones). Although this classification has become modified, still Cuvier gave the method of true classification in animals. One or two points or peculiarities were not to be considered at the expense of others which belonged to organs of great importance to the animal. He asserted that all the structures of the animal must be studied, and physiology as well as anatomy must be considered. The most important structures must be considered first of all, and the grand divisions of classification must rest upon them. In the "Règne Animal" Cuvier commences with man, whom he places in a genus by himself, and recognizes only one species diversified by varieties or races. In 1818 Cuvier visited London, and remained there for about six weeks, receiving every scientific and social honour. He mixed freely in scientific society, and was received by George IV. On being consulted by his Majesty about our national collections, he said that if all the British private collections could be collected into one, they would form a great national museum which would surpass every other. Cuvier was greatly interested in the freedom of English politics; and on the election for Westminster taking place he went on to the hustings. He was intensely amused at the speeches and the violence of the mob, who pelted their political opponents after the fashion of the day with bad eggs, dead cats, cabbages, and mud. He went to Oxford, and then all the party were invited to Windsor. Sir Joseph Banks asked everybody in the scientific world to meet Cuvier, and Sir Everard Home also. The great naturalist, once a half-starved student and a tutor, became the guest of the most honoured amongst men, and was very sensible of the kindness shown him. He could not, however, reconcile himself to the long dinners and long sittings at table, which were then, as now, fashionable in England. Not only did Cuvier study the national and private natural history collections in this country, but he also paid much attention to the system of education and to the nature of our political constitution.

Returning to Paris, Cuvier was elected a member of the Academie Française, and in the following year was made president of the Comité de l'Interieur, and created a baron. He resigned his temporary grand mastership of the University, so as to accept without salary the grand mastership of the Faculties of Protestant Theology, and vice-president of the Bible Society.

In 1824, as president of the Comité, or one of the councils of state, Cuvier took part in the coronation of Charles X., on which occasion he was made grand master of the Legion of Honour. In 1827 he was appointed censor of the press, an office which his love of liberty of thought soon made him resign. Sacrificing all his leisure to the greater educational matters, and ever labouring at science, Cuvier also formed a great library, which was always open to naturalists who desired to visit and use it. Cuvier's orderly and critical mind enabled him to fulfil the office of secretary to the institute with great success; and he especially shone in writing the interesting lives of the distinguished men who died during each year. Moreover, he reported on each memoir which was submitted to the institute for reading and publication. Cuvier was great as a public lecturer, and had a flexible and sonorous voice, which resounded far and wide in the room. His audiences were always enthusiastic; and many a student waited long to get a good seat before the professor began. He taught, chalk in hand, and drew well on the black board, his artistic power remaining to the last.

Cuvier came to England a second time, and it is tolerably clear that it was to escape the inevitable revolution which was caused by the tyranny of Charles X. and his advisers. His carriage passed out of Paris, and five hours afterwards firing began, which led to the dethronement of the king and the restoration of liberty. In London Cuvier used to enjoy the political and other caricatures in the shops, and loved to go down to such places as Richmond to see the scenery.

After a six weeks' visit, Cuvier returned to Paris, and occupied his former positions and dignities.

Cuvier was slightly built in his young days, and moderately tall; but the sedentary nature of his work and his carelessness about taking proper exercise, produced corpulence in his later years, and his extreme near-sightedness brought on a slight stoop in his shoulders. His hair had been light in colour, and to the last it flowed in fine curls over one of the noblest heads ever seen. He was handsome and had regular features, with an aquiline nose, a broad forehead, and keen eyes. The love of order, which was his very peculiarity in his work, was seen in little things, for Cuvier was almost feminine in his attention to dress. He even took in hand the costume of the University, and designed the embroidery of his court suits. Cuvier's manners were dignified and yet not ceremonious; for accustomed to mingle with the highest of all classes and countries, and naturally desirous of paying a just tribute of respect and good will to everybody, he was likely to be generally polished and courteous. He was stately enough sometimes, and his reserve with strangers who were not open with him was mainly—as is usually the case with others—from mere shyness and timidity. To the young he was always kind and sympathizing. When at the Institute Cuvier's manner was always stately, for he was with his peers there, and perhaps he might have occasionally felt it necessary to retain an appearance of reserve during the sometimes not very scientific discussions of that mixed assemblage.

Cuvier, notwithstanding his great patience when he was at work, and his singular placidity when on the face of a difficult point in natural history or anatomy, was what is called a "Turk" at home, and with others. Accustomed to most minute exactitude, and to regulate his hands by his rapidly working brain, he was singularly impatient with other people who had to serve under him. He used to hasten his workmen, so that his orders were often performed with difficulty. He was hard to bear with, and any waste of time the result of carelessness, put him in a rage. Anything wrong at table in his house, to be kept waiting, or some trifling disobedience, would rouse an absurd amount of anger. His irritability was excessive, and he frequently forgot himself in his scoldings, and had to make reparation afterwards. But he was always ready to testify that he had been wrong, and to do his best to make amends; nevertheless, he did not improve in this particular, and he never had great control over his feelings. No labour, however minute and prolonged, irritated him when he believed that it was requisite for the attainment of an object; still he could not listen to a few pages of a book which taught nothing, without expressing himself very decidedly. From what has been written of Cuvier's domestic life, it could not have been very enjoyable by those around him, and yet it was the kind of life which has to be led by most prominent men in science, art, and literature. Work, everlasting work, with but little relaxation. He certainly wasted no time. Before and after breakfast he saw anybody who wished to have an audience of him. By seven in the morning he was dressed, and began preparing his day's work and that of his assistants, so that by ten o'clock, when he breakfasted, he had time to look at the newspapers, to read correspondence, and look over any particular works. After breakfast he dressed for the day and began work. His carriage was punctual to a moment, and no one was allowed to keep him waiting. When the ladies were to accompany him, they made a point of being as exact to time as was possible; and he seems to have enjoyed the sight of his womankind rushing downstairs with their shawls streaming after them and their gloves half on their hands. The instant he had given his orders he would thrust himself into a corner of the carriage and set to work reading, but suffered the ladies to talk as much as they pleased. The family dinner hour was half-past six; and if Cuvier had a few moments to spare before that time, he would occasionally join his friends in Madame Cuvier's room, but more frequently he seems to have given even this short time to study. One or two intimate friends joined the circle at dinner, and then Cuvier's conversation was delightful. On proceeding to the drawing-room Cuvier sometimes gratified his friends by an hour's stay amongst them before he retired to his occupation or his visits, but so untiring was his industry, that he often set the whole party to work aiding him in his researches. If he had any foreign works he would often amuse his friends by verifying the figures in them, one after the other. It must be said that this everlasting work was trying to people who were with Cuvier, for no sooner did friends come to stay with him than he began to use them in tracing drawings on paper. He kept them at work, for when he returned from his labours he generally asked for the tasks he had thus set. Nevertheless, many found it a real pleasure to work for him, for he was very grateful for such assistance. Cuvier's hours of relaxation were few. Change of employment afforded him relief, and conversation still greater. At the close of the day's labour, when he found it impossible to work any longer, he was accustomed to throw himself on a sofa, hide his eyes from the light, and listen to the reading of his wife or daughter, and sometimes of his secretary, M. Laurillard. These nightly readings lasted two hours, and thus Cuvier became more or less acquainted with the current literature and good works of the day. Very likely he did not listen, and went to sleep, but that is not stated of him by those who wrote his domestic habits.

Cuvier was so downright that he did not like any one who indulged in satire, or who ridiculed the conduct of others. He never did this sort of thing, and he carefully discouraged it in those about him, even when embellished with sallies of wit and drollery, and his rebukes to those who indulged in sarcasm were accompanied by a sharpness of expression generally very unusual to him. He bore but little malice, and it is said that the annoyances and disappointments of his public career left no trace of bitterness of spirit; and he was always willing to lay the fault on the ignorance rather than on the bad feeling of the offenders.

When in the full swing of his career, Cuvier gave very interesting *soirées* on Saturday evenings, and it is said that they were the most brilliant and interesting meetings of their kind in Paris. They were much frequented by the scientific world of the time, and the rooms were as much open to the prince as to the last young student who had just begun to study natural history. In this society Cuvier was an amusing conversationalist, a great asker of questions; and as he could talk well on a variety of subjects, he made his guests at home, and gave the meetings a character for freedom of expression of opinion. A light repast concluded the evening, and a select few remained to partake of it. The chat was amusing, curiosities were shown about, and the last anecdotes about nature and the newest ideas were shown and considered, and, reserving himself to the last, Cuvier would relate something that crowned the whole; and all around were struck by the occasional complete change given to the train of thought, or were forced to join in a general shout of laughter. The period of these brilliant *soirées* was that of the prime of the lovely daughter who was so fondly loved by Cuvier. A perfect lady, of great grace and goodness, was Clementine Cuvier. She was a highly-gifted girl, and her resemblance to her father was remarkable. She had a delicate constitution, and gradually faded away, dying of rapid consumption at last amidst the joyful preparations for her marriage. A great change then took place in Cuvier, who mourned his daughter greatly. Society was given up for a long time, and when the evening meetings were resumed, the life of them seemed to be gone, and the dejection of Madame Cuvier added to the feeling. After the death of his own daughter, Cuvier became more than ever attached to his step-daughter, and his care and anxiety on her account manifested itself on all occasions. If she were ill he would be up and down stairs over and over again, and worried himself about even the most trivial symptoms. Although so greatly occupied and so often absorbed in scientific pursuits, he never neglected the opportunity of doing good in his way. His private charities were large and well bestowed. His purse was ever open to the needy and unfortunate of all countries and stations, and the miserable inhabitants of the dens of Paris and the modest student struggling under adversity were alike the recipients of his bounty. Many hotels in the neighbourhood of the colleges and institutions had students in them, living in the top stories, who were so poor that they had to subscribe to get a book or two between them. They would occasionally be surprised by a visit from their great teacher. He came to offer, with the greatest courtesy, the assistance he knew they required; and if they were ill he did not rest satisfied until he had obtained advice and nourishment for them. Himself keenly alive to the slightest rudeness or neglect, and grateful for the smallest proof of affection, he knew how to give, not only with a liberal hand, but with a delicacy which never wounded the most sensitive temper. The year 1832 was a melancholy one for Paris; for political disturbances and cholera prevailed. The disease raged around Cuvier's neighbourhood, and he saw many cut off from it in the midst of their youth and strength. At this time he gave up his evening visits and the few relaxations he permitted himself to enjoy. Secluding himself from society, except that of his own family, he had no sooner performed his daily routine of public duties than he returned to his studies with a zeal and closeness of application that was doubtless injurious to his health, though he himself said that he had never worked with such enjoyment. On Tuesday, May 8th, he opened the third and concluding part of his course of lectures at the College of France on the history of science, and it was his last discourse. Strangely enough, it was as if it were to be his last, so impressive, so grandly comprehensive, was the diction; and he treated the subject in a manner which proved that he had been thinking much about the mysterious and supernatural environment which most men of great experience can recognize in nature. Cuvier in this lecture dealt with the meaning of the changes which had occurred on the surface of the earth in relation to the succession of animals and plants on the globe and the present creation. He stated the manner in which he proposed to view the present in relation to the past, a task which was to lead his hearers, independently of narrow systems, back to that supreme intelligence which rules, enlightens, and vivifies, and which gives to every creature the especial conditions of its existence. He noticed how each being contains in itself an infinite variety, an admirable arrangement for the purposes for which it was intended: that each being is good, perfect, and capable of life, according to its order and species, and in its individuality. He concluded by saying, "These will be the objects of our future investigations, if time, health, and strength are given to me to continue and to finish them with you." The lecture hall was slowly left by Cuvier's hearers and students, and an undefined sadness seemed to weigh upon his late hearers, who seemed to linger with the impression that his days were numbered. On the evening of the same day, Cuvier felt some pain in his right arm, which was supposed to proceed from rheumatism. The next morning he presided over the

Committee of the Interior with his usual ability and activity; but at dinner that day he felt some difficulty in swallowing, and the numbness in the arm increased. When he felt himself thus ill, in order to take away the attention of Madame Cuvier, he said, "I must eat more soup," swallowing bread even being impossible. Advice was sought, but during the next day both arms became paralyzed, and the swallowing was worse. He made his will with perfect calmness, and it evinced the tenderest solicitude for those whose cares and affections had comforted his life, and for those who had aided him most in his scientific labours. He could not sign the will, but it was attested by four witnesses. Convinced that all human skill was in vain, he nevertheless submitted to treatment by his medical men. Paralysis crept on, and the legs were attacked, his speech was affected, and he muttered, "It is the nerves of volition that are affected." He spoke of his last lecture, and said to a friend who called, "Behold a very different person to the man of Tuesday; nevertheless I had great things still to do. All was ready in my head, after thirty years of labour and research; there remained but to write, and now the hands fail and carry with them the head." Cuvier gradually sank, but kept his intelligence nearly to the last. It was his wish to be buried privately, interred in the cemetery of Père le Chaise, under the tombstone which covered his beloved child; but it was not possible to avoid the public demonstration of respect. The funeral procession was followed by the representatives of all the great learned bodies of France.

Cuvier was too generous, and too desirous for the advancement of his branch of natural history knowledge, to die very rich. He had several important sources of income, and there is no doubt that, had he chosen so to do, he could have saved much money. He spent largely when it was necessary to procure specimens from abroad, and to dig out fossils at home, and his private charities were numerous. He only left about the sum of four thousand pounds sterling, a library worth about the same sum, and a house for his family. There is no doubt that Cuvier was, in his private life, a very estimable man, and that in his public life he upheld the teachings of his conscience to his disadvantage. It was to be expected that a man whose work proved the great antiquity of the kinds of animals now living on the surface of the earth, and the existence of a great philosophy in nature which linked the past and present animals in a scheme which showed that life had been continuous for ages, would be abused and called an atheist by some ignorant people or other. His true character has been written as follows:—" He promoted the cause of true religion by every means in his power, both public and private; he was a warm supporter of the Bible Society, and caused the Old and New Testaments to be widely disseminated in every part of Protestant France.

In his letters to the heads of colleges and masters of schools, he strongly recommended them to teach for the love of God, himself pointing out their duties according to that great rule. He adhered consistently and persistently to the Protestant faith, when it was well known that a change to the Roman Catholic would have been the surest step to the attainment of the highest honours in the state. He caused a number of chapels to be established, in order to give facility for attending divine worship; and he never would receive a salary for attending and administering to the interests of the Protestant religion. He discharged faithfully all the duties of his office, with a zeal which showed that he had a much higher motive than that of gain or reputation. Humility and forgiveness marked his character; he was thankful for the correction of errors; he gloried as much in the discoveries of another as his own; and in the triumph of joint labours, unhesitatingly gave the preference to his colleague. He suffered his servants to expostulate with him, and the very nature of his amusements was social and cheerful. He felt ingratitude keenly, and also unkindness and injustice, but they made him sad rather than angry. His antagonists openly indulged in the most irritating and violent taunts, or secretly intrigued against him; the former never excited him beyond a clear, firm, and dignified reply, wrung from him only when reply was absolutely necessary; and the latter nothing but candid remonstrances. To these high attributes we may add charity. The failings of others were never trumpeted forth by Cuvier; he did not even tolerate playful satire, however disguised by wit; his earnest desire was to make all happy around him, even by a sacrifice of his own convenience; and his resignation was great, under calamities which bereaved him of the dearest objects of his affection; all these things appear to establish his character as a Christian."

The character of Cuvier was hardly equal to this panegyric, for he held his own boldly enough, and faced his enemies with no feeble humility; moreover, the details of his everyday life prove that he was sufficiently exacting, and that everything had to give way to his will. Nevertheless, it is true that that will was to advance knowledge in the right direction, and that it was stimulated by an earnest desire for truth. Men like Cuvier are very apt to be misunderstood by their most intimate friends. When studying the collections of animals, and when comparing the forms of ancient and modern life, Cuvier mentally recognized a divine wisdom and the work of the God he worshipped. That was his worship, and he probably cared all the less for the oratory of the pulpit, which he was expected to listen to. He was not a constant attendant at his church, and this seems even to have afflicted his daughter when on her deathbed, according to some reports. But in all probability she knew her father's worth and real religion, better than outside friends and detractors, and prayed that he might receive that support which alone could enable him to bear the heaviest of sorrows with resignation.

Judging the man by his fruit and life, it must be admitted that Cuvier was one of the greatest students and teachers of nature that have lived, his work, being true, lasts; moreover, there is no doubt that he had but few failings, and a great amount of wisdom and virtue. Certainly he was a staunch friend to religious education, and if one could have known his heart, it is very possible that his apparent ambition and desire of social greatness and position may have been influenced by the knowledge that influence and dignity would further his work both as an anatomist and zoologist, and as a responsible promoter of education.

The lives of these heroes have been mainly taken from the life of John Ray in the Ray Society's publications, and from an excellent little book, by an anonymous author, called "Cuvier and Zoology," and from the "Memoires de L'Academie des Sciences."

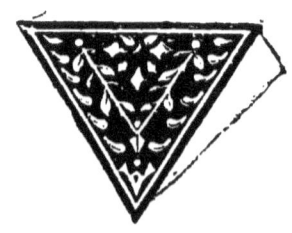

CHAPTER IX.

HEROES OF GEOLOGY.

The rise of the science which treats of the ancient history of the earth—Students of the present changes, which are the examples by which the past may be comprehended—The Greeks—The life of Pythagoras; a notice of the geology of Aristoteles—Strabo's life—The nature of fossils and the life of Steno.

As was the case in the other branches of natural history already noticed, the Greeks knew much more about geology than did the nations of the rest of Europe, subsequently, for nearly seventeen hundred years. The first recorded teacher of the ancient history of the earth was Pythagoras, who was born on the island of Samos, about the year 570 B.C. By his mother's side he was connected with the principal families of the island, and his father appears to have been a Phœnician or a Tyrrhenian of Lemnos. There is nothing known about his childhood, and it is evident that he studied under the great philosophers of his age in Greece. But he wanted further information, and therefore travelled into Egypt, and thence into Chaldæa. Polycrates, the ruler of the island in which Pythagoras was born, appears to have assisted him with the Egyptians by introductions. The traveller noticed not only the habits and customs of the people he visited, but also the aspect of the countries, and the method by which nature wore the earth, and produced changes on the surface of the ground. He appears to have been much struck with the periodical nature of many natural events, such as the succession of the seasons, the time of rain and inundation, and of great heat, and of all the common examples with which everyone is familiar at the present day. Returning home he soon became aware that he could not teach, unreservedly, what he had learned and discovered during his travels, for fear of Polycrates, and he left the island. Finally he settled at Croton, in southern Italy, and he appears to have chosen the locality, in order to propagate his moral and political, as well as scientific opinions. Unfortunately, this ardent scholar and teacher did not write any books, but left that task to his pupils and successors, so that much good sense is mixed with much nonsense in the so-called doctrines of Pythagoras which came from them. Some of his opinions are very remarkable and striking, and he introduced into his own country the statements of the Eastern nations, that there has been a gradual deterioration of the human race from an original state of virtue and happiness. But his principal work regarding the earth has descended to us through the poet Ovid, and it is most interesting. Pythagoras insisted that there was a perpetual and gradual system of change, inherent in the earth. This idea, which came into his mind from the results of observation, he did not apply to very remote ages, or to what is now called the ancient history of the globe. He simply insisted on modern changes. Really this limiting of his thought was in the true scientific spirit, and he dealt with what was true and proveable so far as he was concerned. It might be supposed that the present changes cannot come within the studies of the geologist, but they really do so, because, as will be noticed further on in considering the life of Hutton, the past history of the earth can only be comprehended by studying the present state of things. Pythagoras cleared the way, and made a path for the geologist. He is said by Ovid to have taught as follows :—

"Nothing perishes in this world, but things simply vary and change their form. To be born means simply that a thing begins to be something different from what it was before; and dying is ceasing from being the same thing. Solid land has been converted into sea. Sea has been changed into land; marine shells lie far distant from the deep, and the anchor has been found on the summit of the hills. Valleys have been excavated by running water, and floods have washed down hills into the sea. Marshes have become dry ground. Dry lands have changed into stagnant pools. During earthquakes some springs have been closed up, and new ones have broken out. Rivers have deserted their channels, and have been reborn elsewhere; as the Erasinus, in Greece, and Mysius, in Asia. The waters of some rivers, formerly sweet, have become bitter, as those of Anigrus, in Greece. Islands have become connected with the main land, by the growth of deltas and new deposits. Peninsulas have been divided from the main land, and have become islands, as Leucadia; and according to tradition, Sicily, the sea having carried away the isthmus. Land has been submerged by earthquakes. The Grecian cities of Helice and Burris, for example, are to be seen under the sea, with their walls inclined. Plains have been upheaved into hills by the confined air seeking vent, as at Trœzene, in the Peloponnesus. There are streams which have a petrifying power, and convert the substances which they touch into marble. Volcano vents shift their positions. There was a time when Etna was not a burning mountain, and the time will come when it will cease to burn; whether it be that some caverns be closed up by the movements of the earth and others opened, or whether the fuel is finally exhausted."

Of course there are several errors in these statements, and especially those which relate to the causes of volcanic vents are absurd. Pythagoras also noticed the changes in the animal kingdoms, such as the metamorphoses of insects. Besides being a naturalist this great man taught some most extraordinary doctrines for his time of the world and nation. He stated that virtue was with him and his followers, a harmony, unity, and an endeavour to resemble the Deity. The whole life of man should be an attempt to represent, on earth, the beauty and harmony displayed in the order of the universe. The mind should have the body and the passions under perfect control; the gods should be worshipped by simple purifications and offerings, and above all by sincerity and purity of heart. Pythagoras, by his good teaching and example, established a great school of philosophy, which influenced the world subsequently in a marked manner. A political riot dispersed his followers, and he died about 504 B.C.

A notice of the life of Aristoteles as botanist and zoologist has already been given, and now a few words must be said about the opinions held by this very remarkable man regarding changes in the earth. He progressed beyond Pythagoras, for he refers to many examples of changes now constantly going on, and insists, emphatically, on the great results which they must produce *in the lapse of ages*. The changes of the earth, he says, are so slow in comparison to the duration of our lives, that they are overlooked, and the migrations of people after great catastrophes, and their removal to other regions, cause the event to be forgotten. In one work Aristoteles wrote: "The distribution of land and sea, in particular regions, does not endure throughout all time, but it becomes sea in those parts where it was land, and again it becomes land where it was sea; and there is reason for thinking that these changes take place according to a certain system and within a certain period. Everything changes in the course of time."

There was a great geographer called Strabo, about whose life little is known, except that he travelled far and wide in Europe and North Africa, and wrote largely on the earth. He did not content himself with simple geography, however, for he entered into a discussion, which was a very common one in those days, as it has been since, concerning the nature of the fossil shells which are found in strata or layers of the earth remote from the sea. He attributed the collecting of the shells where they are found to the former subsidence of the land, and not to the rising of the sea. It is not, he said, because the lands covered by seas were originally at different altitudes, that the waters have risen or subsided or receded from some parts and inundated others, but the reason is, that the same land is sometimes raised up and sometimes depressed, so that it either overflows or returns to its own place again. We must therefore ascribe the cause to the ground, either to that ground which is under the sea or to that which becomes flooded by it, but rather to that which lies beneath the sea, for this is more moveable, and on account of its humidity can be altered with greater celerity. This philosopher clearly laid down the law that the general level of the sea has remained the same, but that it has been and is the land which has been or is upheaved or subsided. It is a fundamental truth on which much of the science of geology depends. He moreover asserted that volcanoes were safety-valves, and were the result of subterranean convulsions.

These were the principal writers which influenced geology in the days before the Christian era, and it is to be noticed that they did not treat of the construction of the rocks, of the succession of the layers or strata, or of much concerning the ancient history of the globe. But they taught, wisely and admirably, the nature of modern changes, and believed that these and the older ones they could comprehend, were part of a scheme, and were produced by natural causes, in the course of events.

Aristoteles, Strabo, and Plinius wrote about the changes which were progressing on the surface of the earth, and compared them, in their reasoning, with changes they presumed had been, but still no great advance was made.

In the early part of the sixteenth century a remarkable discussion sprang up about the nature of shells and bones, which were found in layers of earth remote from the sea. The celebrated painter Leonardo da Vinci had seen some of these fossils during his youth, when he planned and carried out some important canals in the north of Italy. He laughed at the fancies of the day about the shells, for some people said that they were made by the stars, and others that they were brought forth naturally, in the layers of earth in which they were found. He wanted to know where the things were being made in the hills, by the stars, at the present time, and stated that, like the rounded stones of gravel, the shells had been in the sea, and that they were of different ages and kinds, and were once alive. But the former living condition of fossils, and the possibility of their being understood, by comparing them with recent or living things, was, perhaps, most strongly put by Steno, a Dane.

In 1638, a goldsmith, Steno by name, living at Copenhagen, who was a tradesman of the King Christian IV. of Denmark, had a son. The young Nicholas was brought up carefully, evidently was well educated, and was destined for the medical profession. A strict Lutheran, he naturally went to Holland for a part of his education, and studied at Leyden under the very distinguished anatomists there, after he had taken his degree. Nothing is known about his person or habits, but the results of his constant labour prove him to have been a most industrious student, and also an investigator of the human frame in his early days of manhood. At first the medical profession was everything to him, and he studied human anatomy and physiology with great success, making some important and interesting discoveries. He discovered the duct or channel by which the saliva runs into the mouth from the salivary gland beneath the skin on the cheek, and in 1664 he published some researches on the manner in which the chick is nourished in the egg. Moreover, he examined the structures of the eye of the calf, the nature of the mucous secretion, and wrote on the heart. While engaged in these researches at Amsterdam, he heard of the death of his mother, and returned to Copenhagen. After a short stay there, he set out for Italy, taking France on his way; and he began a series of researches on the structure of the brain at Paris in 1664. Here a great change occurred, which influenced his future life in a remarkable degree. Steno, well known then as a successful investigator, came under the notice of a great French geographer, Thévenot, and, what was more important, became the friend of Bossuet, one of the greatest preachers and teachers the Roman Catholic Church has ever produced. Steno was so influenced by Bossuet, that he became converted to the Roman Catholic faith, and left the Lutheran Church. Going subsequently into Italy, Steno pursued his studies, and settled in Florence, in 1667, being well received by the Grand Duke Ferdinand II. de Medici. In spite of the somewhat natural jealousy of the medical men of the city, Steno was appointed physician to the Grand Duke, and prosecuted his anatomical studies under his influence. Then he came across a subject which directed his attention to geology, or rather to that part of the science which relates to extinct animals. In a letter to Thévenot, Steno describes the dissection of a shark which had been captured off Leghorn in 1666, and especially discussed the mode of growth of the teeth of the animal. At this time many fossils were picked up and gathered out of layers or strata, which were called by many curious names, and believed to be anything but what they really were. They were distinguished by Steno at once as shark's teeth, and he insisted that sharks lived during the former ages of the globe, and that they had become entombed in the deposits which were then forming a stratum or layer of earth, the result of deposition in water, being the burial-ground of the time of its collection or formation.

Fossils were thus shown by Steno to be mineralized or petrified organic remains, and he gave the hint or method to future investigators, that the example of the existing animals must be taken, in order to learn the nature of those creatures whose remains are more or less perfectly preserved in the fossil condition.

Following out this subject, Steno wrote on the manner in which deposits accumulate, and accumulated in past ages; and he concluded that if we found a deposit containing sea-salt and the remains of marine animals, planks of ships etc., we should believe that the sea had once been there, whether the bed was exposed in consequence of the sea having retired, or because the land had been raised. He showed that although the lowest beds deposited over any area, must conform to the shape of the underlying rock, the tendency of all sediment must be to occupy the horizontal position; and so when we find them highly inclined, as in mountains, for instance, we must refer this to subsequent movement. He noticed that mountains are made up both of horizontal and inclined strata, as may be seen along their flanks. He infers that mountains were once not in existence, and that they do not grow, but that their regions are raised and depressed and subject to rending and fissuring. Steno clearly showed that the land had sunk and had been again elevated in the geological ages, and in considering the causes he seems to have grasped the idea that the internal heat of the earth becoming less, the mass cools, and that the movements on the surface have had to do with the cooling. His most important work was removing fossils out of the category of marvels, sports of nature, and as things which grew in the earth, to the proper truth that they are preserved parts of animals and plants which were formerly alive. In 1688, Steno was appointed to the chair of anatomy at Copenhagen; but he had to suffer from jealousy, and doubtless some religious persecution influenced his desire to leave his native country and to return to Florence again. This he did, and Cosmo III. entrusted him with the education of his son. Steno then began to give up science and to study theology, and wrote several works on the subject by which he hoped to convert his old natural history friends. One of these involved him in a controversy with the reformed clergy of Jena. The Pope, Innocent XI., rewarded Steno in 1677, by making him a bishop and apostolic vicar of Northern Europe. Steno went to reside at Hanover; but he had to leave, and returning to Schwerin, he died there. His body was, at the request of the Grand Duke Cosmo, carried back to Tuscany in 1687.

CHAPTER X.

THE LIFE OF HUTTON.

The rise of the modern school of geology—The continuity of the operations of nature and their sameness—The necessity of studying the existing state of things in order to comprehend the past—The denial of catastrophes—Hutton's theory of the earth the foundation of scientific geology.

MANY facts had been recorded regarding the ancient history of the earth, and a host of ideas, more or less absurd, had been given forth on geology, during the years which preceded and followed the reformation. Several Italian geologists had examined into the truths discovered by Pythagoras, and, as stated in the preceding pages, the nature of fossils had become understood by a few liberal minded men. The age of Newton, and the years which followed his time, were consumed, however, so far as the history of the earth was concerned, by vain attempts to form cosmogonies, to account for the origin of the globe and visible universe. There was also a fierce struggle between two great geological factions, one asserting that all rocks were the product of heat, and the other denying this *in toto* and deciding that water was the originator. Many, and indeed nearly all, geologists taught that nature had acted during the past, by fits and starts, and that great convulsions had occurred, bringing the earth at last to its present condition. The common sense of mankind was opposed to many of these beliefs, and there was moreover a very great indisposition, on the part of many educated men, to credit that the earth was more than six thousand years old. Not a few believed that the hills and dales, mountains and plains, cliffs and valleys, were first formed as they are now.

A Scottish gentleman, a quiet retiring man, having some means of his own, studied the structure of the rocks and taught himself physical geography. He mastered a great number of undoubted facts, and reasoned upon them, and produced a theory which made geology a science, instead of a jumble of guesses flavoured with the love of the marvellous.

James Hutton was the son of William Hutton, a merchant living in Edinburgh, and was born in that city on the 3rd of June, 1726. His father, a man highly respected for his good sense and integrity, and who had held the important office of city treasurer, died whilst the boy was young. The mother was a woman of considerable ability, and she determined that her child should have a good education. He went, consequently, to the High

School, and subsequently was entered at the University at the early age of fourteen. James was a thorough student, and loved work, and his tastes were directed rather to natural science than to classics and the higher mathematics. He studied mathematics under Maclaurin, and used to say in after years that although he enjoyed Professor Stevenson's teaching of logic, still he thought more of him because a hint that was given in a lecture led him to take a passionate interest in chemistry. The fact that gold is dissolved in aqua regia (a mixture of nitric and hydrochloric acids), and that two acids, which can each of them dissolve any of the baser metals, must unite their strength before they can attack the most precious, was mentioned by the professor, in illustration of some general doctrine. Hutton was much impressed with this fact, and was led to study it further, and he got all the books on the subject. This led to his love of chemistry, which never forsook him, and which really decided the course of his career. But Hutton was destined for a profession, and his mother did not intend him to occupy himself solely with science. Consequently he was articled to a writer to the signet, with a view of becoming a lawyer. He had hard work to do, and plenty of it; it was mere routine work, that of a clerk, and there was a possibility that he would forget his scientific pleasures. His desire for knowledge persisted, in spite of his monotonous work, and occasionally he endeavoured to teach his fellow clerks a little, and he was found amusing himself and them with chemical experiments, when he should have been copying papers or studying the forms of legal proceedings. His master soon saw that the young man's mind was not that which would suit a lawyer, so, with much kindness and good sense, he released his young friend from his obligations. Young Hutton at once began to study medicine, as that science which was the most closely allied to chemistry. He attended lectures, and studied well from 1744 to 1747. Then, as the teaching at Edinburgh was not sufficient in all the parts of medical studies, he went, as was usual, to Paris, where he studied chemistry and anatomy with great ardour. He was there for nearly two years, and then went to Leyden, in Holland, where he took his degree in September, 1749. On his return to London at the end of that year, he began to think seriously about settling in the world. Edinburgh afforded no flattering prospect for his establishment as a physician. The business there was in the hands of a few eminent practitioners, who had been long established; so that no opening was left for a young man whose merit was yet unknown, who had no powerful connections to assist him on his first outset, and very little of that patient and circumspect activity by which a medical man pushes himself forward in the world.

Full of anxiety about the future, Hutton wrote to a friend of his own age on the subject. This was Mr. James Davie, with whom Hutton had been on most intimate terms before leaving Scotland. They had both a great love of chemistry, and had experimented together, especially on the nature and production of ammonia. Their experiments had led to some valuable discoveries, and had been pursued by Mr. Davie during his friend's absence. They had afforded a reasonable expectation of establishing a profitable manufacture of some salt of ammonia from coal-soot. The project of this establishment was communicated by Mr. Davie to his friend, who was still in London, and it appears to have lessened his anxiety about settling as a physician, and, probably, was one of the main causes of his laying aside all thoughts of that profession. Perhaps, too, on a nearer view, he did not find that the practice of medicine would afford him that leisure for pursuing chemical and other scientific objects which he fancied it would do, when he saw things at a greater distance. In fact, Hutton found himself in the same position as many other men of genius who have pursued as successfully the peculiar studies requisite for an accomplished medical man. Anatomy, physiology, chemistry, and botany have often been much more attractive to the aspirant for medical fame than surgery, practical medicine, and the study of drugs and their uses. Many a good doctor has been spoiled by over-education, and science has gained an enthusiastic student. It would appear, however, that there was another cause which was influencing Hutton. He had inherited a little property in land in Berwickshire from his father; it was possible to live on it, and farm and work at chemistry without risk, whilst if he sold it, or used the rent in advancing his position as a medical man, he might fail after all.

Certain it is that he returned to Edinburgh, and in the summer of 1750 he abandoned his intention of practising, and resolved to apply himself to agriculture. He had as a friend Sir John Hall, of Dunglass, a man of ingenuity and taste for science, and also an agriculturist. As he was never destined to do anything by halves, Hutton determined to study farming in the school which was then reckoned the best, and the manner which is undoubtedly the most effectual. He went into Norfolk, and fixed his residence for some time in that county, living in the house of a farmer, who served both for his landlord and his instructor. This he did in 1752. He always spoke well of John Dybold, who made him comfortable, and whose practical lessons in husbandry he much valued. He appears, indeed, to have enjoyed this situation very much: the simple and plain character of the society with which he mingled, suited well with his own, and the peasants of Norfolk could find nothing in the stranger to set them at a distance from him, or to make them treat him with reserve. It was always true of Dr. Hutton that to an ordinary man he appeared to be an ordinary man; possessing a little more spirit and liveliness, perhaps, than it is usual to meet with.

He enjoyed Norfolk life very much, and doubtless it was the very different soil of that county which made the young Scotchman think, for the first time, about the construction of the surface of the earth which he hoped to till and profit by. While his head quarters were thus established in Norfolk, he made journeys, on foot, into different parts of England; and though the main object of them was to obtain information in agriculture, yet he never passed a pit, or a cliff, or a river-side, without studying the structure of the soil, so that in 1753, Hutton was incontinently making himself a geologist, a pursuit which his knowledge of chemistry and mineralogy rendered easy to him. What agriculture he learned in Norfolk was of the greatest use to him, and he visited Flanders to learn more. He travelled from Rotterdam through Holland, Brabant, Flanders, and Picardy, and was highly delighted with the cultivation of the small holdings of those countries. Though his principal object in this excursion was to acquire information in the practice of husbandry, he appears to have paid much attention to the mineralogy of the countries through which he passed. Then he returned and took up his own farm in Berwickshire, bringing with him a Norfolk ploughman. He set to work and farmed, using every known improvement, and he has the credit of being one of those who introduced the new husbandry into a country where it has since made more rapid advances than in any other part of Great Britain. From 1754 to

1768 he resided on his farm, visiting Edinburgh occasionally. He seems to have led a tranquil country life, succeeding as a farmer; and yet there was, during all this time, a slow yet progressive growth of a science in his mind. Cautious, persevering, observant, and truly logical in his method of thought, Hutton was accumulating facts upon which to reason in geology, whilst the so-called geologists of the day were forming theories without facts. He took a tour to the north of Scotland, through Ross and Caithness, and returned by way of Aberdeen to Edinburgh, and he studied the mineralogy and geology of the districts. Returning home, he still went on farming, and at the same time he became a partner with his friend Davie in a manufactory of ammonia. By the year 1768, being forty-two years of age, Hutton had matured his plans; he let his farm at a very advantageous rent, and, untroubled about his affairs, having his three sisters as his companions, he went to Edinburgh, and entered the singularly interesting scientific society of that time. His biographer, Playfair, writes that Hutton, "employed in maturing his views and studying nature with unwearied application, now passed his time most usefully and agreeably to himself, but in silence and obscurity with respect to the world." "Free from the interruption of professional avocations, he enjoyed the entire command of his own time, and had sufficient energy of mind to afford himself continual occupation." A good deal of his leisure was now employed in the prosecution of chemical experiments. In one of these he made an interesting discovery which relates to the changes that go on in apparently most unchangeable rocks, and which are due to the action of percolating water on them. He noticed that in the midst of dense masses of hard, cold, volcanic rock, called basalt, crystals of great beauty are found in cavities. They can be fused under the blowpipe easily, and that is not the case with the surrounding rock. On adding hydrochloric acid to one of these zeolites, as they are called, a gelatinous substance is formed out of the crystal, and on evaporation, sea salt or chloride of sodium is found. "This was the first instance," writes his biographer, Playfair, "of an alkali being found in a stony body." He went to Cheshire to see the salt mines, went to Birmingham, and then set out for Wales. His desire was to trace the hard gravel of granular quartz which is found in such abundance in the soil about Birmingham and elsewhere, to its origin, and to find out whence it came and how it was distributed. He found none of the rock in Wales; but on returning he found it in places, in a body of old rocks which stand out of the country between Bromsgrove and Birmingham.

Then Hutton wrote a little book on the "Nature, Quality, and Distinction of Culm and Coal." The result was more economical than scientific, for it led to the abolition of a duty on the small coal of Scotland. He read hard, and every book on travels which referred to physical geography was carefully studied, so that at last no man of the age was so fit to deal with the great problem he had been revolving in his mind for thirty years. All his studies of nature, all his examinations of the surface of the earth, were with a view of ascertaining the changes that have taken place on its surface, and of discovering the causes by which they have been produced. He was impressed with the belief that the former changes in the earth's surface have been of the same kind as those now in progress; that the ancient history of the earth could only be studied by taking the example of modern changes, and that the past could be studied from the present, because there was uniformity and constancy and law in nature. The same energies and forces have always been and have acted by law in much the same manner as at the present time. With his true scientific spirit Hutton would have nothing to do with convulsions or with the origin of the globe; he did not want to guess or speculate, but to argue logically on facts which anybody could observe. He took geology out of the age of the marvellous and laid the foundations of the present aspect of the science. He was in no hurry to publish his views, possibly because his temperament was cautious, and possibly he was aware what a furious fuss there would be made about it; how he would be abused, scolded, and anathematized. There is no doubt that the lights of the age and public opinion were perfectly incompetent to judge the merits of such a theory; they were sunken in prejudices, and resisted any change of opinion. He was aware that a great outcry would be made by men whose religious opinions were his own, and whom he respected greatly. In fact, the world, just before the appearance of Hutton's "Theory of the Earth," was less prepared for it than ordinary opinion was for the doctrines of Charles Darwin one hundred years afterwards. The appearance of the work of this last great naturalist made, and is still making, a great stir, but that of Hutton's work was received, as he anticipated, with incredible opposition, by the teachers of the day; and its slow acceptation by the scientific world was remarkable. No abuse could efface its effects; it was true, and the true alone lasts; it was reasonable, and it was to the glory of God.

In this book, geology was, for the first time, declared to be in no way concerned about the origin of things. It was the first in which an attempt was made to dispense entirely with all hypothetical causes, and to explain the former changes of the earth's crust by reference exclusively to such natural agents as still exist. Hutton laboured to give fixed principles to geology, as Newton had succeeded in doing to astronomy. He wrote: "The ruins of an older world are visible in the present structure of our planet, and the strata which now compose our continents, have been once beneath the sea, and were formed out of the waste of pre-existing continents. The same forces are still destroying, by chemical decomposition or mechanical violence, even the hardest rocks, transporting the materials to the sea, where they are spread out and form strata analogous to those of more ancient date. Although loosely deposited along the bottom of the ocean, they become afterwards altered and consolidated by volcanic heat, and then turned up, fractured, and contorted." He showed that many hard crystalline rocks, such as basalt, were of igneous origin, and that some of them had been injected in a melted state through fissures in the older strata. He proved, by examining Glen Tilt, that granite was once in a state of fusion, and had cooled. He wrote: "In the economy of the world I can find no traces of a beginning, no prospect of an end," a declaration all the more startling when coupled with the doctrine that all changes on the globe had been brought about by the slow agency of existing causes. Sir Charles Lyell, writing on this, stated, "The imagination was first fatigued and overpowered by endeavouring to conceive the immensity of time required for the annihilation of whole continents by so insensible a process; and when the thoughts had wandered through these intermediate periods, no resting place was assigned in the remotest distance. The oldest rocks were represented to be of a derivative nature, the last of an antecedent series, and that, perhaps, of one of many pre-existing worlds."

Most unfairly was Hutton attacked, and he was thus defended by his friend Playfair: "In the planetary motions, where geometry has carried the eye so far, both into the future and the past, we discover no mark either of the commencement or termination of the present order. It is unreasonable, indeed, to suppose that such marks should anywhere exist. The Author of nature has not given laws to the universe, which, like the constitutions of men, carry in themselves the elements of their own destruction. He has not permitted in his works any symptom of infancy or of old age, or any sign by which we may estimate either their future or their past duration. He may put an end, as He no doubt gave a beginning, to the present system at some determinate period of time; but we may rest assured that this great catastrophe will not be brought about by the laws now existing, and that it will not be indicated by anything which we perceive."

Hutton studied meteorology, and gave to the world the first reasonable theory of the cause of rain. He described the formation of invisible vapour by evaporation, the production of visible mist and cloud, and finally rain. And he investigated the reasons of the cause of rainfalls differing in amount in the tropics and temperate zones of the earth. In 1793 serious illness attacked Hutton after he had been writing his speculations regarding matter. On his recovery he republished his work on the "Theory of the Earth," and replied to many of the attacks upon it, and later on wrote a work which was not published in the "Elements of Agriculture." Illness again seized him, and he died in 1797.

Hutton was such an observer of facts that he rarely read any books of a theoretical nature, and he never would concede anything to mere authority. He was indefatigable in study, and wrote largely, expressing his thoughts constantly with his pen. He rose late, and began to study at once, and until early dinner. He rarely dined from home, and was a most sparing eater, and he drank no wine. After dinner he resumed his studies, or, if the weather was fine, walked for two or three hours, when he could not be said to give up study, though he might, perhaps, change the object of it. He rarely departed from this kind of life, except when he was travelling. To his friends his conversation was inestimable; as great talents, the most perfect candour, and the utmost simplicity of character and manners, all united to stamp a value upon it. His slender, active figure, thin countenance, high forehead, and somewhat aquiline nose, gave him the appearance of being acute and vigorous in body and mind. He was full of ardour and enthusiasm, gay and humorous, and most forcible in argument. The man's simplicity, determination, and desire for truth, his carelessness of the opinion of men, and his great regard for his fellow labourers who were not led away by prejudice and authority, were his great characteristics.

Hutton founded geology as a logical science; and although he was ignorant of the succession of the forms of life on the globe, yet his method of studying the past from the present has been, and still is used as the way in which the extinct animals and plants can be comprehended in the scheme of nature. Hutton's works were carefully studied by, and in after years they were the mainspring of the toil of Lyell.

There is a very interesting notice of the life of this great man in the "Encyclopædia Britannica," by Professor Geikie, and in an essay by Playfair in the "Transactions of the Royal Society of Edinburgh" to which the author of this memoir is indebted.

CHAPTER XI.

THE LIFE OF WILLIAM SMITH.

The succession of the strata recognized—Strata known by their fossils, position, and mineral contents—England surveyed by Smith and made the type of the results of the succession of changes studied by geology.

THE ancestors of William Smith were a race of farmers who owned small tracts of land, and had been settled in Oxfordshire and Gloucestershire for many generations.

William Smith was born at Churchill, a village in Oxfordshire, on the 23rd of March, 1769, the year which gave birth to Cuvier. Of his parents he always spoke with great regard, but there is little in the recollections which he has preserved of them, to show in what degree they contributed to form his remarkable character. His father he described as "a very ingenious mechanic," and mentions as the cause of his death a severe cold caught while engaged in the erection of some machinery. Deprived of this parent before he was eight years old, it was fortunate for him that his mother was a woman of ability, of gentle and charitable disposition, and attentive to the education of her children. An expressive pencil sketch and a characteristic description, both from memory, record his devotion to his mother.

According to his own account, however, not only were the means of his instruction at the village school very limited, but they were in some degree interfered with by his own wandering and musing habits. The rural games in those "merrie daies" of England might sometimes attract the wayward and comparatively unrestrained scholar from his books; but he was more frequently learning of another mistress, and forming, for after-life, a habit of close and curious contemplation of nature.

After his father's death and his mother's second marriage, the person to whom he was principally to look up to for protection, was his father's eldest brother, to a portion of whose property he was heir. From this kinsman, who was but little pleased with his nephew's love of collecting the "pundibs"* and "poundstones," or "quoit-stones,"† and had no sympathies with his fancies of carving sun-dials on the soft brown "oven-stone" ‡ of the neighbourhood, he with great difficulty wrung, by repeated entreaty, money for the purchase of a few books fit to instruct a boy in the

* Terebratulæ.
† A large Echinite (*Clypeus sinuatus* of Leske), not unfrequently employed as a "pound-weight" by the dairywomen.
‡ Named from its frequent use in the construction of ovens.

rudiments of geometry and surveying. But the practical farmer was better satisfied when the youth manifested an intelligent interest in the processes of draining and improving land; and there is no doubt that young William profited in after-life by the experience, if it may be so called, which he gathered in his boyhood while accompanying his relative ("old William") over his lands at Over Norton.

Whatever he saw, was remembered for ever. To the latest hours of life he retained a clear and complete recollection of almost every event of his boyhood and often interested young and old by his vivid pictures of what he had seen when a child. These notices would be swelled to an unreasonable degree by introducing the pleasant stories of "the narrative old man;" but the following recollections, written in his seventieth year, of events which had passed fifty-six years before, are worth preserving as evidence of this peculiar circumstantiality of memory.

"I was early a tall and strong-grown boy, and in my way to London, between twelve and thirteen years of age, I particularly noticed the great work of cutting down the chalk hill at Henley-upon-Thames, and how the loaded carriages on an inclined plane were made to bring up the empty ones.

"I was in London shortly after the riots of Lord George Gordon; and at the time when news of Rodney's defeat of the French fleet arrived.

"There was then a halfpenny toll for foot-persons passing over Blackfriars Bridge; the Albion Mills (worked by steam power) had just before been burnt down.

"Criminals were hanged at Tyburn, where there were cow-houses with wood seats on top for persons to see the executions.

"From Manchester Square to the Edgeware Road and Paddington, there were footpaths entirely across open fields. The buildings on the side of the square were unfinished; but, as more connected with what relates to the earth, I saw how the ground was made in Manchester Square, for a poor fellow, in turning his cartload of slush, had let his horse and cart slip down, so that he was up to his middle in mud, endeavouring to extricate his horse just as I passed by. This was on the east side of the square."

In 1783, and from this time to 1787, the young man, without instruction or sympathy, prosecuted irregularly, but with ardour and success, the studies to which his mind was awakened. He began to draw, attempted to colour, became tolerably versed in the geometry and calculations then thought sufficient for engineers and surveyors, and by these acquirements, at the age of eighteen, so strongly recommended himself to Mr. Edward Webb, of Stow-on-the-Wold, who had been invited to make a complete survey of the parish of Churchill, for the purpose of enclosure, that he became assistant to that most able and excellent man, and was taken into his family.

This was the critical moment; from this event flowed all the current of his useful life, and to the same origin may be ascribed many of the peculiar habits and feelings, the contrasted lights and shades, which diversified his character.

Edward Webb was, like his pupil, self-taught, and very slightly acquainted with languages and general literature, but possessed of great ingenuity and skill in mechanics, mensuration, logarithms, algebra and fluxions. His practice as a surveyor included many things now conceded to the engineer, such as the determination of the forces of water, and planning machinery. His instruments were commonly invented, often made and divided by himself; peculiar pentagraphs, theodolites, scales, and even compasses and field books, of new construction enriched the office at Stow, and stimulated the young men who were fortunate enough to be placed in it, to thought and exertion. "I admired," says the subject of this memoir, "the talent of my master, his placid and ever unruffled temper, and his willingness to let me get on, for I required no teaching."

Speedily entrusted with the management of all the ordinary business of a surveyor, Mr. Smith traversed, in continual activity, the oolitic lands of Oxfordshire and Gloucestershire, the lias clays and red marls of Warwickshire; visited (1788) the Salperton tunnel on the Thames and Severn Canal, and (1790) examined the soils and circumstances connected with a boring for coal in the

New Forest, opposite the Shoe alehouse at Plaitford. All the varieties of soil, in so many surveys in different districts, were particularly noticed, and compared with the general aspect and character of the country, and the agricultural and commercial appropriations. The arrangement of the lias limestone beds in Warwickshire contrasted with the neighbouring red marls at Inkborough, the boring for coal in some dark lias clays on the road to Warwick, the absence of arenaceous beds from the limestones of Churchill—these were some of the points treasured in a mind capable of combining them at a future time.

In 1793 we find him engaged in executing surveys and complete systems of levelling, for the line of a proposed canal. In the course of the operations which he performed in the summer and autumn, a speculation which had come into his mind regarding a general law affecting the strata of the district, was submitted to proof and confirmed. He had *supposed* that the strata lying above the coal were not laid horizontally, but inclined; that they were all inclined in one direction, viz., the eastward, so as to successively terminate at the surface, and thus to "resemble, on a large scale, the ordinary appearance of superposed slices of bread and butter." This supposition was now proved to be correct by the levelling processes executed in two parallel valleys, for in each of the levelled lines the strata of "red ground," "lias," and "freestone" (afterwards called "oolite"), came down in an eastern direction and sunk below the level, and yielded place to the next in succession.

But at the same time it was known to Mr. Smith that the position of the strata of coal in Somersetshire was not generally conformed to that of the "red earth" "lias," and other beds above; the same thing was proved to him by an inspection of the colliery at Bucklechurch, in Gloucestershire; he knew besides that the great faults which divide *all* the coal strata underground, were in general found not to divide *any* of the superincumbent rocks which formed the surface.

Geologists who, at the present time, notwithstanding the devoted attention which has been paid to the phenomena of local displacement, find a difficulty in understanding the causes, may imagine the perplexity in the mind of a *discoverer*. Mr. Smith felt this perplexity severely, but not long. The Canal Bill, on which he was engaged, received the sanction of Parliament in 1794; and one of the first steps taken by the judicious committee of management was to depute two members of their body to accompany Mr. Smith, "their engineer," on a tour of inquiry and observation regarding the construction, management, and trade of other navigations in England and Wales.

The tour extended altogether nine hundred miles, and occupied between one and two months; by one route the party reached Newcastle, and by another returned, through Shropshire and Wales to Bath. Mr. Palmer and Mr. Perkins were gentlemen well acquainted with coal-working, and they willingly stayed to inspect every new invention applied to canals and collieries; but Mr. Smith's treasured object of consideration on the road, that which occupied all his thoughts in the intervals of professional inquiries, was the aspect and structure of the country passed through, in order to determine if his preconceived generalizations of a settled order of succession, continuity of range at the surface, and general declination eastward, were true on a large scale.

It is needless now to say that his general views were justified; he found the strata from the vicinity of Bath and Bristol prolonged into the north of England, in the same general order of succession with the general eastward dip. There is, however, one part of the conclusions adopted in this rapid survey from a postchaise, which merits particular attention. He passed through York on the high road to Newcastle, and saw at a distance of from five to fifteen miles to the east the hills of chalk and oolite. He was satisfied of their nature by their *contours* and *relative position*, and by their position on the surface in relation to the lias and "red ground" occasionally seen on the road. This is, in fact, the only authority he could rely upon for drawing, in 1800, the continuations of the chalk of Wiltshire, and the oolite of Somersetshire, through the eastern parts of Yorkshire, but he drew them with a considerable approximation to accuracy.

Engaged for six years in setting out and superintending the works on the Somersetshire Coal Canal, Mr. Smith found but few opportunities of making known to scientific persons, the peculiar generalizations which had taken possession of his mind. But in the execution of these works he was putting his thoughts into practice, informing the contractors what would be the nature of the ground to be cut through, what parts of the canal would require unusual care to be kept water-tight, what was the most advantageous system of work. Another singular advantage attended this engagement. The notions which up to this time he had obtained regarding the distribution of organic remains were comparatively vague. He found peculiar plants in the "clift" above the coal, particular shells in the lias and oolites, but none in the red ground, and he had combined these simple facts so far as to see that "each stratum had been successively the bed of the sea, and contained in it the mineralized monuments of the races of organic beings then in existence." But it was the necessity of possessing an accurate knowledge of the different sorts of rock, sand, and clay, which were to be cut through on the line of the canal, which led him to examine minutely and scrupulously into the distribution of the "fossils" which he had been in the habit of collecting. The result was a proposition which he proved to be locally true, and of practical value, and which has now a world-wide application, " that each stratum contained organized fossils peculiar to itself, and might, in cases otherwise doubtful, be recognized and discriminated from others like it, but in a different part of the series, by examination of them." In other words, he discovered that strata are to be recognized by their fossils. He now remarked also the contrast between the rounded state and mixed condition of the fossils which lay in gravel deposits and the sharply preserved specimens lying in natural associations in the strata, and thus acquired a notion of the distinction between what were afterwards named diluvial and stratified deposits.

The possessor of all these generalizations, now (1795) twenty-six years of age, was still shrouded in the obscure village of High Littleton, but in this year he removed to Bath, and took up his abode in the central house of a short range of buildings called the Cottage Crescent, which occupied a picturesque and elevated site south of that city. "From this point," says he, "the eye roved anxiously over the interesting expanse which extended before me to the Sugar-loaf mountain in Monmouthshire, and embraced all in the vicinities of Bath and Bristol. Then did a thousand thoughts occur to me, respecting the geology of that and adjacent districts continually under my eye, which have never been reduced to writing." He continued to direct all the operations on the Somerset Coal Canal, and very copious note-books attest the constancy and exactitude of his attention to that occupation. To this cause, indeed, may be ascribed the extreme rarity of any essays, or even memoranda, from which the progress of his geological studies can be gathered.

That in January, 1796, he had begun to commit his thoughts to paper, in a lucid arrangement for publication, the written proofs remain. In 1797 he drew a larger general plan for such a work; but not till 1799, after his engagement ceased with the Coal Canal Company, did he make public his intention to compose a general work on the stratification of Britain, or enter on the prosecution of an actual survey of the geological structure of the whole of England and Wales.

In the execution of the canal, Mr. Smith had found the means of applying his newly acquired knowledge to useful practical problems, such as how to draw the line through a country full of porous rocks, so as best to retain the limited supplies of water which frequent mills left to the navigation, where to place bridges on a good foundation, how to intercept and conduct the springs, and where to open quarries of proper stone. We find him also engaged, as early as 1796, in the short intervals which could be snatched from the main business before him, in putting to practical proof his theoretical views of the earth's structure and the properties of the mixed calcareous and argillaceous strata in the hills near Bath, by a new and successful process of land-draining.

The earliest connected remarks which have been found, bear the date of January, 1796, and relate to organic remains and their distribution in the different strata. The vicinity of Bath is rich in fossils, and fine collections were formed there previous to Mr. Smith's researches. It might be after inspecting some of these treasures, whose full value was so entirely unknown to their owners, that the following reflections, which strikingly illustrate the enlarged state of his own views at that period, were penned :—

"Dunkerton, Swan, Jan. 5, 1796.

"Fossils have been long studied as great curiosities, collected with great pains, treasured with great and at a great expense, and shown and admired with as much pleasure as a child's hobbyhorse is shown and admired by himself and his playfellows, because it is pretty; and this has been done by *thousands who have never paid the least regard to that wonderful order and regularity with which nature has disposed of these singular productions, and assigned to each class its peculiar stratum.*"

Gifted in a very uncommon degree with that philosophical faith in the generality and harmony of natural laws which is a characteristic of discoveries in natural science, Mr. Smith was at the same time remarkably disinclined to indulge in himself, or even to tolerate in others, mere speculations in geology. Whatever of this nature he found in the circle of his reading, was severely judged by a close collocation of the hypothesis which had been advanced with the phenomena of stratification which he had entirely established,

These judgments might be erroneous in cases which required the knowledge of other data, not then collected, for a true and general solution; but the very unreasonableness of raising the standard of his own discoveries in a limited region, for condemning a speculation perhaps founded on other truths occurring elsewhere, shows how firmly these discoveries, and the influences belonging to them, were established and fortified in his mind. The following passage, written in January, 1796, might have been acknowledged by the author to contain his real opinions forty years later:—

"Therefore every man of prudence and observation who has paid the strictest attention to mineralogy, the structure of the earth, and the changes it has undergone, will be very cautious how he sets about to invent a system which nature cannot conform to without having recourse to subterraneous fires, volcanic eruptions, or uncommon convulsions, by which every hill and dale must have been formed and every rock must have been rent to form those chasms, which, in comparison to the strata they are found in, are no more than sun-cracks in a clod of clay; yet such has been the language of ingenious men, who have set their theoretical worlds a-going without either tooth or pinion of nature's mechanism belonging to them."

In October and November of this year (1796), we find him returning to the contemplation of organic remains; discussing the circumstances which attend the sparry substance occupying the place of the shell, which has been removed, in the lias, and the empty cavity, where the shell was, surrounding a loose stony cast of the interior, in the freestone (oolite).

That his mind was now actively employed in tracing out the bearings of the extensive subject before him, will be evident from the following extract, dated August, 1797 :—

"*Locality of plants, insects, birds, etc., arises from the nature of the strata.*

"Where art has not diverted the order of things and nature is left to herself, a considerable locality may be observed in many animals and vegetables as well as mineral productions, by which they evidently attached to particular soils to such a degree that, if this subject were studied with attention, it would form one of the principal external characteristics of the strata underneath. Though it may seem mysterious to some, that birds, beasts, insects, etc., which have the liberty of roving at pleasure, should feel any particular attachment for this or that soil, yet the wonder ceases when we consider how the chain of natural things is linked together, and how these creatures are taught to cull their food from insects that are lodged in, or seeds that are produced from, particular plants that grow upon particular soils."

Smith had seen layers of limestone crowded with shells succeeded by others containing corals. He found ammonites and oysters in some, and insect remains in others, and his speculations assumed the curious phase of the sentences just noticed. But he soon became aware that accident had much to do with the presence of certain organic remains in strata, and that, whilst some fossils, like corals, once lived where they are now preserved in strata, others were carried there as the deposit collected.

A manuscript, dated December 2, 1796, Dunkerton, Swan Inn, headed "Strata in general, and their position," and evidently intended for publication, commences thus:—

"The strata being found as regular on one side of a rivulet, river, deep valley or channel as on the other, over an extent of many miles, when proper allowance is made for the inclination, and for the variation of the surface, is it not reasonable to suppose that the same strata may be found as regular on one side of the sea or ocean as on opposite sides of a deep valley upon land, and if so, and the continuation of the strata is general, what is their general direction or drift? Is it in straight lines from pole to pole, or in curved lines surrounding the globe regularly inclined to the east?"

After hinting at a general cause for such an assumed regularity, he adds, "But all theories are best built on practical rules, which will enable any one to make such observations for himself as must carry conviction along with them; for a work so novel as this must expect to find some who will hardly believe what is plain to be seen; for all men do not see alike, nor can patiently trudge through the dirt to search for truth among the stubborn rocks where nature has best displayed her. . . . Shall, therefore, describe a number of quarries, cliffs, etc., at a great distance, etc. See Book—— "

In what seems to be the continuation of this paper, we see the predominant desire of the author to establish the certainty and generality of the inclination of strata, which he had proved on a limited scale near Bath.

"If the strata lay horizontal, every part of the sea-shore would present the same beds at the water edge instead of that wonderful variety which is found on the coast and banks of every river and rivulet in the kingdom, especially those that run in an east and west direction, or nearly so. In such situations the young mineralogist may soon be convinced of that wonderful regularity which nature has adopted, especially if the shores are rocky; he will there find that, independent of partial and local dips which appear in different quarries of the same stone, the outlines, or top and bottom layers of each complete stratum or class of stones or earth, considered as a mass, have a general tendency towards the eastern horizon."

By the term "dip" is meant the inclination that strata make with the horizon. Mr. W. Smith constantly brought forward his well worked out fact that the strata of England dip from west to east more or less. The oldest strata come to the surface in Wales and the lake districts, and because they were upheaved the newer strata were tilted and curved, and the slope is to the east.

In February, 1798, we find as part of the introduction to this contemplated work, an interesting notice of some of the steps by which the author was conducted to his general conclusions.

"It will be readily admitted by all classes of men, from the most accurate observers of nature to the simplest peasant, that there is some degree of regularity in the strata from whence our building materials are generally collected. Masons, miners, and quarrymen can identify particular beds of stone dug many miles apart; indeed, every cliff and quarry presents a true section of a great many beds of stone, which may be found of the same quality and in the same position in all or most of the neighbouring cliffs and quarries. And this regularity is nowhere more conspicuous than in the lias quarries of Somersetshire, from whence these observations first took their rise, about seven years since.

"For the stratification of stone struck me, who had not been accustomed to such appearances, as something very uncommon, and till I had learned the technical terms of the strata, and made a subterraneous journey or two, I could not conceive a clear idea of what seemed so familiar to the colliers; but when these difficulties were surmounted, and an intelligent bailiff accompanied me, I was much pleased with my peregrinations below, and soon learnt enough of the order of the strata to describe on a plan the manner of working the coal in the lands I was then surveying.

"Being engaged soon after to survey the lands and take the levels of a canal that was proposed to be made from the collieries to Bath, I observed a variation of the strata on the same line of level, and soon found that the lias rock, which about three miles back was full three hundred feet above this line, was now thirty feet below it, and became the bed of the river, and in that direction did not appear any more at the surface. This induced me to note the inclination of the same rock, which I knew was to be found at the head of two other valleys lying each about a mile distant from, and in a parallel direction to, the one just described, and accordingly found it to dip the same to the south-east, and sink under the rivers in a similar manner.

"From this I began to consider that other strata might also have some general inclination as well as this (though I had been frequently told by the colliers that there was no regularity in the strata above ground), yet, by tracing them through the country some miles, I found the inclination of every bed to be nearly the same as [that of] the lias; and notwithstanding the partial and local dips of many quarries which varied from this rule, I was thoroughly satisfied by these observations that everything had a general tendency to the south-east, and thence concluded there could be none of these beds to the north-west, the truth of which conjecture was soon verified by a tour of observation through the northern parts of this kingdom."

In March, 1798, Mr. Smith purchased a small but beautiful estate, in a deep valley, within three miles of Bath, almost overgrown with wild wood, hiding in its bosom a sheet of water and a small mill. Through this retired possession the canal was cut, without greatly injuring its remarkable beauty; and, under Mr. Smith's fond and tasteful attention the scene was partly cleared, the pond expanded to a lake, the cottage became a comfortable home, in which he passed many happy and thoughtful hours. He did not, however, at any time reside long in this favourite retreat, but took up his station for about a year at the village of Mitford, near Bath, and engaged in the last duties which he performed as resident engineer to the Coal Canal.

Owing to a misunderstanding with the Company, this occupation ceased in June, 1799, and Mr. Smith felt and acknowledged that a new era in his life had arrived. He was not only at liberty, but placed under the necessity to consider the best means of making known his geological system, and of founding upon it a professional practice, which might provide the expense of travelling to verify and extend his knowledge, and fill up the outline of a geological map of England and Wales.

In these objects, which were ever closely associated in his own mind, he was successful; the most valuable portions of his discoveries soon became public property, and he quickly acquired extensive employment in the practical applications of these discoveries to mineral surveying and draining of land on a large scale. The extensive diffusion of his fame and opinions, which now began, was owing to no actual and authorized publication, but to continual discussions and explorations with several active friends, oral communications and exhibitions of maps at agricultural meetings (then frequent), and circulation of manuscript copies of tabular expositions of the series of strata at that time determined.

His views at this epoch appear by the following notice:—

"During my five years' close confinement to practical engineering on the Coal Canal, my much-wished-for opportunity of collecting observations enough from the ranges of the different strata to make an accurate delineation of the stratification throughout England were suspended.

"I had seen enough by my tour of August, 1794, to satisfy myself of the practicability of doing it, and often wasted much time in poring over maps, in contriving how the ranging edges and planes of different strata could best be rendered intelligible: models were thought of, and one small map was cut along the edges of some of the strata with a view of defining their extent, and of showing how one stratum was successively covered by another.

"I drew in colours, on a map of the vicinity of Bath, and on 'Day and Masters' county survey,' all [that had been observed] very accurately to a certain extent, which embraced an interesting but intricate variety of strata in hills around Bath; and some small maps of England were spoiled by speculating on the ranges of stratification without sufficient data. The intricacies in their marginal edges were such that I found, to mark point by point, as the facts were ascertained, was the only way in which I could safely proceed.

"My experience in what I had done upon the Somersetshire map was sufficient to convince me that to make a map of the strata on a scale as large as Cary's England (five miles to an inch), with sufficient accuracy, much of it should first be drawn on a larger scale."

It was fortunate for Mr. Smith, and for the progress of his views, that he gained at this time the friendship of a man singularly competent to estimate the truth and value of these views, and both able and willing to advocate the merit of their author. The Rev. Benjamin Richardson was at this time living in Bath, and possessed a choice collection of local fossils, mostly gathered by his own diligent hands. Extensively versed in natural history, and generally well acquainted with the progress of science, he was perfectly enthusiastic in following out, and liberal in enabling others to prosecute, new and ingenious researches, especially if they tended to practical and public good. He knew accurately the country in which Mr. Smith had principally worked, and was acquainted with the views entertained on the subject of fossils, which had been recorded in books, or were adopted by the collectors, who were even then celebrated in the vicinity of Bath. He had no knowledge of the laws of stratification and the connection between the forms of organic life and the order of superposition of the strata; while, on the other hand, his new friend had very little knowledge of the true nature of these organic forms, and their exact relation to analogous living types. The result of a meeting between two such reciprocally adjusted minds was an electric combination; the fossils which the one possessed were marshalled in the order of strata by the other, until they all found their appropriate places, and the arrangement of the cabinet became a true copy of nature.

That such fossils had been found, in such rocks, was immediately acknowledged by Mr. Richardson to be true, though the connection had not before presented itself to his mind; but when Mr. Smith added the assurance, that everywhere throughout this district, and to considerable distances around, it was a general law that the "*same strata were found always in the same order of superposition and contained the same peculiar fossils,*" his friend was both astonished and incredulous. He immediately acceded to Mr. Smith's proposal for undertaking some field examinations to determine the truth of these assertions, and having interested in the object a new and learned associate, the Rev. Joseph Townsend (author of "Travels in Spain"), they at once executed the project. Among other places visited with this view was the detached hill on which Dundry Church is conspicuously elevated. From its form and position in respect of the lias of Keynsham, Mr. Smith had inferred that this hill was capped by the lowest of the Bath "freestones" (inferior oolite); and, from his general views, he expected to find in that rock the fossils which the freestones contained near Bath; that is to say, on the westward rise, which he believed to affect all the strata near Bath above the coal. It is needless now to say, that examination confirmed both the inference of the character of the rock and the conformity of its organic contents. The effect of this and other illustrations of the reality of Mr. Smith's speculations was decisive. In general literature, and especially in natural history, Mr. Smith was immeasurably surpassed by his friends, but they acknowledged that, from his labours in a different quarter, a new light had begun to manifest itself in the previously dark horizon of geology, and they set themselves earnestly to make way for its auspicious influence.

What a step was made from the old ideas that fossils were sports of nature to the proof that during the long ages of the earth's history every deposit of river mud, sea-shore sand, and marine collection contained relics of its age of accumulation; and that there has been a succession of animals and plants on the earth foreshadowing those that now exist.

One day, after dining together at the house of the Rev. Joseph Townsend, it was proposed by one of this triumvirate, that a tabular view of the main features of the subject, as it had been expounded by Mr. Smith, and verified and enriched by their joint labours, should be drawn up in writing. Richardson held the pen, and wrote down, from Smith's dictation, the different strata according to their order of succession in descending order, commencing with the chalk, and numbered, in continuous series, down to the coal, below which the strata were not sufficiently determined, according to the scheme already noticed.

To this description of the strata was added, in the proper places, a list of the most remarkable fossils which had been gathered in the several layers of rock. The names of these fossils were principally supplied by Mr. Richardson, and are such as were then, and for a long time afterwards, familiarly employed in the many collections near Bath. Of the document thus jointly arranged each person present took a copy, under no stipulation as to the use which should be made of it, and accordingly it was extensively distributed, and remained for a long period the type and authority for the descriptions and order of superposition of the strata near Bath.

Years rolled on, and Smith's wanderings over England and their results were laid down by him on a map, which was to be published. With regard to this map of the strata, it may be said that it was very trying work for the publisher as well as the author. The basis of the map, as already explained, was in many respects peculiar; the colouring of it was more so. Instead of the *flat colouring* ending in narrow defined edges usually employed for maps, Mr. Smith introduced a peculiar style of *full tints* for the edges of the strata, *softened* into the paler tint employed for the remainder of the area which they occupied on the surface. This new style of colouring gave a picturesque effect to the map, but required more than usual skill and patience to be correctly executed, and occasioned great trouble in examining the copies. The colouring of the map was thus rendered more expensive than had been anticipated, and notwithstanding the labour was well paid for, it was not always at first properly performed.

At length the difficulties inseparable from such a task were so far overcome, and this enormous labour was so far completed, that a coloured map of the strata of England and Wales was submitted to the consideration of the Society of Arts, supported by various testimonials of its general accuracy and value, in April and May, 1815. The result was the award of the premium of £50, which had been in vain offered for very many years for a work of this description — a reward which Mr.

Smith might have claimed long ago, had not an honest desire to produce his work complete withheld the attempt. The map was published on the 1st of August, 1815, dedicated to Sir Joseph Banks, and from that hour the fame of its author as a great original discoverer in English geology was secured. Would that this epoch of his revived and enlarged reputation had also been the dawn of more prosperous fortunes, or that, satisfied with the degree in which he had accomplished his gigantic task, he had left to others the completion of his work, and devoted himself for a time to even the humblest of those professional labours by which he had been at least supported through oppressive difficulties, and by which he must have already grown comparatively rich but for the incessant drain of money in following up discoveries which no living man could reasonably hope to complete.

Science, indeed, is a mistress whose golden smiles are not often lavished on poor and enthusiastic suitors. The time for a strenuous exertion was indeed come. Geology had kept him poor by consuming all his professional gains; the neglect of his employers too often left these unpaid; in such a condition one unfortunate step was ruin, and that step was made. On the property which he had purchased near Bath, and which he had greatly improved, he was tempted to lay a railway for bringing the freestone of Comb down to the Coal Canal, to open new quarries of this stone, and to establish new machinery for cutting and shaping it for buildings. The project, which looked well at first, failed utterly by the unexpected deficiency of the stone, on whose good quality the whole success depended. The abandonment of this cherished scheme was followed by the compulsory sale of the still more cherished property, a load of debt remained to be discharged, and the miserable effects fell heavily on others besides himself. But there were not wanting persons of station, knowledge, and humanity, who, esteeming Mr. Smith and admiring his solitary and ceaseless industry, exerted themselves to save him from the sad fate which seemed to await him.

Such things are common in the lives of men, but they are not often encountered by so resolved and patient a spirit as that of Mr. Smith. One who saw the struggle may boldly say this, because there can be no other motive for mentioning private and personal griefs but to show forth the character of the mind which could firmly bear and overcome them. As a mean of reducing his difficulties he proposed to sell that geological collection which had been so much prized, and through the assistance of some friends a communication was opened with the Treasury. Two gentlemen being deputed to examine the collection, reported favourably, and their lordships were pleased to authorize the purchase, in order that the specimens might be fitted up in the British Museum. There was also some defined notion of engaging Mr. Smith's services at the museum to take charge of and explain the geological principles which this collection was intended to illustrate ; but this project came to nothing.

In the winter of 1818–19, Mr. Smith revisited, after an absence of ten years, his native village, re-examined the unforgotten localities where in childhood his "pundibs" and "poundstones" were gathered, and collected "marlstone" fossils from an excavation at Churchill Mill, nearly at the same points where he had noticed them in 1787. In one whose life had been one long wandering, and who had earned for himself an immortal name, this return to the haunts of his childhood and the simplicity of village occupations, must have excited many interesting reflections. He had sold his patrimony, and what had been the modest dwelling of his ancestors for two hundred years ; he had disbursed in travelling for what he deemed a public object all that he had earned ; while one of his two brothers, quietly prosecuting trade in his native village, had grown a rich and prosperous man.

In the autumn of 1819 Mr. Smith gave up his house in London, after fifteen years' occupation, and was compelled to submit to the sale of his furniture, collections, and books, preserving in fact, only his papers, maps, sections and other drawings, through the kindness of a most faithful friend. While this happened, he was in Yorkshire busily engaged, apparently oblivious, perhaps sternly regardless, of what seemed to others an insupportable misfortune. He deemed it an inevitable corollary to his irretrievable losses in the unlucky speculation already mentioned near Bath, and armed himself with what seemed more than fortitude to meet it.

One more used to monetary arrangements would have foreseen and averted this occurrence; but on the practical geologist the blow fell with stunning effect. He surrendered with deep regret his interest in the much-loved and really valuable little property near Bath, quitted London, and consented to have no home. From this time for seven years he became a wanderer in the north of England, rarely visiting London, except when drawn thither by the professional engagements which still, even in his loneliest retirements, were pressed upon him, and yielded him an irregular, contracted, and fluctuating income.

In the winter of 1819-20, Mr. Smith, having perhaps more than usual leisure, undertook to walk from Lincolnshire into Oxfordshire. The object proposed was to pass along a particular line through the counties of Rutland, Northampton, Bedford, and Oxford, but the ultimate destination was Swindon, in Wiltshire.

"Leaving the great road at Colsterworth, with some reflections on the birthplace of Newton,[*] we crossed in a day's easy walk, the little county of Rutland, its hills of oolite and sand, its slopes of upper lias, and its valleys often showing marlstone, and reached the obscure village of Gretton, on the edge of Rockingham Forest. Whatever

[*] Written by his biographer.

may now be the accommodations at this village, they were very wretched in 1819 (December), but the odd stories of supernatural beings and incredible frights which were narrated by the villagers assembled at the little inn, greatly amused Mr. Smith, and reminded him of exactly parallel tales which circulated around Whichwood Forest in his boyhood.

"The next morning we walked to Kettering, noticing on the road the peculiar characters of the Northamptonshire oolite. In this walk Mr. Smith had somehow sprained or over-fatigued himself, and he chose to proceed to Wellingborough in a chaise. From this point, situated on sand of the oolite series, we resumed our geological proceedings on foot, and passing by Irchester, Woolaston, and Boziate, traversed in the next hills the oolite, the forest marble, the cornbrash, and an outlier of Kelloway's rock. The road up Boziate Hill was mantled with fossiliferous stone, some of which, obtained from the hill-top, was believed to be Kelloway's rock, and was found to contain *Ammonites sublævis* and other fossils. A fine specimen of this ammonite was here laid by a particular tree on the road side, as it was large and inconvenient for the pocket, according to a custom often observed by Mr. Smith, whose memory for localities was so exact, that he has often, after many years, gone direct to some hoard of this nature, to recover his fossils. This road, however, over Boziate Hill, he was not to travel again.

"From Olney to Buckingham the route was performed in chaise. The stone dug here in clay attracted much attention, and Mr. Smith doubted whether to rank it as forest marble or cornbrash. We now crossed the oolitic country to Aynhoe, celebrated for its fossils, on foot; next day continued the walk to Deddington, Chapelhouse, and Churchill, and after a few days walked to Burford, and then travelled in the ordinary way to Swindon, Oxford, and London. In passing through Oxford, Mr. Smith, for the first time in his life, had the pleasure of seeing Professor Buckland, at the house of Mr. Bliss, the bookseller, with whom he walked over Shotover Hill, on his way toward London."

This little tour is thus briefly narrated, because it appears in all respects a fair example of the usual way in which Mr. Smith explored the country, walking when the object he had in view required this mode of examination, travelling as fast as possible in all other cases, but always recording in note-books or on maps, the observations he made.

Up in the north of England on the east coast Smith loved to wander beneath the cliffs, noting the minutest variations in the stratification, detecting the slightest marks of dislocation, watching the peculiarities of the sea's action on materials of unlike qualities, and inferring the causes which had anciently modified the outline of the land, and covered the low cliffs of the oolitic series with fragments of the lias from Whitby, of the coal and limestone from Teesdale or Swaledale, and of the granite and syenite from the Shap Fells and Carrock Pike. In numerous papers dedicated to the local geology of Scarborough, his reflections on these subjects are recorded; his exertions in examining one curious case of dislocation on the north side of the Castle Hill, brought on rheumatic, or rather a paralytic affection of the muscles of the lower extremities, which bound him a prisoner in bed in the early part of 1825.

Previous to this accident, he had taken part in a course of lectures to the Literary and Philosophical Society of Hull; after it had occurred, and before its effects were removed, while yet he was incapable of walking, and was actually lifted into the carriage which took him away, he accepted and executed a similar engagement proposed by the Literary and Philosophical Society of Sheffield. It was a singular spectacle, to witness the delivery of lectures which required continual reference to large maps and numerous diagrams, by a man who could not stand, but was forced to read his address from a chair, to an audience of several hundred persons in a room not very well adapted for the voice. But it was far more extraordinary to witness during all the severity of the disorder, the unpretending patience and fortitude of the sufferer, who, had he then permitted his mind to dwell too curiously on the state of his health and the state of his finances, might have added the bitter foretaste of want and privation to the actual difficulty of the moment. Such reflections and such anticipations might sadden the hearts of those who surrounded him, but Mr. Smith would have thought it unworthy of his resolved mind and firm trust in Providence, to have abated one jot of his accustomed cheerfulness, shortened one of the innumerable playful stories which were always springing to his lips from the rich treasure-house of his memory, or turned his meditations from his favourite subjects.

At Sheffield, while slowly recovering the use of his limbs, he busied himself in arranging a body of information which he had gathered concerning the neighbouring coal districts; and on removing soon afterwards to his old quarters at Doncaster, he worked much on the large "Old Survey of Yorkshire," thinking to complete the colouring of it. By degrees he recovered entirely from his painful disorder, and from this year (1825) to 1839, nothing of the kind ever affected him again.

But these years were fruitful of events interesting to the friends of William Smith. In February, 1831, the Council of the Geological Society of London honoured him by awarding to him the first Wollaston medal; and the terms with which the gift was accompanied render this act on the part of the society and the president extremely memorable. Dr. Wollaston's services to physical science were well known and duly honoured in his lifetime; geology has felt, and will long feel the benefit of his dying bequest. He invested one thousand pounds in the three per cent. Reduced Bank Annuities, in the joint names of himself and the Geological Society, and directed that after his decease, "the society should apply the dividends in promoting researches concerning the mineral structure of the earth, or in rewarding those by whom such researches should hereafter be made; or in such manner as should appear to the Council of the said society for the time being, conducive to the interests of the society in particular, or the science of geology in general." He afterwards enjoined the society "not to hoard the dividends parsimoniously, but to expend them liberally, and, as far as might be, annually, in furthering the objects of the trust." The first year's income from this fund was appropriated to the acquisition of a die for a medal bearing the head of Dr. Wollaston, and this having been undertaken by Mr. Wyon, the society was prepared in 1831 to fulfil the trust with which they were charged. The council accordingly passed unanimously the following resolutions, Jan. 11, 1831:—

"1. That a medal of fine gold, bearing the impress of the head of Dr. Wollaston, and not exceeding the value of ten guineas, be procured with the least possible delay.

"2. That the first Wollaston medal be given to Mr. William Smith, in consideration of his being a great original discoverer in English geology; and especially for his having been the first, in this country, to discover and to teach the identification of strata, and to determine their succession by means of their imbedded fossils."

The announcement of this award was made by a congenial spirit. The chair of the Geological Society was then filled by one of its most honoured members, an original thinker and faithful observer, well qualified to appreciate the originality of Mr. Smith's discoveries, and well acquainted by actual research with their extent and their value. In his address on this occasion, Professor Sedgwick, speaking in the name of the Geological Society, sketched a brief but satisfactory history of Mr. Smith's career, demonstrated the entire justice of the award of the Council of the Geological Society, and added his personal testimony in favour of Mr. Smith's claims in terms of no ordinary value.

"I for one can speak with gratitude of the practical lessons I have received from Mr. Smith. It was by tracking his footsteps, with his maps in my hand, through Wiltshire and the neighbouring counties, where he had trodden nearly thirty years before, that I first learned the subdivisions of our oolitic series, and apprehended the meaning of those arbitrary and somewhat uncouth terms, which we derive from him as our master, which have long become engrafted into the conventional language of English geologists, and through their influence have been, in part, also adopted by the naturalists of the continent.

"After such a statement, gentlemen, I have a right to speak boldly, and to demand your approbation of the council's award. I could almost dare to wish that stern lover of truth, to whose bounty we owe the "Donation Fund," that dark eye, before the glance of which all false pretensions withered, were once more amongst us. And if it be denied us to hope that a spirit like that of Wollaston should often be embodied on the earth, I would appeal to those intelligent men who form the strength and ornament of this society, whether there was any place for doubt or hesitation? whether we were not compelled, by every motive which the judgment can approve and the heart can sanction, to perform this act of filial duty, before we thought of the claims of any other man, and to place our first honour on the brow of the father of English geology?

"If, in the pride of our present strength, we were disposed to forget our origin, our very speech bewrays us: for we use the language which he taught us in the infancy of our science. If we, by our united efforts, are chiselling the ornaments and slowly raising up the pinnacles of one of the temples of nature, it was he who gave the plan, and laid the foundations, and erected a portion of the solid walls by the unassisted labour of his hands.

"The men who have led the way in useful discoveries, have ever held the first place of honour in the estimation of all who in after times have understood their works or trodden in their steps. It is upon this abiding principle that we have acted; and in awarding our first prize to Mr. Smith, we believe that we have done honour to our own body, and are sanctioned by the highest feelings which bind societies together.

"I think it a high privilege to fill this chair on an occasion when we met, not coldly to deliberate on the balance of conflicting claims, in which, after all, we might go wrong, and give the prize to one man by injustice to another; but to perform a sacred duty, where there is no room for doubt or error, and to perform an act of public gratitude, in which the judgment and the feelings are united." *

On this occasion Mr. Smith presented to the society the original Table of Stratification drawn in 1799, and a circle-map of the vicinity of Bath, which had been geologically coloured about the same period.

The British Association, founded at York in 1831, held its second meeting at Oxford in June, 1832; and on this occasion the Wollaston Medal, awarded in the previous year, was put in Mr. Smith's possession; and he was further gratified by the announcement that a pension of one hundred pounds, solicited by the united voice of English geologists, had been assigned him by the Government of His Majesty William the Fourth.

The meeting of the British Association was this year (1839) appointed to be held at Birmingham, on the 26th of August, and Mr. Smith received

---

* Address to the Geological Society, at the Anniversary Meeting, Feb. 18, 1831, by the President, the Rev. Adam Sedgwick, M.A., F.R.S., etc.

from Mr. Joseph Hodgson (one of the secretaries of the meeting) a special and very cordial invitation to be present. He stopped on his journey to Birmingham, at the house of friends at Northampton. Here the kindest welcome awaited him; and in addition to the pleasure of contemplating the beautiful series of Northamptonshire fossils which had been collected, he was gratified by several excursions into the neighbouring country, which had always been interesting to him since, in earlier days, he had opened the curious volume of Morton's "Northamptonshire." While thus tracing the boundaries of the minor divisions of the oolitic rocks which he had been the first to distinguish, a slight cold by which he was affected seemed to the eyes of his friends, to deserve more attention than he bestowed on it; medical assistance became immediately advisable. William Smith had for many years been successful in guarding his own usually robust health, and he was slow and reluctant to admit of advice better suited to the disorder which now attacked him, and which on a former occasion had so prostrated his strength that he recovered with difficulty. He began to feel the attack serious, and to perceive the alarm in the faces of his friends.

It was difficult to believe, that under that calm, thoughtful, and pleased expression of countenance, those animated descriptions of the country which he had visited a few days previously, those plans of further and strenuous exertion, which asked years of active life for completion, lurked pain and fatal disease. At first it seemed as if the remedies applied were producing beneficial effects, but this hope failed ; the uncomplaining sufferer sank continually in each succeeding hour, till his eyes lost their bright and kindly light and the ever-varying features became fixed in serene and awful tranquility (Aug. 28, 1839).

His life, written by his distinguished relation the late Professor John Phillips, F.R.S. of Oxford, has been the source of these pages. William Smith's portrait hangs in the most distinguished position, over the president's chair at the Geological Society of London. He was a great genius, and suffered much toil and poverty, in order to produce the truth ; but he led a very happy life on the whole for his thoughts about nature were his great and good riches. He proved that there is a regular succession of strata which are characterized by their fossils, each stratum being the burial ground of its time of collection.

CHAPTER XII.

THE LIFE OF MURCHISON.

The older rocks of the globe studied accurately and surveyed—The general similarity of the succession of strata in many parts of the world decided—The geology of Wales and Scotland described—The commencement of accurate geological surveys.

RODERICK IMPEY MURCHISON was the descendant of a very old Rossshire family, who were great supporters of the Stuarts in the wild western country of the north of Scotland. His great-grandfather fell at Sheriffmuir, and his grandfather, a tenant farmer, had to struggle with slender means during a long life. But long before this fine old man died, at the age of ninety-nine, he saw the fortunes of his family retrieved by his eldest son, whom he outlived.

This son, Roderick Impey Murchison's father, was born in 1751, and, thanks to the cheap and good education which was to be got at Edinburgh and Glasgow, he became a surgeon. Passing the examination at the Royal College of Surgeons in England, the young man was sent out to India, and living at Lucknow for seventeen years, made a fortune. He came home to the old country, and bought the estate of Tarradale, in the eastern part of Ross, kept up the old Highland customs, and made himself useful as a medical man when aid was required. He married, in 1791, the daughter of Mackenzie, of Fairburn, lineal representative of the Rory More, or Big Roderick Mackenzie, to whom the estates had been granted by James V. Their younger son, Roderick Impey was born in February, 1792, and was reared by the "sonsie" miller's wife of Tarradale, who hushed him to sleep with gaelic lullabies, and gave him an occasional taste of the famous whiskey distilled on the adjacent lands of Ferrintosh. But the father got delicate and moved to the south, carrying with him his household. On the way an end nearly came to the future geologist, for his father, wishing to make the boy "stand fire," presented what was thought an empty pistol at him. The mother snatched the child away, and instantly a charge of shot rattled through the window. The father died when Murchison was only four years of age, and the boy wrote in after years his sad memory of the last of his father: "The opening of the red damask curtains of the lofty old-fashioned bed, the last kiss of my dying parent, and the form of the old-fashioned edifice to which the invalid had been removed, have been stereotyped in my mind."

The father was an accomplished gentleman, and the mother a young and attractive lady. A second marriage gave Murchison a good step-father in Colonel Robert Macgregor Murray, a friend of the deceased; but home life was broken up when the colonel was ordered off to Ireland during the rebellion. So Murchison was sent to the Durham Grammar School in 1799. He had a bitter parting from his mother and from Sally, the Devonshire lass, who gave him his English accent, which he retained through life. Six years were passed at school, and he was as full of mischief as most boys; picking up at the same time some of the so-called rudiments of learning.

He was ringleader in most of the exploits of the school, and during the holidays led a very active life with the assistance of his pony and terrier. One day his uncle told him that in due time he would make a good soldier, and from that day Murchison read of nothing but military heroes.

At the early age of thirteen he was sent to the military college at Great Marlow, and, after one pluck, was admitted as cadet. There he became conspicuous as a daring leader of fun and frolic, and as a moderate student; nevertheless he was great at drill. A gift which decided in after years much of his success was fostered at Great Marlow. His exercises in military drawing led to the future rapidity and correctness of his "eye" for "country" in geological surveying.

At fifteen years of age Murchison was gazetted as

an ensign in the 36th regiment, and at Edinburgh he took lessons in French, Italian, German, and mathematics. He learned to ride and fence, and went in for debating. So having, as he said, done so much in the way of having a good opinion of himself, he was ordered to join his regiment at Cork in the winter of 1807-8. He was wonderfully surprised to find the officers anything but dandies, and, in fact, true old soldiers, quiet, well disciplined and associated with a first-rate fighting regiment. His chief, Colonel Burne, was a cool and gallant officer, and a favourite of Sir Arthur Wellesley's. In 1808 the regiment was prepared for service in South America, and was suddenly ordered to Portugal, and on August 1st he landed, and saw the future Wellington put his foot on Portuguese soil, followed by his aide-de-camp, the future Lord Raglan.

A battle was soon to be fought, and at Vimiera.

Professor Geikie's charming "Life of Murchison," from which this little history is compiled, gives the following graphic description of Murchison's first fight, at Vimiera:—

"To return to our own part of the battle, *i.e.*, to our left wing, the fire of the enemy soon became very hot, and even though the 36th were lying on their breasts under the brow, our men were getting pretty much hit, whilst the regiment in our rear, the 82nd, which at that time could not fire a shot, suffered more than we did. General Spencer, who commanded the division, when moving about to regulate the general movements, was hit by a ball in the hand, and I saw him wrap his handkerchief round it, and heard him say, 'It is only a scratch!' Soon after the light infantry in our front closed files and fell in; our guns we pulled back, and then came the struggle. General Ferguson waving his hat, up we rose, old Burne (our colonel) crying out, as he shook his yellow cane, that he would knock down any man who fired a shot.

"This made some merriment among the men, as tumbling over was the fashion without the application of their colonel's cane. "Charge," was the word, and at once we went over the brow with a steady line of glittering steel, and with a hearty hurrah, against six regiments in close column, with six pieces of artillery, just in front of the 36th. But not an instant did the enemy stand against this most unexpected sally within pistol shot. Off they went, and all their guns were instantly taken, horses and all, and then left in our rear, whilst we went on chasing the runaways for a mile and a half, as hard as we could go, over the moor of Tourinhâo. They rallied, it is true, once or twice, particularly behind some thick prickly-pear hedges and a hut or two on the flat table-land; but although their brave General Solignac was always cantering to their front, and animating them against us, they at last fled precipitately, until they reached a small hamlet, where, however, they did make a tolerable stand.

"Here it was that Sir Arthur Wellesley overtook

us after a smart gallop. He had witnessed from a distance our steady and successful charge, and our capture of the guns, and he now saw how we were thrusting the French out of this hamlet. Through the sound of the musketry, and in the midst of much confusion, I heard a shrill voice calling out, 'Where are the colours of the 36th? and I turned round (my brother ensign, poor Peter Bone, having just been knocked down), and looking up into Sir Arthur's bright and confident face said, 'Here they are, sir.' Then he shouted, 'Very well done, my boys! Halt, halt—quite enough.'

"The French were now at their last run, in spite of every effort of Solignac to rally them. Several of our bloody-minded old soldiers said in levelling, 'they would bring down the —— on the white horse,' and sure enough the gallant fellow fell, just as the 71st Highlanders, who were on our left, being moved round *en potence*, charged down the hill, with their wounded piper playing, sitting on the ground, and completed the rout of the enemy, taking General Solignac of course prisoner."

Subsequently Murchison's regiment joined the expedition of Sir John Moore, and participated in the disastrous retreat upon Corunna. "Murchison (writes Professor Geikie) suffered much, although he was strong and in good health, from the excessive fatigue. On one occasion, after a fruitless midnight march against the enemy, who was supposed to be advancing to the attack, Murchison, commanding that night an outlying picquet, threw himself into a corner of a farmer's yard, and soon fell asleep. Day had scarcely broken when the cry of 'Picquet, turn out!' roused him from his rest, but not in time to escape the notice of the vigilant Colonel Packe, who, however, allowed him to escape with a severe reprimand. But after the halt at Tugo, when having vainly offered battle to the French, the British army retreated by a forced march to Corunna, the young lieutenant fairly broke down. The mule, which had hitherto carried himself or his kit, was lost; his old soldier servant had gone back to seek among the snow for his wife and child." Of this sad time he has preserved the following recollections:—" Never shall I forget the night which followed the abandoning of our position in front of Tugo. We marched through that city at dusk, and then blew up the bridge, which was to check for awhile our foe. In darkness, with no food, and after sleepless nights, with worn-out shoes, and thoroughly disgusted with always running off and not fighting, this army now fell into utter disorder. Starved as they were, the men soon became reckless, and all the regiments got mixed together; in short, the soldiers were desperate, in spite of the exertions of the few mounted officers. For my own part, I walked on, usually in my sleep, with the grumbling and tumultuous mass, until awakened by the loss of my boots in one of the numerous deep cuts across the roads, which were like quagmires, so that with my bare feet I had some twenty miles still to march. Many of the soldiers got away from the road to right and left. Marching all that dreadful night my young frame at last gave way, the more so as I was barefoot, cold, and starved, and already the great body of troops had got ahead of me. In short, I was now one of a huge arrear of stragglers when day broke and the little hamlet was in sight.

"Seated on a bank on the side of the road, and munching a raw turnip which I had gathered from the adjacent field, and just as I was feeling that I never could regain my regiment and must be taken a prisoner, a black-eyed drummer of the 96th came from the village, whither the young fellow had been to cater. Seeing I was exhausted, and almost as young as myself, and not yet a hardened old soldier, he slipped round his canteen, which he had contrived to fill with red wine, and gave me a hearty drink. He thus saved me from being taken prisoner by the French, who were rapidly advancing, and who, if they had had a regiment of cavalry in pursuit, might at that moment have taken prisoners, or driven into the mountains, a good third of the British forces.

"With the draught of wine I trudged on again, and came in, at eleven o'clock of the 10th, into the town of Betanzos, and rejoined my regiment, which had marched in about fifty men only, with the colours, though ere night it was made up to its strength of six hundred and odd men. This fact alone shows better than a world of other evidence, what forced night-marches with a starving and retreating army must infallibly produce. At Tugo the 36th regiment was fit to fight anything; in two days it was a rabble.

"Happily for me I tumbled into a shoemaker's house. His handsome young wife washed my feet with warm water, and furnished me with stockings, while her husband came to my further aid with shoes. But my swollen feet had no time to recover. On the following day the whole army, such as it was, passed over the river, blowing up the bridge and taking up its last position.

"There, remnant as it was, the army formed a respectable line—Corunna within two miles of us, and our fleet ready to back us. Provisions and shoes were served out to us, and with such luxuries the bivouac, even in the month of January, was well borne. In truth, the army got into comparative good spirits, and on the 15th the French crossed the last bridge we had blown up, and were defiling at a respectable distance along our front. We were quite refreshed, and ready to repel them. The picquets, indeed, of our (Hope's) division had a sharp encounter in that evening, and when looking through the colonel's glass, I saw Colonel Mackenzie, of the 5th regiment, fall dead from his grey horse whilst leading an attack on two of the enemy's guns.

"On the 16th, just after our frugal repast, and whilst leaning over one of the walls where we lay, my old colonel, after looking some time with his glass, suddenly exclaimed to me, 'Now, my boy, they're coming on;' and when I took a peep to the hills beyond on the right and south-west, I perceived the glitter of columns coming out of a wood. Scarcely had the colonel given the word to fall in, when a tremendous fire opened from a battery of seventeen to twenty pieces, under cover of which the enemy was rolling down in dense columns from the wooded hills upon our poor fellows, who were in a hollow with their arms piled, like our own, until they were assaulted.

"For our cavalry was extinct, as the horses and men, as well as most of our artillery, were embarked on the 13th and 14th; yet never since Englishmen fought was there a more gallant fight than was made by the 4th, 42nd, and 50th regiments (Lord W. Bentinck's brigade), who rushed on with the bayonet, and, supported by guards, held their own against a terrific superiority, until General Paget was ordered to move his brigade towards the enemy's flank, and compelled them to withdraw; not, however, before poor Moore, galloping out from the town, fell while encouraging the troops, and Baird, who marched his division out of the town, had lost his arm. My own brigade had much less to do, our front line and picquets being alone engaged.

"As night fell, and after the firing had ceased, the enemy having returned to his own ground, we received the order to march into Corunna and embark. Our fires were left burning to deceive the enemy, and make him believe that he must fight us again next morning if he hoped to beat us.

"Silently and regularly we moved on this our last short night-march in the dark, tranquil night of the 16th, and, passing through the gates, reached the quay. The names of our respective transports had previously been explained to us, my own being the brig *Reward*, which I found to be from Sunderland. I was on deck as light dawned, and then at once saw the danger of the position of this miserable little transport, as well as of a dozen or more of the same craft. They had been foolishly allowed to anchor immediately under the tongue of high land which forms the eastern side of the harbour, and on which there were no land defences. Knowing that this ground was only a continuation of the hilly track on which my division had marched a few hours before, and being certain that the French would with the peep of day pass over our old bivouac to this promontory, I at once urged our skipper to get up his anchor betimes. But the grog had, I suppose, been strong that night. He exclaimed, 'Why, I tell you, the brave Highlanders are there; they have not come away like you folks.' Scarcely had he spoken when a battery of field-pieces opened their fire and sent some balls through our rigging. Turning pale as death under the fire of these mere field-pieces, and seeing that his crew were ready to run below, he applied the axe to the cable, and in a few minutes we were drifting away as we best could. The wind being from the east, we were fast approaching the rocks on which the Castle of Antonio stands, and on which at least five transports similarly circumstanced to my own were wrecked, the men being saved with difficulty, after losing their arms, colours, and baggage.

"I have often reflected on the extraordinary want of all due arrangement on the part of our admiral, in command of a splendid fleet, who allowed those miserable transports to anchor in such a position without placing a frigate or two near them to silence the puny battery and prevent the dismay which seized the skippers.

"Not missing stays, the *Reward* floated away, and was soon going fast before a strong nor'-easter, with the rest of the fleet helter-skelter for the Channel."

In 1815 Murchison met Charlotte Hugouin, the daughter of General Hugouin, and as she was attractive, piquante, clever, and higly educated, she made a conquest of the gallant soldier. They were soon married, at Buriton, in Hampshire.

Hitherto he had lived at his own free will. From this time he came under the influence of a thoughtful, cultivated, and affectionate woman. Quietly and imperceptibly that influence grew, and she led him, with true womanly tact, into a sphere of exertion where his uncommon powers might find full scope. To his wife he owed his fame, as he never failed gratefully to record; but years had to pass before her guidance had accomplished what she had set before her as her aim.

Tired of the army, and possessing a great amount of energy and physical power, Murchison longed for a profession, and at one time seriously contemplated entering the Church. But money was scarce, and he went with his wife to live economically in Italy. This was an epoch in his life, and he went by way of Paris, and there he heard Cuvier lecture. At Geneva he met De Candolle, and as his wife had relatives at Vevay, they spent some time there, and Murchison began taking walking tours. On one occasion he walked four hundred and thirty-two miles over mountain ground, in fourteen days, finishing with a last day's walk of thirty-seven miles. In another excursion to Mont Blanc he walked one hundred and twenty miles in three days. This was characteristic of the man. But it was not simple exercise that he took, for his retentive memory and eye for landscape were occupied; and such walks always produced good results in after years.

Arrived at Rome they went into lodgings, and Murchison became a confirmed visitor of galleries, museums, and churches. Then Mrs. Murchison fell ill, and they went, on her recovery, to Naples, where, of course, Vesuvius was seen, but oddly enough, his written impressions of the scene do not tell of any geological tastes. Two years glided away, and they founded his intellectual life, and impressed him that it was better than gaiety. When returned to England, Murchison sold his Scotch estate and went to live in a most out of the way old mansion at Barnard Castle, in Durham. Then there was no art, and therefore Murchison became a sportsman, and for five years rode as hard and as well to the front as any of his foxhunting friends. Every now and then some intellectual society was enjoyed at some of the great houses of the neighbourhood, and Murchison made the acquaintance of Sir Humphrey Davy. Mrs. Murchison did not care about the everlasting hunting, and tried, in her wise manner, to wean him from the purposeless life he was leading. She knew botany, and tried to interest her husband in it, but he did not care for it; then she tried to learn mineralogy to get him to help her. But Murchison got deeper and deeper into the love of field sports, and took a house at Melton Mowbray and hunted six days in the week. Murchison got tired at last, and having met Sir Humphrey Davy again, was advised by him to interest himself about chemistry. So Murchison sold his horses and gave up his establishment, really intending to settle in London. But probably want of means prevented his having an establishment in the West End at first, so he led a less active but still sporting life in the south of Scotland for some time.

Murchison was now to change his method of life completely, and the summer of 1824 saw the last of his rambles, wherever the rocks around him made no direct and urgent appeal to him. Bringing his wife to London, they rented a house in Montague Place, and Murchison began to attend scientific lectures, and especially those on geology, which was at that time much talked about. Hutton's admirable views of the causes of the changes on the surface of the earth, and their possible comparison with those of the present day, was making progress, but was still antagonized by the notions of sudden convulsions and great underground movements. He went to the Geological Society, a young and ardent one, which had sprung into active work in spite of the opposition of the nursing mother of science, the Royal Society.

With hearing lectures on science, scientific papers and discussions, attending evening soirées, and the opportunity of hearing and talking to men who had already made themselves famous, Murchison found enough fully to fill up his time, and to make London life a very different thing to him from what it had been in the old days, when he used to escape to town from the monotony of a country barrack. With his characteristic ardour, he had not completed his first winter's studies in geology before he longed to be off into the field to observe for himself.

"My first real field work," he says, "began under Professor Buckland, who having taken a fancy to me as one of his apt scholars, invited me to visit him at Corpus Christi College, Oxford, and attend one or two of his lectures. This was my true launch. Travelling down with him in the Oxford coach, I learned a world of things before we reached the Isis, and, amongst other things, I enjoyed a lecture on crustacea, given whilst he pulled to pieces on his knees, a cold crab, bought at a fishmonger's shop at Maidenhead, where he usually lunched as the coach stopped.

"On repairing from the Star inn to Buckland's domicile, I never can forget the scene which awaited me. Having, by direction of the janitor, climbed up a narrow staircase, I entered a long corridor-like room (now all destroyed), which was filled with rocks, shells, and bones in dire confusion, and, in a sort of sanctum at the end was my friend, in his black gown, looking like a necromancer, sitting on the sole rickety chair not covered with some fossils, and cleaning out a fossil bone from the matrix."

The few days spent at Oxford were memorably pleasant. Buckland's wit and enthusiasm glowed all his scientific sayings and doings, and he had a rare power of description, by which he could make even a dry enough subject fascinatingly interesting. Murchison heard one or two brilliant lectures from him, but what was of still more importance, he accompanied the merry professor and his students, mounted on Oxford hacks, to Shotover Hill, and for the first time in his life had a landscape geologically dissected before him. From that eminence his eye was taught to recognize the broader features of the succession of the oolitic rocks of England up to the far range of the Chalk Hills, and this not in a dull, text-book fashion, for Buckland, in luminous language, brought the several elements of the landscape into connection with each other, and with a few fundamental principles which have determined the sculpturing of the earth's surface. His audience came to see merely a rich vale in the midst of fertile England, but before they quitted the ground, the landscape had been made to yield up to them, clear notions of the origin of springs and the principles of drainage. This was the very kind of instruction needed to fan the growing flame of Murchison's zeal for science. He returned to town burning with desire to put his knowledge to some use by trying to imitate, no matter how feebly, the admirable way in which the Oxford professor had applied the lessons of the lecture-room to the elucidation of the history of hills and valleys.

Murchison started with his wife in the middle of August, on a tour of nine weeks along the south coast, from the Isle of Wight into Devon and Cornwall. Taking a light carriage and a pair of horses, he made the journey in short stages, lingering for days at some of the more interesting or important geological localities. Driving, boating, walking, or scrambling, the enthusiastic pair signalized their first geological tour by a formidable amount of bodily toil.

Mrs. Murchison specially devoted herself to the collection of fossils, and to sketching the more striking geological features of the coast-line, while her husband would push on to make some long and laborious detour. In this way, while she remained quietly working at Lyme Regis, he struck westward for a fortnight into Devon and Cornwall, to make his first acquaintance with the rocks to which, in after years, Sedgwick and he were to give the name by which they are now recognized all over the world. It was in the course of this tour that he met with a man, whom he has the merit of having brought into notice, and who certainly amply requited him by the services rendered in later years. William Lonsdale had served in the Peninsular war, and retired on half-pay to Bath. With the most simple and abstemious habits, his slender income sufficed not only for his wants, but for the purchase of any book or fossil he coveted, and so he spent his time in studying the organic remains, and especially the fossil corals, to be found in his neighbourhood. Murchison met him accidentally in some quarries, "a tall, grave man, with a huge hammer on his shoulder," and found him so full of information, that he stayed some days at Bath under Lonsdale's guidance.

With the enlargement of view which so instructive a ramble had given him, Murchison prepared and read to the Geological Society, on 16th December, 1825, his first scientific paper—"A Geological Sketch of the North-western Extremity of Sussex, and the adjoining parts of Hants and Surrey." This little essay bore manifest evidence of being the result of careful observation of the order of succession of the rocks in the field, followed by as ample examination of their fossils as he could secure, from those best qualified to give an opinion upon them. In these respects it was typical of all his later work. Having shown by this first publication his capacity as observer and describer, and being further recommended by the leisure which his position of independence enabled him to command, he was soon after elected one of the two honorary secretaries of the Geological Society. "Lyell being then a law-student, with chambers in the Temple, could only devote a portion of his time to our science, and was glad to make way as secretary to one who, like myself, had nothing else to do than think and dream of geology, and work hard to get on in my new vocation."

In the spring of 1826 he was elected into the Royal Society—an honour more easily won then than now, and for which, as the President, his old friend Sir Humphry Davy told him, he was indebted, not to the amount or value of his scientific work, but to the fact that he was an independent gentleman, having a taste for science, with plenty of time, and enough of money to gratify it.

Murchison next investigated, at the instance of Dr. Buckland, the geological age of the Brora coal-field, in Sutherlandshire. Some geologists maintained that the rocks of that district were merely a part of the ordinary coal, or carboniferous system; others held them to be greatly younger, to be, indeed, of the same general age with the lower oolitic strata of Yorkshire. A good observer might readily settle this question; Murchison resolved to try.

Again he prepared himself by reading and study of fossils to understand the evidence he was to collect and interpret, and in order to do full justice to the Scottish tract, he went first to the Yorkshire coast, and made himself master of the succession, and leading characters of the rocks so admirably displayed along that picturesque line of cliffs. The summer had hardly begun before he and his wife broke up their camp in London and were on the move northwards. At York he made the acquaintance of two men, with whom he was destined in after life to have much close intercourse and co-operation—the Rev. William Vernon (afterwards Vernon Harcourt) and Mr. (subsequently Professor) John Phillips.

Murchison's own record of the meeting is as follows:—" Phillips, then a youth, was engaged in arranging a small museum at York. He recommended Murchison strongly to his uncle, William Smith, who was then living at Scarborough, and had little intercourse with the Geological Society. From the moment I had my first walk with William Smith (then about sixty years old), I felt that he was just the man after my own heart; and he, on his part, seeing that I had, as he said, 'an eye for a country,' took to me, and gave me most valuable lessons. Thus he made me thoroughly acquainted with all the strata north and south of Scarborough. He afterwards accompanied me in a boat all along the coast, stopping and sleeping at Robin Hood's Bay. Not only did I then learn the exact position of the beds of poor coal which crop out in that tract of the eastern moorlands, but collecting with him the characteristic fossils from the calcareous grit down to the lias, I saw how clearly strata must alone be identified by their fossils, inasmuch as here, instead of oolite limestone like those of the south we had sandstones, grits, and shales which, though closely resembling the beds of the old coal, were precise equivalents of the oolitic series of the south. Smith walked about stoutly with me all under the cliffs from Robin Hood's Bay to Whitby, making me well note the characteristic fossils of each formation."

Though the main object of this summer tour was to work out the geological problem which had been assigned to him in Sutherlandshire, he sketched a most circuitous route, partly for the sake of showing Mrs. Murchison something more of the Highlands than she had yet seen, and partly with the view of putting to use his new acquirements in geology; so that after reaching Edinburgh, and having its geology expounded to him by Jameson, instead of striking north at once, he turned westwards to the island of Arran, and spent many weeks among the western islands from the Firth of Clyde to the north of Skye. The hills of his native country had now acquired an interest for him which they never possessed even in the days when they drew him off in eager pursuit of grouse and black cock. At every halt his first anxiety was to know what the rocks of the place might be, and how far he could identify their geological position. In Arran he filled his note-book with observations and queries about granite, red sandstone, limestone, and other puzzling matters, on which his previous experience in field-work in the south of England and in Yorkshire could throw no light, and for the elucidation of which he wisely resolved to secure, at some future time, the guidance and co-operation of an older geologist than himself. It was in the fulfilment of this resolution that Sedgwick and he first became fellow-workers in the field.

In the wildest of the western islands he and his wife did excellent work in collecting fossils, and thereby obtaining materials for making more detailed comparison between the secondary rocks of the west of Scotland and those of England than had been attempted by Dr. Macculloch. The actual fossil-hunting was mainly done by Mrs. Murchison, after whom one of the shells (*Ammonites Murchisoniæ*) was named by Sowerby, while her husband climbed the cliffs and trudged over the moors and crags, to make out the order of succession among the secondary strata. But the tour was not merely geological; many a halt and detour were made to get a good view of some fine scenery, or to make yet another sketch. Friends and highland cousins, too, were plentifully scattered along the route, so that the travellers had ample experience of the hearty hospitality of those regions. An occasional shot at grouse or deer, varied the monotony of the hammering; but even when stalking, Murchison could not keep his eyes from the rocks. Amid the jottings of his sport he had facts to chronicle about the gneiss or porphyry or sandstone through which the sport had led him. This characteristic, traceable even at this early period of his life, remained prominent up to the last autumn of his life in which he was able to wield a gun or hammer.

The summer had in great part passed before he reached that part of the eastern coast of Sutherlandshire where the scene of his special task lay; but that task proved to be eminently easy. From Dunrobin, where he was hospitably entertained, he could follow northwards and southwards a regular succession of strata, and he recognized in them the equivalents of parts of the oolite series of Yorkshire. The Brora coal, therefore, instead of forming part of the true carboniferous system, was simply a local peculiarity in the oolitic series. He made a collection of the fossils, which offered a means of satisfactory comparison with the oolitic rocks of England.

The rapidity with which this piece of work could be done left time for a prolongation of the tour northwards through Caithness, even up into the Orkney Islands, but at length the tourists had to prepare for a southward migration again. Reaching Inverness, they turned eastward to

Aberdeen, and thence down the eastern coast by Peterhead, by Buller's of Buchan, Arbroath, and St. Andrews. The immediate result of this summer's work was seen in the preparation of a paper for the Geological Society.

Professor Sedgwick had already distinguished himself in the difficult labour of unravelling the structure of some of the older rocks, and Murchison suggested that they should visit Scotland and examine and describe part of the country together. They desired to ascertain if possible the position and general relations of the Old Red sandstone. This journey, intensely amusing in its anecdotes, led to much united work and good fellowship.

Having learned the principles of the science, Murchison went to study geology in the field on the continent. Accompanied by Mrs. Murchison, he visited the extinct volcanoes of Auvergne, the South of France and Italy, and finally Germany. Next year the Alps were explored, and subsequently Austria. At Vienna, Murchison indulged a little in what he always liked, and which did good to science, good society, and then started for Styria, and got much puzzled about the rocks and fossils at Gosau. On his return to England Murchison became secretary to the Geological Society, and held the position for five years, and then he became the president of the society. Subsequently he began seriously to attempt the description of the geology of Wales which ended in the establishment of the Silurian system of rocks.

Then the Devonian and old red sandstones were considered, and the merits of the paleontologist, Lonsdale, who really established the great geological division of the Devonian, were fully conceded. About this time Murchison and his wife settled in the well known mansion in Belgrave Square, which was such a home for scientific men, British and foreign, for many a long year to come.

Russia was the next country to be explored, and Murchison spent a long and very pleasant time there; and his description of the Ural Mountains was of great importance. He was the first to sketch out broadly the geological construction of that very monotonous country, and to point out the existence there of a formation which covers the coal-bearing rocks of England, and which he called the Permian. Returning to England, after receiving the thanks of the Emperor Nicholas, Murchison again became President of the Geological Society, and with increased experience endeavoured to work out more fully than before, the old rocks of Wales, which he and Sedgwick had laboured over in common. Murchison and Sedgwick, however, began at this time to misunderstand one another, and those admirable men, the one having recognized the higher strata, and the other the lower, began to differ regarding the line of separation of their work. It is an unsettled point even at the present day, notwithstanding all the knowledge that these great men have left to us, and all that has come to science since their time. Ever enthusiastic in the cause of science as he had been in war and in the field, Murchison allowed himself no rest, but started for Germany *via* France to examine the red sands and clays in those countries which, overlying the carboniferous formation, resemble in position the Permian of Russia. The geologist was treated like a prince by kings, emperors, and a host of titled people who were glad to welcome the perfect gentleman so full of good genial temper and amiability.

At the same time Murchison did not forget the British Association for the Advancement of Science, with which he was officially connected. In 1843 he began to interest himself in the then little Geographical Society, which had been founded in 1830, chiefly by members of the Rayleigh Travellers' club. Murchison was chosen its president, and he read an address to the fellows in 1844. This society, now of great utility to science and civilization, was fostered mainly by Murchison, and passed through years of steady progress under his management. In the same year, our geologist visited Scandinavia, where he found science more honoured than anywhere else on earth, and went on to St. Petersburg. Returning to England, Murchison and his fellow labourers, Von Keyserling and De Verneuil, published the great work on "Russia, and the Ural Mountains," and our hero became a recognized pillar in geological science.

Knowing the geology of the Ural Mountains thoroughly, and having paid much attention to those parts of them where gold is found, Murchison was impressed, when he read of the nature of the Australian Alps, that they ought to be auriferous. In 1845, and 1846, Murchison spoke and wrote on this subject, and kept on directing the attention of the colonists to the necessity of searching for the precious mineral. In 1846 Murchison advised the unemployed tin miners of Cornwall to emigrate and dig for gold in Australia. In 1847 a Mr. W. T. Smith, of Sydney, acquainted Murchison that he had discovered gold, and a Mr. Phillips, of Adelaide, wrote announcing the same fact. Finally, in 1848, Murchison impressed on Her Majesty's Secretary of State for the colonies the necessity of having Australia surveyed, for the purpose of gold finding. Three years afterwards a Mr. Hargraves came forward as the real Simon pure, and was acknowledged by the ignorant legislature of New South Wales as the discoverer of gold in Australia. Count Strzelecki, a geologist, sent Murchison specimens of rocks from Australia, and positively found gold, not by inference, as in Murchison's case, but in reality. But at the request of the colonial authorities it was kept a secret ! ! ! The Rev. W. B. Clarke, F.R.S., a capital geologist, found gold in places, and settled what rocks it was in. This was in 1841. So that Murchison, although not the first discoverer, or the first who inferred the existence of gold in the Australian rocks, must have great credit given to him.

Twenty years had passed away since Murchison sold his horses and gave up fox hunting, and he had done more than any man to establish the grand features of the outside structure of the earth, and to prove the succession everywhere of the same great formations. He was knighted in 1846, an honour which was appreciated in those days, but which is not compatible with the proper simplicity and nobility of science at the present time. Everybody was glad of the honour being given, and received by Murchison, and "Sir Roderick," for the future came as aptly to the thoughts of his friends as "Mr. Murchison" had done of old. There is no doubt that at this time this experienced geologist believed that great lapses of time had occurred, involving great distinctions and new creations between the successive geological formations, that great changes had happened, universally, in the physical geography of the land and sea before a new formation was produced, and that the vast majority of fossils found in one were not recognized in a succeeding formation. He believed much in grand and sudden catastrophic changes in nature. The presidency of the British Association was given to the new scientific knight, and he worthily occupied the chair at the meeting at Southampton in 1846.

In 1848, the year of revolution in Europe, Murchison enjoyed foreign politics and Alpine geology, and made the acquaintance of most of the young Swiss geologists, whose names are now so celebrated. An essay on the geology of the Alps was written, and our hero received the Copley

Medal of the Royal Society. But the many years of close and hard work had told even on Murchison's iron frame; and his wife was an invalid. So they spent the summer of 1849 at Buxton, much to the disgust of the geologist, however. He attended the meeting of the British Association at Birmingham, however, and relapsed into a state of perpetual "liver," suppressed gout and "stomach attacks." After awhile the invalid went abroad and enjoyed rambling over the extinct volcanoes of Auvergne, and had his trip over the same ground twenty-two years before, brought before his mind. But he did not accept the theories of Lyell about the formation of the valleys and the denudation of the district. He stuck, unfortunately, to the violent in nature, and dismissed the truth of the former uniform and slow action of the same forces as now prevail, from his mind. In the next year Murchison was happy again with his old friend Sedgwick, and they geologized in the highlands, and enjoyed the hospitality of the young Duke and Duchess of Argyll. Then the southern uplands of Scotland were examined; and Murchison, stimulated by the great progress of the writings of Lyell, came out in strong opposition to the Huttonian philosophy. Murchison contended in favour of great oscillations and ruptures of the earth's crust leading to the sudden breaking up and submergence of tracts of land; but he did not explain how all this took place or could take place. He believed in many superficial deposits, such as drift, being the product of violent convulsions and floods. His frame of mind was not difficult to account for. He had found, in investigating the Alps, that movements amongst the strata had occurred on a vast scale, and that whole series of them, hundreds of feet thick, had not only been bent, but positively turned upside down. In 1851 Murchison visited Ireland, and geologized there, and gradually began to complete his great work, entitled "Siluria ; or a Description of the Geology of the Silurian Rocks of the World and of their Fossils." This was published in 1854. The next great act of Murchison's was the assisting and promoting the success of the geological survey of the United Kingdom, and the establishment of the museum in Jermyn Street. This led to the establishment of the Royal School of Mines. Murchison became the director of the survey, and went into the subject with heart and soul, and found himself surrounded by the most distinguished teachers in England.

Murchison worked personally at the Scottish rocks from 1855 to 1858, and it is a matter of interest that at the present day his admirable work relating to the order of the older rocks is a vexed question. In 1860, Murchison went to the highlands for the fourth time, and came to the same conclusions as before.

Year after year the grand old man laboured on for the benefit of the sciences of geology and geography, and kept the geological survey in capital order. He obtained the sanction of the Government for colonial surveys, and was, in fact, the main stay of science in relation to the state. For ten years he did all this, and occasionally indulged in a trip to the north and west, and also into Bohemia. In 1862, Murchison was terribly troubled by the sudden ill-health of his wife, to whom he owed so much. She became more and more of an invalid, and died in 1869. It was the greatest blow possible, and it brought the kindest letter from his old friend Sedgwick, eighty-four years of age. In September, 1870, Murchison's time was coming to an end. A slight attack of paralysis warned him to retire from active life. In the spring of 1871 he prepared his last address as president of the Royal Geographical Society, and resigned the chair he had so ably filled for fifteen years. He lingered on, and passed quietly away on October 22nd, 1871, full of years and well merited honours. Murchison's name will live for ever as a clear, keen-eyed, careful observer of nature, and as a master of the facts relating to much of the ancient history of the earth. He was a great stimulator of men of science, assisted the weak, and helped the good worker. He had a great personal character, religious, honest, truthful, open and generous; he was a gentleman indeed. His biographer, Professor A. Geikie, F.R.S., whose most charming book has been so freely quoted by me, writes about his good old friend as follows: "A man's face and figure afford usually a good indication of the general calibre of the spirit which lodges beneath them. The picture which rises to the mind when one thinks of Murchison, is that of a tall, wiry, muscular frame, which still kept its erectness even under the burden of almost fourscore years. It seemed the type of body for an active geologist, who had to win his reputation by dint of hard climbing and walking, almost as much as by mental power. It was, moreover, united in his case with a certain pomp and dignity of manner, which at one time recalled the military training of the Peninsula days, at another the formal courtesy of the well-bred gentleman of a bygone generation."

CHAPTER XIII.

THE LIFE OF LYELL.

The study of existing nature and its changes undertaken in order to comprehend the past changes during geological ages—The uniformity of natural operations under law—Catastrophes abolished—The succession of life on the globe, and that of the tertiary ages explained—The antiquity of man and of the great ice age considered.

CHARLES LYELL was born in Forfarshire, at Kinnordy, on November 14th, 1797. His father was an able, wealthy, well-educated gentleman; and his mother, a Yorkshire lady, had the usual good sound sense of the women of that county. He was the eldest of ten children, the whole of whom grew up; and he, as is commonly the case in large families, was a good son and brother, and a most independent man in mind and action.

Charles Lyell's family resided, for years, in the south of England after his birth, and the boy was sent to school early; and in his amusing history of his schoolboy days, which is given in the "Life of Sir Charles Lyell," edited by his sister-in-law,

Mrs. Lyell, he went through all the fun and trouble, the games by day and the bolsterings by night, the keeping of pets, and the petty warfares of the English schoolboy. When eleven years of age, Lyell got into indifferent health at school after measles, and this necessitated his being less pressed at his lessons. He was fond of study, however, and this enforced idleness made him take to some of his father's amusements, that of entomology.

Young Lyell studied butterflies, and chased them in the fields and woodlands of the New Forest in Hampshire. He soon began to study the changes of form which insects undergo in their short lives, and to watch, hour after hour, the habits of the water-beetles and other aquatic insects. After spoiling a considerable number of hats in chasing butterflies, Lyell was supplied with a net and a cabinet in which to place his stores of insect wealth. Oddly enough, some of the varieties of the butterflies which young Lyell collected were of use in after years to Curtis the entomologist. The boy had no companions in these "un-English" amusements, and was very grateful for the assistance of his father's head servant, who knew a few plants by sight, and helped his young master. "Instead of sympathy," wrote Lyell, "I received from almost every one beyond my home, either ridicule, or hints that the pursuits of other boys were more manly. Whether did I fancy that insects had no feeling? What could be the use of them? The contemptuous appellation of 'butterfly hunting' applied to my favourite employment always nettled me." However, Lyell persisted, and when he got back to school he used to work at his favourite subject out of school hours.

Finding a number of expensive books in his father's library on entomology, with beautiful plates in them, the boy's common sense told him that somebody prized all this knowledge, and that it must be valuable. Oddly enough, he took to reading Linnæus for descriptions of insects, and hunted up pictures of his captured butterflies in the plates of the more modern authors. Recovered in health, and fairly strong, Lyell was sent at thirteen years of age to school at Dr. Bayley's, preparatory to being sent to the great school at Winchester. The new school was at Midhurst, in Sussex, and it had all the demerits of the schools of the day, fighting, fagging, and bullying being rampant. Lyell came off well, although a weak and short-sighted boy. Nevertheless, he stated that the method of teaching got rid of "most of my natural antipathy to work and extreme absence of mind, and I acquired habits of attention, which were, however, painful to me, and only sustained when I had an object in view."

It is evident that at this time, 1811–1813, Lyell's heart was not altogether in his classics and mathematics, and that he was reading other subjects which were more pleasing to him. At the early age of seventeen, Lyell entered Exeter College, Oxford, and whilst working fairly well at his studies, cultivated music, and entered thoroughly into all the politics and literary fellowships of the undergraduates. His love of nature persisted, and he began to direct his thoughts to the past, and to learn something about fossils. Thus he found out the house of Sowerby, the conchologist, by finding at the door an ammonite, well known to Oxford geologists. Subsequently, when on a visit to Mr. Dawson Turner, of Norwich, he met a Javanese traveller, Dr. Arnold. Mr. Dawson Turner had a fine collection of Norwich and Suffolk fossils. Lyell writes to his father to say, "I have copied for Buckland, part of his paper, being a list of those which are described, and shall copy the rest." It appears that the seed was sown by attending a course of lectures on geology, at Oxford, given by the celebrated Dr. Buckland, and it is no little thing for that great university to be able to assert that its teaching developed the greatest system of geology ever brought forward. Lyell geologized over Norfolk, and in his conversations with his host and Dr. Arnold, it appeared that he had got hold of the idea, the elaboration of which is at the very bottom of his future great work. Lyell studied what is now in progress in nature so as to comprehend what occurred in the past times of the earth. Modern changes are the examples by which ancient changes can alone be studied. He quotes in a letter to his father, the following saying of Buckland and of White : "Local information, from actual observation, tends more to promote natural history science, than all that is done by the speculations and compilations of voluminous authors." Dr. Arnold made collections of Norfolk fossils, and catalogued them, whilst his young friend endeavoured to make a geological map of the county. In the vacation Lyell and two friends went to Staffa, and his description of the grand columns of the old volcanic stone shows how he enjoyed and comprehended the scene.

In 1818 the family of the Lyells made a tour in France, Switzerland, and Italy, and the notes, letters, and diaries of the eldest son have been preserved, and they show how gradually, yet surely, he was educating himself for that path which he, subsequently, never deserted. France was not very lively, but he noticed the country more than the people, and observed the country changed with the soil. He spent his first Sunday at Paris, and went to the Jardin des Plantes the first thing on Monday morning, but was disappointed by not hearing Cuvier lecture. In the evening he went to see the great fountains at Versailles, where Wellington was dining with some French marshals. Day after day the wonderful sights of Paris were visited; but Lyell, whenever he had the opportunity, slipped off to the Jardin des Plantes. He was much struck with the collection of comparative anatomy, which he said might tempt anyone who had the opportunity of staying in Paris, to take up ardently the study of anatomy. He studied Cuvier's work on fossil remains, and on the geology of the country round Paris. One of his visits was to Cuvier's lecture room, which he described as filled with fossil remains, among which are those glorious relics of a former world. Leaving Paris, Lyell travelled by post, and noticed the geology and rocks of the monotonous country to the Jura Mountains. He was mightily puzzled about the rocks of the Jura, and enjoyed that magnificent scene of the Alps from the top of the hills over which he was travelling. He wrote, "In descending the Jura from Lavatey to Gex, we had a most magnificent view of a vast extent of country. Below us the Lake of Geneva and the Canton de Vaud ; before us the Savoy Alps towering up to the clouds, and in spite of their great distance and the height on which we stood, extended in a long line before us like an army of giants, Mont Blanc rising high above all in the middle as their chief. We saw the Dent du Midi to our left, shooting up his two remarkable peaks, with many more of extraordinary and picturesque forms." On visiting the Valley of Chamouni, we find Lyell naming the rocks of the different well known scenes, according to the accepted terms of the mineralogists of the day, and this is a satisfactory proof that he had been studying geology very effectually, by himself, before he left England. He saw his first glacier, of any importance, and was immensely struck with the changes it was producing in the valley.

Many books have been written about Mont Blanc, its botany and its glaciers, but none have ever equalled, in truthfulness and freshness of description, the diary of Lyell. He seized upon all the remarkable points to be noticed, and shone both as a botanist and geologist. He, moreover, did not forget his old entomological tastes, for he chased butterflies in the valley of the Arve, and was delighted with the Alpine rhododendrons, and the little *ranunculus glacialis*. On the Grimsel Lyell saw "some extraordinary large bare pieces of granite-rock, which I could not account for," and was puzzled by the redness of the snow in some places. Afterwards on the Wengern Alp, he saw a fine avalanche fall over a precipice on to a ledge below. He went to the Valais to see the result of the great flood the previous June, and witnessed the results of the enormous force of running water, carrying with it sand and stone, on everything against which it came in contact.

Lyell then crossed the Alps and visited the Italian lakes and the principal towns of Italy, but more as an antiquarian than a geologist.

The long journey bore fruit, for the constant proofs of changes ever progressing in nature, which were brought before Lyell's notice, influenced his mind in a very decided manner. He became opposed to the convulsionist doctrines of sudden and violent changes having occurred, and furthered the ideas taught by Hutton, that the alterations on the surface of the earth are slow and constant, and have been uniform for ages. In 1819 Lyell took his B.A. degree at Oxford, obtaining a second class in classical honours, and in the same year he became a fellow of the Geological Society of London, and of the Linnæan Society. On leaving Oxford he was entered at Lincoln's Inn, and resided in London, and studied law in a special pleader's office. His eyes became weak, and he was advised to give up reading for a time, and to join his father in a visit to Rome in 1820. In 1822 Lyell was in full correspondence with the most prominent geologists of the day, and he was doing original work, for his letters show that he was interesting himself about the fresh water strata of the Isle of Wight, and about the bones found in Kirkdale cave, of hyæna, elephant, rhinoceros, etc. His enthusiasm and ability to work were recognized in the very remarkable selection the Geological Society made in 1823. For he was then elected one of the secretaries, and his friends were Mantell and Buckland. The same year he went to Paris to see the French geologists and Cuvier. Cuvier was very polite, and introduced Lyell to Madlle. Duvancel, his stepdaughter, and Lyell spoke very well of her ability and engaging manners. He met Humboldt and Laplace and Arago, the mathematicians and astronomers of the day.

In 1824 Lyell was interesting himself about Dean Coneabeare's discovery of a plesiosaurus at Lyme Regis, and the fossil was brought in triumph to the rooms of the Geological Society, then established at 20, Bedford Street. Then he started on a geological excursion in the west of England with

M. Prévost, and subsequently went to his birthplace and geologized in Scotland.

Lyell was called to the bar in 1825, and went the western circuit for two years, and in 1826 he became a fellow of the Royal Society, and in 1827 he wrote an article in the *Quarterly Review*, showing how thoroughly he identified himself with the school of geology that taught the necessity of studying the past from the modern example of slow and gradual changes on the earth by forces which have always been in existence. In 1828 appeared his papers on the excavation of valleys by ordinary agencies, such as the sun's heat, frost, rain, running water and the atmosphere.

A very remarkable book on the Geology of Central France, with especial reference to the extinct volcanoes and lava flows of the Auvergne, was written by Mr. Scrope, and its criticism was the foundation of the article in the *Quarterly Review* just noticed. Lyell was so impressed with the grand descriptions in the book, that he determined to persuade Mr. and Mrs. Murchison to accompany him on a tour into the region. Two of Lyell's letters to his father are so characteristic that they may well find a place here.

Clermont-Ferrand,
May 26th, 1828.

MY DEAR FATHER,
I have just returned again to Clermont, from an expedition of five days, and we have discovered that there is no end to the work to be

done in this country, and that it is of the most interesting description. The first day was spent in ascending some of the lofty volcanic Puys near here. Mrs. Murchison accompanied us, and then returned to Clermont, where she employed herself, during our absence, in making panoramic sketches, receiving several of the gentry and professors, to whom he had letters, in the neighbourhood, and collecting plants and shells, etc., while Murchison and I, with my man, went on in a patache, a one-horse machine on springs. We first visited Pontgibaud and the Sioule, to see the excavations made by that river in the grand lava-current of the Come, which descended from the central range, and dispossessed the river of its bed. The scenery was beautiful. Just as we were leaving the place, the peasants offered to take us to a volcano farther down the river. As no Puy was mentioned in Desmarest's accurate map, nor by Scrope, we thought their account a mere fable; but their description of the cinders, etc. was so curious, that we had the courage to relinquish our day's scheme, and proceed again down the river.

You may imagine our surprise when we found, within a ride of Clermont, a set of volcanic phenomena entirely unknown to Buckland, Scrope, or the natives here. A volcanic cone, with a stream of basaltic lava issuing out on both sides, and flowing down to the gorge of the Sioule. This defile was flanked on both sides by precipitous cliffs of gneiss, and the river's passage must have been entirely choked up for a long time. A lake was formed, and the river wore a passage between the lava and the granitic schist, but the former was so excessively compact, that the schist evidently suffered most. In the progress of ages, the igneous rock, one hundred and fifty feet deep, was cut through, and the river went on and ate its way, thirty-five, forty-five, and in one place eighty-five feet into the subjacent granitic beds, leaving on one bank a perpendicular wall of basaltic lava towering over the gneiss. In the Vivarrais, where similar phenomena had been observed, Herschel had remarked a bed of pebbles between the lava and the gneiss, marking the ancient river-bed, but Buckland endeavoured to get over this difficulty by saying that these pebbles might have covered a sloping bank when the river filled the valley, and that this bank may have always been high above the river bed; for if the sloping sides of a valley, said the Professor, be covered with pebbles, as they often are, and the valley is filled with lava, and then the lava cut through and partially removed, there will of course be a line of pebbles at the junction of the lava and the rock beneath, but these pebbles will not mark an ancient river bed. Now, unluckily for the doctor in this case, he has no loophole; an old lead mine, said to have been worked by the Romans, happens to have exactly laid open the line of contact, and the pebble bed of the old river is seen going in under the lava, horizontally, for nearly fifty feet. This is an astonishing proof of what a river can do in some thousands or hundred thousand years by its continual wearing. No deluge could have descended the valley without carrying away the crater and ashes above.

Six hundred or seven hundred feet higher, is an old plateau of basalt, and if this flowed at the bottom of the then valley, the last work of the Sioule is but a unit in proportion to the other. There are several of the Clermont savans who, since they discovered how much we were interested with this, have given us to understand they intended to publish on it, but no doubt they will take a year before they launch out in the expense of a patache to Pontgibaud. Murchison certainly keeps it up with more energy than anyone I ever travelled with, for Buckland, though he worked as hard, always flew about too fast to make sure of anything. Mons. Le Coq, the botanist, a clever young man, assures me that the geology of the soils does not affect the botany of Auvergne. I shall get some specimens from him for Dr. Hooker, I expect. None to be bought, at least this year, for it seems there may be hereafter. It is a wonderful fact that *Glaux maritima* grows round some saline springs here. Busset, an engineer, who is mapping Auvergne, has forced us to dine with him to-morrow. As we know his object to be to get geology out of us, of which he knows nothing, M. fears it will be a bore, but the man is evidently clever. We shall get barometric heights from him, and a map of our little volcanic district, and if he pumps unreasonably, I shall find a difficulty in expressing myself in French. We are to meet Count Le Serres there, a gentlemanlike and well-informed naturalist, who has a property on Mont Dore, and knows more geology than anyone we have met here, professors not excepted. He organized a geological society here, and they chose Count Montlosier as president; but the Jesuits took alarm, and, declaring that Montlosier had written a book against Genesis, got the Prefect and Mayor and Government to oppose, and at last put the thing down; at least it merged in the regular scientific Etablissement de la Ville, and Montlosier is just coming out with a book against the Jesuits, a more popular subject in France at present than geology. We are to visit him at his château near Mont Dore. We like the people and the country.

Believe me, your affectionate son,
CHARLES LYELL.

TO HIS FATHER.

Bains de Mont Dore, Auvergne.
June 6th, 1882.

MY DEAR FATHER,

I am at this moment arrived here, after passing three delightful days at Count de Montlosier's, an old man of seventy-four, in full possession of faculties of no mean order, and of an imagination as lively as a poet's of twenty-five. I stayed a day longer than the Murchisons, as I was determined to have one more trial to find a junction between the granite of the Puy chain and the fresh water formations of the Limagne, and I actually found it; and my day's work alone will throw a new light on the history of this remarkable country. I believe most of the granite to have made its appearance at the surface at a later period than even the fresh water tertiary beds have, though they contain the remains of quadrupeds. The scenery of Mont Dore is that of an Alpine valley, deep, with tall fir woods, high aiguilles above, half covered with snow, and cataracts and waterfalls. A watering-place with good views at the bottom of the valley. I shall send Hall back from here, as, although he has been useful, I do not think the advantage will overbalance the additional expense. Le Coq has promised some plants for certain, and Hall has done pretty well in insects.

Believe me, your affectionate son,
CHARLES LYELL.

Lyell was not sparing of criticism so far as his friend Murchison's habits were concerned, as may be gleaned in the following letter :—

TO HIS MOTHER.

Bains de Mont Dore, Auvergne.
June 11th, 1828.

MY DEAR MOTHER,

We have been so actively employed, I may really say so laboriously, that I assure you I can with great difficulty find a moment to write a letter. This morning we got off, after breakfast at five o'clock, on horseback, to return from St. Amand to this: arrived at seven o'clock. But one day we rode fifty-five miles, which I shall take care shall be the last experiment of that kind, as even the old Leicestershire fox-hunter was nearly done up with it. But I have really gained strength so much, that I believe I and my eyes were never in such condition before; and I am sure that six hours in bed, which is all we allow, and exercise all day long for the body, and geology for the mind, with plenty of the vin du pays, which is good here, is the best thing that can be invented in this world for my health and happiness. Murchison must have been intended for a very strong man, if the sellers of drugs had not enlisted him into their service, so that he depends on them for his existence to a frightful extent, yet withal he can get through what would knock up most men who never need the doctor. He has only given in one day and a half yet. On one occasion we were on an expedition together, and as a stronger dose was necessary than he had with him, I was not a little alarmed at finding there was no pharmacy in the place, but at last we went to a nunnery, where Mdlle. la Supérieuse sold all medicines without profit—positively a young, clever, and rather good-looking lady, who hoped my friend would think better of it, as the quantity would kill six Frenchmen. M. was cured, and off the next morning, as usual. The mischief is, that he has naturally a weak though a sound stomach, and if he possessed a more than ordinary share of self-denial, and was very prudent, and after much exercise did not eat a good dinner when set before him—if, in short, he would take the advice which many find it easy to give him, he would be well. He has much talent for original observation in geology, and is indefatigable, so that we make much way, an l are thrown so much in the way of the people, high and low, by means of our letters of introduction, and our pursuits, that I am getting large materials, which I hope I shall find means of applying. Indeed, I really think I am most profitably employed on this tour, and as long as things go on as well as they do now, I should be very sorry to leave off; particularly as, from our plan of operation, which is that of comparison of the structure of different parts of the country, we work on with a continually increasing power, and in the last week have with the same exertion done at least twice as much in the way of discovery, and in enlarging our knowledge of what others had done, as in any preceding. I expect it will be at least three weeks before we can have done with Central France, and then we hope to work south towards Nice, down the Rhone, keeping always in analogous formations, and then to the Vicentin, if possible, though this is very uncertain, as we can never see far before us, either as to time or place, directing our course according to the new lights we are gaining.

We shall leave this place in a day or two. I like

it well enough, but it is certainly too early in the season to enjoy it; and Mrs. Murchison suffers from the cold and damp, though she has not often complained in this tone.

Mont Dore is partially covered with snow, and almost always with clouds, and the transition in coming up here from the low country is violent. Yesterday we rode up from the climate of Italy to that of Scotland. It is the most varied and picturesque country imaginable. There are innumerable old ruins for sketches, with lakes, cascades, and different kinds of wood, so that we wonder more and more that the English have not found it out. The peasantry are very obliging, industrious, well-fed, and clothed, and to all appearance are the very happiest I ever saw. We have crossed the chain of Puys, the Limagne, and the valleys leading from Mont Dore, in all directions. The people in the higher regions begin to talk French—at least there are generally some who have served in the armies, and their children catch some from them. Their own language has a good deal of the old Provençal in it, and a great many of the terminations are Italian. In short, we often find a demand in Italian succeed when French misses fire; but all our ammunition often fails to produce any impression. The population is dense, and bears no other resemblance to other parts of France that ever I saw. In the mountains a large portion do not believe that Napoleon is dead, especially the old soldiers. There is an almost entire want of gentry here, but as it does not arise from absenteeism, but from the great sub-division of property, it evidently produces no ill effects on the character and well-being of the people.

Give my love to all at Kinnordy, and believe me
Your affectionate son,
CHARLES LYELL.

After visiting the south of France with Murchison, Lyell prepared to cross the Alps and to see Vesuvius, he being impressed with the necessity of studying that grand modern example in order to understand, perfectly, the extinct volcanoes they had been studying in the Auvergne. He wrote his father—"I scarcely despair now, so much do these evidences of modern action increase upon us as we go south (towards the more recent volcanic seat of action) of proving the positive identity of the causes now operating with those of former times." This was always his point, and it certainly was not Murchison's.

When at Vesuvius, Lyell recognized the similarity of some very old volcanic dykes of Scotland with those recently exposed in the old crater. Etna was visited, and he was delighted at finding seashells, resembling those now living on the floor of the Mediterranean close by, some three hundred feet above sea level. Whilst at Naples, and in the midst of the highly suggestive scenery of the beautiful neighbourhood, Lyell wrote to Murchison a very characteristic letter, which should be well pondered over even by wealthy men who enter into the studies of nature, and which might be read with benefit by those people who on this not over civilized earth, hold the purse-strings of the world and treat scientific teachers with gross meanness. With all his advantages Lyell could not undertake the research which made him famous, which has tended to elevate our conception of the laws of nature, and which has done so much to lead geologists along the right path, without caring much for pecuniary matters.

He wrote, "I will tell you fairly that it is at present of no small consequence to me to get a respectable sum for my volume, not only to cover expenses for present and future projected campaigns, but because my making my hobby pay the additional costs which it entails, will alone justify my pursuing it with a mind sufficiently satisfied with itself, and so to feel independent and free to indulge in the enthusiasm necessary for success. I shall never hope to make money by geology, but not to lose, and *tax others* for my amusement; and unless I can secure this, it would, in my circumstances, be selfish in me to devote myself as much as I hope to do to it." These sentiments did Lyell great honour. "My work is in part written, and all planned. It will not pretend to give even an abstract of all that is known in geology, but it will endeavour to establish the principle of reasoning on the science. All my geology will come in as illustrative of my views of those principles, and as evidence strengthening the system necessarily arising out of the admission of such principles, which as you know, are neither more nor less than, that *no causes whatever* have, from the earliest time to which we can look back to the present, ever acted, but those *now acting;* and that they never acted with different degrees of energy from that which they now exert." If I can but earn the wherewith to carry on the war, or rather, its *extraordinary costs*, depend upon it I will waste no time in book-making for lucre's sake."

Lyell's long-expected book on the "Principles of Geology" was published in 1830, and it made a very considerable sensation, and was warmly combated and abused. Now it is admitted as the most conclusive and useful of introductory books, fit for a youth, and eminently good in its tone. Then the man, ever on the move, left for the Pyrenees, and studied the formations there, and especially devoted himself to the explanation of ripple-marks in the hundreds of feet of rock, and noticed the effects of water-borne and air-carried sand in accumulating flats of ripples one over the other. In 1831 Lyell accepted the position of Professor of Geology in King's College, London, and he gave courses of lectures there in 1832 and 1833; and he became engaged to Mary, the eldest daughter of Mr. Leonard Horner, a geologist of considerable reputation, and a thoroughly liberal-minded man. Mr. Horner was a great friend of Lyell's before the engagement, and was a most painstaking man and a great manager at the Geological Society. Lyell's letters to Miss Horner are most interesting, and show how admirable a woman she was and how she stimulated him to follow out his great destiny. His work on the "Principles" became a great pecuniary success, and he laboured hard at King's College, and was much annoyed at the decision of the council at the College, not to allow women to attend his lectures, which were a great success. Married, Lyell started for Germany, the Rhine, and Switzerland. Coming home to London, he set to work at his lectures at the Royal Institution, where ladies were admitted, and at King's College, where they were not. He had two hundred and fifty people to hear his introductory lecture at King's College, and it dwindled down to fifteen in a few days, not from any want of care or excellence in Lyell, who was ever bitter against the establishment for their refusal to advance female education. He retired from the professorship as soon as he found that it interfered with his researches, and never again took any part in academical teaching. The trouble he took about his lectures was great, and he went to great expense in having diagrams well drawn. His retirement was a great loss to the College, which now admits ladies to certain lectures. In 1834, Lyell travelled in Sweden and examined into the rise of the land in Scandinavia, and whilst enjoying his hard geological work—for he was well received by everybody, and taken to see everything—his letters show how he missed his gentle and sympathizing wife. On his return home Lyell received one of the Royal Society medals for his work on the "Principles of Geology," and in 1838 became President of the Geological Society. About this time his attention was strongly drawn to the relative numbers of living species found in the strata which had been formed during the last geological or tertiary age. In working at Sicily he had found that in the latest beds in which the shells were hardly fossilised, all the species were still living. That is to say, he collected shells which were of course dead, but they were similar to others which were alive on the floor of the sea close by. The individual had died, but the kind or species was still alive. He examined the latest strata in England, the crag of Norfolk, Suffolk, and Essex, and found that the proportion of recent shells—that is to say, of dead individuals belonging to living species—is great. Some of the shells belonged to kinds which are not now living, and are extinct. He wrote, "I think we may lay it down as a rule, that if any given tertiary deposit in which we have found a few species of shells only, of which one half, or a third, or even less, are recent, and those recent ones inhabit the seas immediately adjoining, the formation will be pliocene." This word was one of three invented by Dr. Whewell, of Cambridge, at Lyell's suggestion to explain the gradual development of the recent animals and plants during the past history of the globe. The other terms were "miocene" and "eocene." The most ancient deposit which was supposed by Lyell to contain evidences of existing genera was at the dawn of the last great geological period, the tertiary. It was called eocene from ηως, dawn, καὶνος, recent. The next deposits overlying these older ones contained, according to his estimate, seventeen per cent. of living species, all the rest being extinct; and they were called miocene, from μεῖον, less, and καὶνος, recent; expressing a minor proportion of recent species to that found in the topmost and most recent tertiary deposits. These last contain a large proportion of recent species, and are called pliocene, πλεῖον, more, and καὶνος, recent. It was a grand theory, which has remained almost unaltered, and it influenced the progress of geology, for it plainly inferred that the living things of the present have been linked with those of the past time by direct descent; that many forms of life have become extinct, and that there is some wonderful law relating to this.

About this time many were the geological heresies, and the lovers of the notion of the violent actions of nature evolved theories about volcanoes and the occurrence of vast waves to account for the presence of the great masses of rock which are found strewn far and wide and away from their sources. These Lyell successfully antagonized. He then published the "Elements of Geology," and his time was fully occupied in the meetings of the Geological Society, in criticising work, and in genial scientific society.

In the autumn of 1841 Lyell crossed the Atlantic, and spent thirteen months in the United States, Canada, and Nova Scotia. He worked hard as an observer and recorder, and his comparisons between the strata in the New and Old World are full of interest. Writing from Philadelphia to his father-in-law, Mr. Horner, he says, "Here I am working away in quarries of greensand and picking up belemnites and other cretaceous fossils;" and then to Dr. Mantell, "After staying two days we went by New York and the Hudson to Albany, where I began my explorings in the silurian strata, and from whence I examined the valley of the Mohawk. The Falls of Niagara were as beautiful as I expected, perhaps scarcely so grand, but in geological interest far beyond my most sanguine hopes. So I shall send a paper on the proofs of their recession to the Geological Society. I will not dwell on them now. After spending some time there, I examined seriatim, all the silurian groups and the old red and coal on the borders of Pennsylvania. Returning to Albany, I went south to Philadelphia, and spent four days in collecting in the different divisions of the greensand, and in New Jersey. The analogy of the genera, and even of the species of the European chalk, is most striking."

One of his duties in the United States, was to give a course of lectures at the Lowell Institute, at which his audiences amounted to two thousand. He also went north, and made some most important investigations with Dr. Dawson, then a comparatively unknown school missionary struggling to learn something about nature, and now one of the most distinguished geologists in the world. They dug out roots called by fossilists stigmariæ, which once supported huge trees called sigillariæ in the days of the coal formation, and they measured foot by foot many hundreds of yards of the cliffs of the now celebrated place called Toggins, in Nova Scotia. There they found rows of trees, one over the other, erect, and indicating that, when the part of the earth now cut into by the sea and exposed as a cliff was formed, there was a series of ages, each having its forest, each of which was overwhelmed, and thus forest after forest accumulated. Amongst the trees were some hollow ones, and they contained little fossils, such as shells and scales. They were objects of interest, but it was not until later on that Lyell and Dawson saw their importance. This subterranean forest exceeds in extent and quantity of timber all that have been found in Europe put together. The new deposit of red sand of the numerous estuaries there afforded them endless instruction. " At this place, Truro, the tide is said to rise seventy-five feet, and we see the bottom of a deep salt-water sea, its rippled sands, shells and holes of *Mya* and *Tellina* and their tracks, footmarks of birds and worms, the manner in which the clays crack and are marked with the rain, and sometimes shells included recently in solid models of claystone. I have also learned more about the geological effects of drifting ice in the last ten days than in all the Canadian tour."

Lyell returned to England, and, after a short rest, started for the north of Ireland. He wrote to his sister: "We have just returned from a walk over the grand pavement (Giant's Causeway), the effect of which was as picturesque as the evening sun and some white breakers rolling and foaming over the black rocks could make it. Much as I have been pleased with the sight, it strikes me that there are parts of Staffa away from Fingal's Cave, and which travellers have seldom leisure to visit, which are even finer in precisely the same style. The geology of Antrim is very interesting—so many formations, such as chalk, green sand, lias, new red —and the coal being represented by such distinctly characterized and yet such thin sets of strata, compared to the same groups elsewhere; and then the grand trap or basaltic mass covering and cutting through them all."

Often slightly political in his ideas, Lyell wrote much about the Irish peasantry, and spoke of them as the quick, obliging, and fine-looking natives of the Green Island. He remarked, in 1843, "One cannot help fearing that the anti-English spirit has sunk deep into the hearts of the millions here, for they read nothing but O'Connell's newspapers, from which he artfully excludes, without appearing to them to do so, every other foreign or domestic topic of interest except repeal and Irish grievances —a great proportion of them now bygone."

He kept steadily at work preparing his American travels for publication, and in a note to a friend regarding the nature of coal, he instanced the swamps of Virginia. "The Virginian morasses allow, under a hot sun, great accumulations of black vegetable matter, nearly like peat, and which might make coal. The shade of *Cupressus distichi*, Thuya, and water oaks shut out the sun, and ferns and mosses draw in the damp air beneath, while the heat causes evaporation, and evaporation cold. One swamp which I saw is forty miles long by twenty broad. Thousands of prostrate trees are in the peat." Some investigators held that the atmosphere must have contained a large amount of carbonic acid gas during the ages in which coal was being formed out of decaying vegetation, but Lyell, adhering to his strictly uniformitarian views, denied this, and considered the Virginian swamps to be explanatory of the formation of coal.

Lyell went to see the skeleton, brought by a German named Koch from the Missouri, of a very large mastodon, and was wonderfully amused to notice how this savant had made it up out of fragments. "He has turned the huge tusks the wrong way—horizontally, has made the first pair of ribs into collar-bones, and has intercalated several spurious dorsal and tail vertebræ, and has placed the toe-bones wrong to prove, what he really believes, that it was web-footed. I think he is a mixture of an enthusiast and an impostor, but more of the former, and amusingly ignorant. His mode of advertising is a thousand dollars reward for anyone who will prove that the bones of his Missourium are made of wood. He is soon to take them to London, when you will have a treat, and see a larger femur (thigh-bone) than that of Iguanodon." He was delighted with the Americans.

Lyell revisited America in 1845, and on returning across the Atlantic in 1846, narrowly escaped shipwreck on an iceberg; but he made an interesting observation about one great berg. "It had a large rock, twelve feet square, on the top, and much gravel and sand on its side. The bergs were from fifty to four hundred feet in height, pyramidal, pinnacled, dome-shaped, single-peaked, double-peaked, flat-topped, and of every form and most picturesque, and only a quarter of a mile off us."

The lesson was not lost, for Lyell had thus ocular proof concerning how stones of huge size and gravity, can travel far from their proper location, And as these icebergs capsize or melt he was confirmed in his views that many deposits of huge stones and gravels in the form of "drift" have been produced in this manner.

Having now attained great eminence, Lyell began to write and agitate about the scientific teaching of the Universities, and his opinion of the decidedly unprogressive character of them was proved to be correct when only four heads of houses out of twenty-four were at Oxford to receive the British Association for the Advancement of Science. He urged strongly the necessity of placing the lay teacher on the same pecuniary level as the clergy. Moreover, he made a vigorous attempt to have truly scientific presidents of the Royal Society, and not only noblemen of high and royal standing. The Queen honoured Lyell with her regard, and Prince Albert used to get him to talk about America and the Americans, listening always with great interest. He was knighted for his distinguished services to science, and the conferring of this dignity pleased the whole scientific world.

In 1849 Sir Charles Lyell was re-elected president of the Geological Society, and the Archbishop of Canterbury, Dr. Sumner, attended at the annual dinner given on the occasion. After the expiration of his presidency, Lyell again went to the United States, and, returning, visited Teneriffe, the Grand Canary, and Palma, arriving in England in 1854.

In 1855 and the two following years Sir Charles and Lady Lyell travelled much on the continent, and always with a view of studying existing nature so as to comprehend the past. He was gratified by finding that most of the rising teachers in Germany were using his books as text books for their lectures, and that the doctrines of Hutton he had elaborated were so much appreciated. In Switzerland, Lyell interested himself more than ever about the great remains of former ice action on the rocks. He was at one time disposed to believe that certain masses of mud containing angular stones, derived from a distance, could have been produced by the sea, but not finding any remains of marine animals, or evidence of such action as the ice would produce in rounding and waterwearing stone, he began to examine the influence of glaciers in wearing rocks and carrying the rubbish down with them. He was of course aware that there had been an age of cold in Switzerland, corresponding to the glacial epoch of Europe to the north, and he was therefore prepared to find some proofs of the former great extension of glaciers beyond their present limits. He was disposed to believe that the Alps were higher than they now are in that age of cold. In order to account for the former action of ice and the production of huge moraines, in comparison with which those now found at the glacier foot are pigmies, Lyell wrote : " In the glacial period, when the weight of ice was enormously greater, when in the region of the Alps there was so little melting, when glaciers at present only ten, fifteen, and twenty miles long, and from three hundred to one thousand feet deep, were fifty to one hundred, and even one hundred and fifty miles long, and four thousand feet deep (and if there is any truth at all in the generally received theory of the old Swiss glaciers, such must have been their gigantic dimensions), one may readily grant that the pressure and friction were so much in excess of what we now see as to explain the contrast between the ice work done in the olden times, and that accomplished in our own days, to say nothing of the probably disproportionate length of the periods compared." He noticed an old terminal moraine, in advance of the new one of the Rhone glacier, covered with wild plants, some in full flower, and cut through in two places by the river; its height was only fifteen feet, and its width ninety feet. He went underneath the Viesch glacier in the Upper Vallais, and beyond it; in consequence of its having melted much, he saw a rounded and domed surface of granite, smooth, and with straight furrows a quarter of an inch deep exactly in the direction of the onward movement of the glacier. On the Ruffelhorn, on the right lateral moraine, that is on the surface of the ice close to the rocks, he saw a splendid mass of granite, angular in shape, and measuring fifty-nine feet long, forty-nine feet wide, and forty-two feet high. Its sides were polished and furrowed. This huge mass was being carried slowly down, by the glacier, and will be deposited at its foot some day or other. Once it formed a part of the valley side, and it fell on to the glacier, whose flanks had scrubbed it for many a long day. He particularly noticed how the glaciers had been advancing of late years (just as they are now receding).

Lyell followed out these researches on the south of the Alps, and he first of all made many excursions, accompanied by Gastaldi, one of the best of the scientific men of Turin, and by Michelotti, in order to compare the shells which are found fossil in the middle tertiary strata on the south of the Alps, with those of the molasse of Switzerland to the north. He found that these strata, separated by the great mass of the mountains, resembled each other somewhat mineralogically as well as in their fossils, but he was not able to make out that they were exactly of the same geological age, although it was highly probable. He wrote on the glaciers ancient and modern of the southern slopes of the Alps, and in relation to the former—" A comparison also of the extinct glaciers of the Italian and Swiss sides of the Alps can better be made from Turin than from any other place. Before my arrival I had seen, on the banks of the Lago Maggiore, some good examples of erratics and of moraines which had come from the Simplon, but these, as you might suppose, *a priori* are far inferior to those which have descended from the Val d'Aosta, or which belong to the mighty glacier derived from the combined snows of the Mont Blanc and the Mont Rosa group of Alpine heights. This glacier, although perhaps of less gigantic dimensions than that of the Rhone, has certainly left, as Gastaldi first pointed out in a memoir on the subject, a far more imposing monument of itself on the plains of the Po, than have the extinct glaciers of the Rhone or the Rhine, in the lower country of Switzerland." He noticed that " J. D. Forbes has well shown in his book on the Alps, that a glacier is a peculiarly sensitive instrument for measuring the average of heat and cold, and that every slight difference of temperature causes it to increase or lessen in height and length." And pursuing the argument, remarks that as geologists had shown from the nature of the fossil remains in lately formed gravels, that arctic animals lived far south in Europe, shortly before the existing state of things, we ought to find evidences of the cold climate which allowed those animals to live so far south. These evidences are at hand in the remains of the glaciers, which in those days extended far lower than they do now, and were grander in extent. Thus a lofty mound or ridge, two thousand feet high, called the Serra, running into the great alluvial flat of the River Po, where maize and mulberries grow, is a huge terminal moraine of an ancient glacier. Ice reigned supreme there in the glacial period, and brought down the stone from the distant hills, and deposited it on the Serra. In Forfarshire, Lyell had noticed the peculiar contorted appearance of the beds of clay, gravel and sand of glacial formation, and also in the mud cliffs of Norfolk. He was anxious to know whether any of the ancient glacial heaps or moraines of the country south of the Alps, showed similar indications of pressure and forcing along by ice. "It happened that a railway was making from Turin to Ivrea, and although they cut through the lowest part of the terminal moraines near Mazzi they have thought it worth while to make a tunnel, through which we walked." Near the entrance, " I was delighted," wrote Lyell, " to see that curious folding of the strata, which will cause the same beds to be here pierced by a perpendicular shaft, yet without the beds having participated in the movement." Full of this important subject he wrote fully on it.

"In order to appreciate the distinctive character of this colossal moraine, you must reflect on the uniformity and evenness of the vast plain of the Po all round it, for, although really inclined from the Alps, it looks as level as the sea; then fancy the great mounds sloping up at angles of 20° and 30° to heights of 500, 1000, 1500 and 2000 feet; then consider that at the very extremity, as near Caluso, there are blocks of protogine which have come one hundred miles from Mont Blanc; also that the whole assemblage of stones is not like that which has issued from the Susa, or from any other valley, but confined to rocks such as now strictly belong to the basin of the Dora Baltea; also that the pebbles and fragments of stone, if of serpentine or any easily striable rock, are all striated, at least nineteen-twentieths of the whole, whereas in a recent glacier which has only travelled ten miles, you might only find one in twenty of the same stone striated; and lastly, think of the narrow vomitory which has disgorged this enormous quantity of material, the ravine above Ivrea being as obviously the source of the whole, as is the crater of Vesuvius the point from which its lavas have issued. When Gastaldi read his paper to the Geological Society at Paris, written jointly by him and Martens, Elie de Beaumont, who had many years before visited the ground, objected entirely to their conclusion that it was a moraine, but I never saw a stronger or more satisfactory case. But in the same paper the authors hazarded an opinion that although the old Alpine moraines stopped short after going a few leagues from the Alps, yet at some former time erratics had been conveyed to the summit of the Collina, just as "Pierre à Bot" and other blocks had been carried by the old Rhone glacier to the flanks of the Jura. Now when I read this at Zurich, I immediately recollected that in the valley of the Bormida, when I passed from Savona to Alessandria in 1828, I had been astonished at some very huge erratics of serpentine in the Miocene. Having never seen blocks of such enormous dimensions in any tertiary formation, I was relieved in 1828 at finding, in some spots on the Bormida, projecting fragments of serpentine in places which the erosion of the valleys had exposed to view. I concluded that they may not have travelled far, and when I saw some large blocks on the Superga (in 1828), I immediately suspected that as that hill consisted of beds of the same formation, the blocks might have been washed out of the Miocene not far off. I therefore now suggested this view to Gastaldi, and found that he was by no means tenacious of his printed theory, although he said that the blocks were many of them angular, of very great size, and accompanied by Alpine loam. We then examined the beds of the Superga, both those dipping to the north-west, and those to the south-east, and on both sides of this anticlinal are strata containing fragments of stone of various kinds, some not known in the neighbouring Alps or Apennines, from two to eight feet in diameter. On our ascent to the Superga I saw a thickness of sixty feet regularly stratified of this conglomerate, in which were fragments consisting chiefly of serpentine, but some of limestone, others of protogine granite, and one of the latter angular and eight feet in diameter. In less than half an hour's search, I found two of the serpentine and one of the limestone pebbles with scratches, which would be called glacial if they were found in a modern moraine, though not such as you would select for examples for a museum. Still I searched this year in some recent moraines quite as long without finding better. As to the age of the beds, there is no doubt of their belonging to the Lower Miocene, the marine fossils of which we collected in strata both below and above them. These enormous blocks, therefore, were brought into their present position by causes which acted in the Miocene age. I know of no agency but that of ice which could have quietly let them down upon subjacent beds of undisturbed fine marl and sand. Hence I conclude that there was floating ice in the Lower Miocene period, and if the few scratches I saw really imply glacial striation, the ice-rafts were probably derived from glaciers which came down from mountains bordering the glacial sea; perhaps from the Alps, for that chain must have existed before the origin of a large part of the Lower Miocene. I have kept the specimens I found of these Miocene striated stones to show Ramsay, who will be interested in hearing, that in spite of some Brazilian genera of trees and insects, and not a few palms, and some reptiles of good size, and many other fossil genera found on both sides of the Alps and supposed to imply a subtropical climate, I am not afraid to appeal to ice as the only known cause capable of stratifying these great masses in the manner in which they occur."

The evidence of former changes in climate was thus strongly impressed on Lyell's mind, and the astonishing truth began to be strongly impressed upon geologists by him, that not only has the area of Europe witnessed ages of tropical heat, but also ages of considerable winter's cold, and that there has been more than one glacial period.

Lyell visited Vesuvius and Etna in 1858, and how carefully he noticed every detail of the mountain structure, and how little he cared about "roughing it" may be gleaned from extracts from his diary sent to his wife:—

"Etna, *Casa Inglese*, Sept. 21, 1858.—Got off with two guides and two muleteers and four mules, at half past seven, in bright sunshine, from Nicolosi, and after a beautiful sunny ride of three hours through wooded craters, protected from the heat by my umbrella, was gradually enveloped in clouds. I saw a lava stream where the oaks had been surrounded by lava, which had taken the form both of upright and prostrate trunks, surrounding them with tuff, and the wood being burned up they are now cylinders of scoriaceous lava. After a couple of hours we got above the clouds, when about eight thousand feet high, but not till my hands were numbed, for I could not believe for a long time in the necessity of my putting on a cloak. After reaching this place, I set out out with Angelo for the top of Etna, leaving Guiseppe to cook. We had now and then a drifting cloud, but on the whole splendid sunshine. I saw the spot at the foot of the great line where the Catanians quarried ice from under a current of lava. My guide saw the same thing some six years ago, while the eruption of 1852 was in progress, in August and September: the sand and lava ten feet thick, and four feet of ice below, and bottom not seen. Not far above the ice I warmed my hands at a fumarole where the steam and some sulphuretted hydrogen were given off at such a heat that I was obliged to be careful how I put my fingers in. This welcome heat enabled me to write. When we reached the edge of the crater the whole of Sicily was hidden except the higher part of Etna, between us and Montagunoli. But Lipari and Stromboli stood out in the sea very conspicuously. I made a rough sketch of the two craters; the smaller one has lately, I believe, fallen, and shows a section of some of the horizontal beds of lava, with which it had been filled nearly to the top. It was a considerable exertion climbing and going half round it after a seven hours' ride, and this makes the Casa Inglese, which is the roughest place I was ever in, seem a hospitable mansion, as it saves our returning. The wind is whistling round and somewhat through it, but Dr. Guiseppe, I hear, has made it weather tight. There is no chimney and we have charcoal burners, but if the wind always blows like this I am not, at any rate, guaranteed from asphyxia."

He got a list of one hundred and fifty shells of the newer pliocene clay on which Etna rests. Nine-tenths of them he found were of species belonging to the present floor of the Mediterranean Sea, and this, to his delight, confirmed what he wrote, and what has already been alluded to, regarding this deposit on a former occasion. At Bronte, Lyell saw the place where a crowd assembled in 1842, to see the lava flow into a great artificial reservoir of water. The torrent of melted stone came forward with a front of more than thirty feet high, and falling suddenly into the water, produced for a while no effect whatever, as if, as in the white hot metal in Butigny's experiment, it required to cool down before it could cause explosion. At length it went off suddenly, and everybody but one or two out of fifty or more in number was killed.

During the years of his journeys in America and Europe, Lyell had paid special attention to the changes which were occurring on the surface of the earth amongst the rocks and hills, valleys, rivers, and sea-shores. He had dealt with inanimate nature largely. About the year 1859 he began to consider the changes which have occurred in the living things of the past, and to direct his attention to the subject of the antiquity of man and to the possible origin of species. He wrote to a friend in his usual half-jesting manner: "I have been much occupied with another geological subject besides that which your niece, Ellen Twisleton, irreverently calls the proving her to be first cousin to a turnip (a violet she should have said); I mean the antiquity of man as implied by the flint hatchets of Amiens, undoubtedly contemporaneous with the mammoth, and also the human skeletons of certain caves near Liége, which I believe to be of corresponding age. I regard the pyramids as things of yesterday in comparison of those relics." Lyell struggled long in his mind against the theory of the great age of man on the earth, and converted himself to the belief in it, and in 1861 he wrote, after examining the associated remains of human art and extinct animals, such as the mammoth and hairy rhinoceros in England, that "the late discoveries at Herne Bay and Reculver convince me that man inhabited England when the Thames was a tributary of the Rhine." He published a work on the antiquity of man, and then began to interest himself about the great age when ice reigned supreme over much of the northern hemisphere. Writing to his nephew he states: "On a hill called Moel Tryfaen (in North Wales), at a height of thirteen hundred feet above the sea, I found twenty species of fossil shells, all of living species, in sand and gravel fifty feet thick. You would have known most of them familiarly." Some of these shells were of kinds now living close by in the sea, but others of kinds now living within the arctic circle. "The shells show that Snowdon and all the highest hills which are in the neighbourhood of Moel Tryfaen were mere islands in the sea at a comparatively late period, or when these living molluscs were flourishing."

The researches of Lyell and Dawson in Nova Scotia have been noticed, and it is interesting to know that they were rewarded by the discovery of an air-breathing mollusc, and of several small amphibians of the age of the coal period, in the hollow of a stump of a tree, which dated back to that very ancient time. After the death of his friend Murchison, although the effects of age and a life of hard study were not unfelt, Lyell followed with great care the researches of Dr. Hicks relating to the oldest rocks of England. Lyell was intensely interested at the discovery of highly organized invertebrate animals in sandstones and shales, which hitherto had only yielded some doubtful worm tracks and impressions of plants, and he recognized the truth that no evidences of the beginning of living things were presented to the geologist. The researches of Carpenter, Thomson, and Agassiz concerning the natural philosophy and natural history of the deep sea were gratefully acknowledged by Lyell, as most important contributions to science, and the author of this memoir has a lively remembrance of Sir Charles's intense excitement when the news first came that the sea was very cold at great depths.

Years passed on, and honours came to the hard-working, truth-loving man. He was elected president of the British Association, and was made a baronet. His sight began to fail, and it was a constant anxiety to many who saw him about London, to witness his constant exposure to danger. Availing himself of an excellent secretary, he still corresponded largely, and attended scientific meetings. But the end was at hand, and he lost his well-loved wife and then his brother. Dying from the results of a fall, Lyell was buried in Westminster Abbey, as a representative man of science. He was a brilliant example of a man who sought out truth, and braved public opinion for its sake, and who enlightened the world, caring little for ease and luxury, and assisting every fellow-labourer in the great science of geology.

www.ingramcontent.com/pod-product-compliance
Lightning Source LLC
Chambersburg PA
CBHW031428230426
43668CB00007B/477